The Record Store of the Mind

By Josh Rosenthal

Published by Tompkins Square
www.tompkinssquare.com

All lyrics are copyrighted by their respective authors.

ISBN: 9781625179135

Printed in the United States of America

Cover illustration by Hazel Gerson-Rosenthal
Cover concept by Emma Gerson-Rosenthal & Hazel Gerson-Rosenthal
Book design by Susan Archie

For my daughters, Emma & Hazel

"Take the hill!"

Table of Contents

Introduction

I was shopping recently at On the Corner Records in Campbell, California, with my older daughter, Emma. On the Corner is my favorite record store in the Bay Area, although I'm a bit hesitant to say so, because I don't want you to go there. Naturally, I want first dibs on all the $6 Yazoo records, the condition-challenged $1 soul LPs in boxes on the floor, the below-market-value yet pricier gems in the New Arrivals box on the counter, and the impeccable rockabilly section.

While perusing the stacks, Emma asked, "How do you know what you're looking for?" Normally I'd muster some mildly irritated dad-grunt as acknowledgment that I'd heard her voice, as she's so accustomed to, especially in record stores. She sensed from a young age that record shopping was very important to me. I dragged her in her stroller to the flea market on 11th Street and Avenue A in sub-freezing temperatures in search of cheap, distressed Blue Notes and Prestiges. I also subjected her to the noise, stench, and all around depravity of the annual WFMU Record Fair. She knows that look in my eyes that says, "We're not going home anytime soon."

I lifted up my head and stared at the wall. "How do I know what I'm looking for?" I went back to looking at records. She had asked a probing philosophical question—one I'd never bothered to ask myself. She had interrupted my shopping.

A few minutes later, Emma pulled an LP out. "What about this?" It was a record by Philippe Bruneau. Giving it a quick once-over, I tabulated and itemized certain attributes that made the LP promising: I'd never heard of the artist, nor seen the record; the cover showed a gray-haired guy wearing a plaid shirt, holding an accordion; the record looked to be from the early '70s. 1973, to be exact. It had the original shrink-wrap on it with the original price sticker: $1.99. It also had a new price sticker on it: $1.99. (Adjusted for inflation, the record should have been $10.60.) It was on a reputable label, Philo; it had an air of authenticity emanating from the liner notes and song descriptions; it had spare instrumentation, listing only accordion, bass, and piano; the LP was in perfect condition.

The record was disappointing: on the commercial end of traditional French Canadian dance music, the sort of monotonous, cloyingly whimsical stuff you hear on a carousel, sans the barrel organ. The music makes me think of carousels, and carousels make me think of vomit. So, the record is bad. But it doesn't matter, because Emma did a very surprising thing. She tapped right into my aesthetic, presenting in one 12x12 square many of the attributes she sensed I'd be searching for.

Maybe you think it's bad parenting that I watched my kids' lips turn blue while I read the back-cover liner notes of an Ike Quebec LP, but I beg to differ. I was demonstrating to my kids that I *really* cared about something. My passion was certainly way more important than where their next snack was coming from.

My daughter Hazel was obsessed with Littlest Pet Shops for a couple of years. She had about a hundred of those things. It was her passion, and I wondered if she had picked up a collector gene from me. She would beg to go to Walgreens to get that special LPS she had never seen before. Her mom and I would often point out to her that she already had a lot of these; did she really need another? It was the same question my mom asked me when I hauled my entire record collection off to college. "Hell yes, I need all of these!"

You might say that's bad parenting too, that Hazel was spoiled. Yet I never hesitated to buy her LPSs, because, honestly, how much longer is she gonna want those fucking things? Besides, experts say free-form play with toys is great for developing creativity in the mind. She still likes to play with them at my house, although it hurt my heart a little when she recently told me that she never plays with them with her friends anymore—because she's too old.

Everything in life seems the result of randomness, chance encounters, and the unexpected. It's The Quest that makes collectors crazy in the head, whether it's stamps, LPs or LPSs. You go to the flea market because you never know what might be there, and the possibilities are infinite. As I sit here in San Francisco on this Saturday morning, I wonder what I'm missing over at Groove Yard, Groove Merchant, Grooves, Stranded, the Beat Museum, 1-2-3-4-Go!, Bird & Beckett, Mod Lang—and what about the former owner of Village Music who sells only on Saturdays in Mill Valley?—Amoeba x2, Aquarius, Rasputin x3, Streetlight, Recycled, Rooky Ricardo's, Alemany Flea, Alameda Flea, Dave's, Jack's, Walden Pond, Explorist International, Down Home, Red Devil, Vinyl Solution, Mill Valley Music, Green Apple Books, Book Bay in Fort Mason (where I found an original copy of the Art Farmer Quintet's *When Farmer Met Gryce* on Prestige for $6). Maybe I should drive up to Petaluma to the Thrifty Hippy. There's even what I consider the extreme-sports version of record shopping—more like an endurance test—at places like 101 Music in North Beach, with thousands of LPs down in that damp dungeon. You literally can't turn around, and you need a Hazmat suit, or at the very least, a dust mask. Think the West Coast equivalent of equally nasty the Thing in Brooklyn or Music Inn in NYC. I'm surprised they don't make you sign something before you walk in there. These are places where you're just as likely to contract histoplasmosis or dengue fever as you are to find some coveted private-press folk record.

A bit farther afield, there's Needle to the Groove in Fremont, near Niles (best known as the site of several Charlie Chaplin movie shoots), which has the largest selection of '70s major-label LPs I've never seen I've ever seen [sic]. There's even a not-for-profit record store in San Rafael: Bedrock Music & Video. The place is stuck in the '90s, with its plastic keepers on CDs and a VHS rental business. I recently went in there and found a Charlie Feathers LP, Mickey Newbury's *His Eye on the Sparrow* (no one does lonely like Mickey, and this may be his loneliest), and a Maddox Brothers & Rose LP, all for $9. I said, "How's business?" The guy said, "Slow to nonexistent, but we're a not-for-profit—that's the only way we stay open." The store is run by young adults, ages 18 to 28, through a local "emancipation" home, Four Winds West.

Oh, and there are the annual sales. The Record Man down in Redwood City has a parking lot sale in October—everything is $1. That's where I found the mega-rare Vanguard LP by '60s psychedelic band Elizabeth. I gave it to my buddy David Katznelson, cuz I knew he'd appreciate it more than me. Or the San Francisco Public Library Book Sale, which takes place in an airplane hangar at Fort Mason. Crabby old guys line up hours before the opening with big shopping carts and fill them up with $1 records, leaving nothing but Burl Ives LPs and *Flower Drum Song* soundtracks in their wake.

When I look at a map of the USA, I see record stores. I look at a state and think about the stores I've visited there, and how I can't wait to go back someday. Given how our world has changed since the '70s, when I was a kid, it's heartening to see so many of these points of light still beaming out across our nation. The soul and character of a city or town is reflected by the record store (and/or the bookstore), a central point of community for the culturally engaged. A place like Stereo Jack's in Cambridge, for example. The banter that goes down in there between the employees and customers is the musical equivalent of *Car Talk*, except much funnier. These places are oases in our increasingly alienating digital society.

At various times in my life, the record store has served as an escape hatch or safe harbor, a place to cut Hebrew school or cool out a domestic conflict. But mainly it's about The Quest: the bottomless pit of recorded music that awaits you in all its gloriously untidy randomness at the church sale or the garage sale; in the cardboard box next to a garbage can on Mercer Street, where I found an original mint copy of Bill Evans' *Waltz for Debby*; or at Val's Halla in Oak Park, where Ryley Walker discovered guitar maestro John Hulburt's unknown 1972 LP *Opus III*.

Chance visits to record stores have changed the trajectory of my work and life. Picking up a gospel compilation, *Life Is a Problem*, led to the release of four multi-disc black gospel sets on my label. When I worked for a major label, I bought a CD by a band I'd never heard of, Lamb of God. I was intrigued by the band's name and the album cover. I brought the band to the attention of the A&R guy who signed them, and they went on to sell millions of albums. I bought a record I'd never seen before by Bill Wilson—for a quarter—and wound up reissuing it. I walked into a store in San Diego in 2014 and walked out with the phone number of a local guy with a stash of old archival live tapes, which led to my releasing an unheard concert recording by old-time legend Roscoe Holcomb. So for me, the record store isn't just a place to idly dawdle. It's a place where magic can happen.

Emma asked, "How do you know what you're looking for?" I guess I've spent my whole life figuring that out. It's great that I still can't fully answer her question. In this book, I write about some stuff I've done in and around music over the past thirty years; records that I found or that found me; and records, people, and live music experiences that have forever changed the way I listen.

I hope you'll be inspired!

[r-l] Richard Dobson, Townes Van Zandt, Ron Davies
(Photo courtesy of Gail Davies)

Chapter 1:

Ron Davies

Ron Davies was born Ronny Wayne Dickerson on January 15, 1946, in Shreveport, Louisiana. His father, country singer Tex Dickerson, appeared on the *Louisiana Hayride* radio program. Ron grew up as the oldest of three children in Broken Bow, Oklahoma, until the age of seven, when his mother moved the family out to Bremerton, Washington, to escape her husband's abusive ways. She married a shipyard worker, Darby Davies, and the children took his surname.

Ron's younger sister, Gail Davies, an accomplished singer/ songwriter and producer based in Nashville, published her 482-page memoir, *The Last of the Outlaws: the Music & Memoirs of Gail Davies,* in 2010. She describes growing up in the abusive household in Oklahoma: "My brothers and I lived in what was the equivalent of a war zone. We witnessed bloodcurdling events that no child should ever see."

Gail and Ron sang together from an early age. Ron received a guitar for Christmas when he was eleven and, inspired by the Everly Brothers, he began to write and perform his own songs. He also studied the blues and classical guitar. "Self-expression without intrusion was the perfect answer for an introverted boy who just wanted to sit in his room and be left alone," Gail recalls in her book.

Even after the discord back in Broken Bow was over, there was plenty of upheaval. The family moved around Washington multiple times—Bremerton, Tacoma, Silverdale, Port Orchard, Gorst, Kitsap County, Port Townsend. Ron dropped out of high school and joined the Army at age 17, only to receive an Undesirable Discharge on the grounds of "emotional immaturity," having refused to yell "KILL" while running with a bayonet. He returned home to find that his 15-year-old girlfriend, Vicki Lynn La Force, was pregnant with his child. Back in the early '60s, an underage child could marry with parental consent in certain states, so Ron and Vicki crossed into Idaho and got hitched, amidst much turmoil on both sides of the aisle. Their first child, Desiree, was born in August, 1964, followed by another daughter, Michelle, in 1966.

The Pacific Northwest rock scene of the mid '60s was popping, with bands like the Sonics, the Ventures, and the Kingsmen drawing major label prospectors to the region. Gail brought her big brother to the attention of the Wailers, who formed in 1958 and are often credited as one of the earliest garage-rock bands. Ron would write ten songs for their 1966 United Artists album *Outburst*.

Gail and Ron recorded a session together in Tacoma that wound up on the desk of Frank Weber, owner of Trident Records in San Francisco, who then offered Ron a publishing deal. Soon thereafter, Weber sold his publishing outfit to Irving/Almo, a division of A&M Records. Jerry Moss, the "M" in A&M, signed Gail and Ron to a recording contract as a duo. However, Ron instead chose to record his first solo album with his wife Vicki on vocals. The resulting album, *Silent Song Through the Land*, was produced by Chad Stuart of pop duo Chad & Jeremy and released on A&M in 1970.

The album opens with "It Ain't Easy," but first, a gritty solo slide-guitar intro that was recorded separately—though it's not separately banded on the LP. Leon Russell plies the 88s, Jim Keltner lays down the kick drum, and Ron Davies' wily vocal comes over the top like some crazy old cracker emerging from his barn to chase you off his property. And when the groove kicks in, you hear a snare sound so impossibly in-the-pocket it makes your head swim.

It's all over so fast at only 2:29. You just want it to go on and on.

Instead, Davies immediately pours ice water over the red-hot coals with "What Life Must Be for Some," a plaintive solo acoustic ballad.

If you play acoustic guitar, you probably know the sensation of fingering a chord, using the body of the guitar as a percussion instrument, and then hearing that chord's echo ring out. I've never heard anyone do it on a record, but Davies employs this technique here and also on "The Clown." Hot session players offer accompaniment throughout: Larry Knechtel (organ), Doug Dillard (banjo), Merry Clayton (of "Gimme Shelter" fame), and Clydie King (backing vocals). There's a heavy gospel flavor to tunes like "Silent Song Through the Land," with its swelling organ and choir-charged arrangement. "Yesterday Is All I Want" is an intricately fingerpicked solo acoustic duet with Vicki Lynn.

What's remarkable about this song is the vulnerability in Davies' voice, almost like that of a frail old woman. Is this the same guy with all that cocky swagger on "It Ain't Easy"? As you dig deeper into his work, you find these personas are connected. "Open Road, the Open Sky" was written by a teenaged Davies about his mother, and a recurring theme of breaking free is delivered in his lyrics in a measured, Dylanesque cadence:

Do you recall all that you did

To the one who was closest at hand

The album closes with what we call a "burner" these days: the smoldering 6:05 "Lover and the Loved," which has all kinds of cool production choices, including a lo-fi solo piano intro that fades into a crisp, full-bodied band opening; a woozy, T. Rex–sounding chorus; an *Abbey Road* guitar lick; and a super-long fade at the end that clocks in at about a minute and a half.

After hearing "It Ain't Easy," you spend the rest of the album wondering where the unhinged funk has disappeared to. It's kind of a tease. It's hard not to wonder what would have happened had Davies recorded multiple songs in this vein, of this quality, on the debut. The material is a bit too stylistically scattered to have taken hold in the marketplace, but maybe it wouldn't have mattered. The album didn't sell. In fact, it's now hard to find copies of his two A&M LPs that aren't radio promo copies or cutouts.

There was more swampy funk to come on Davies' second album, *U.F.O.*, and he really excelled with these kinds of songs. He could also write a ballad. But the debut is uneven. With flashes of greatness, its charms rest in Davies' uniquely cracked vocals and his clear disinterest in "fixing" anything.

Davies found success in the early '70s when his songs were covered by Three Dog Night, Dobie Gray, Helen Reddy, and, most famously, David Bowie, who recorded a version of "It Ain't Easy" for his 1971 *Hunky Dory* album. The song eventually wound up on *The Rise and Fall of Ziggy Stardust and the Spiders from Mars*, released in 1972. It's unclear how Bowie came upon the song, although we can speculate that it may have been guitarist Mick Ronson who first heard Davies' album. The indelible ascending opening guitar line of the title track, "Silent Song Through the Land," is strikingly similar to that of Bowie's song "Andy Warhol" from *Hunky Dory*, a lick played by Ronson.

While he was glad someone of Bowie's stature was recording his song, Davies expressed displeasure with the star taking lyrical liberties with "It Ain't Easy." The last verse of Davies' version is a pretty vivid depiction of fellatio, which Bowie changed, presumably to make it more (ahem) palatable. Also, the song was credited to "R. Davies," leading some to mistakenly believe the Kinks' Ray Davies had composed it.

Davies co-produced his second A&M album, 1973's *U.F.O.*, with Tommy Vicari. Vicari gets the best out of Davies and some top-shelf session players, including soul singer Claudia Lennear (the inspiration for the Rolling Stones' "Brown Sugar"), Billy Preston, Andy Newmark, and even jazz trumpeter Harry "Sweets" Edison. This is a more full-blown, studio-conscious effort than the debut. They were really making a record this time. Although the production is a little overcooked in places, with its period string and horn arrangements, *U.F.O.* remains the best example of Davies' uncanny art.

"I Wonder" is an exuberant Leon Russell-type strut. Davies can't help but stuff a delightfully inscrutable lyric somewhere in the corner of almost every song:

I wonder just why it is you want a
Fancy progression and a ten-cent word

His excited chuckle mid-song is one of the greatest recorded laughs in rock and roll history. "Long Hard Climb," one of several songs written for Vicki, veers close to MOR territory, but it is delivered convincingly, with its lilting string arrangement and electric piano. The song was later recorded by Maria Muldaur and again by Helen Reddy. "Flapjack" is like a cross between a Muscle Shoals workout and Harry Nilsson's "Coconut." Davies tosses in a line from the Rolling Stones' "I Just Want to See His Face" off their then-new release *Exile on Main Street*—"Don't wanna walk and talk about Jack, just wanna see his face"—swapping "Jesus" for "Jack" during the vamp at the end. Side One closes with a faithful cover of Tim Hardin's "Misty Roses." Davies had been introduced to Hardin by Frank Weber, and considered Hardin a friend and mentor, according to Gail.

U.F.O. keeps coming at you on Side Two with "It's a Lie," another gospel-tinged tune. A down-home backbeat with soul singers—this is Ron's best turf, and where he ultimately sets himself apart from his '70s singer/songwriter peers. Saints and sinners collide as Ron trades verses with Claudia Lennear and the other background singers:

It's a lie, well it's a dirty lie
It's a goddamn dirty lie

And then:

It's the truth, well it's the gospel truth
Well it's God's own gospel truth

Interesting that the printed lyrics in the gatefold say "*the* God's own gospel truth," but Ron drops the "the" when he sings it. I wish Ron were here so I could ask him about his intent. Either way, it's powerful, rousing, playful, and searching. Davies was no Bible thumper, but he was definitely diving into fire-and-brimstone with these lyrics. He must have been pretty enamored with "I Just Want to See His Face," because he references it once again as he sings these words with the same meter as the original:

Well, all your friends may walk and talk about you

His Okie and Louisiana roots shine on these tunes. This is lowdowndirty Southern music with an LA-studio-setting vibe. "Can I Count on You" is a gorgeous duet with Vicki Lynn featuring some unorthodox chord changes. Somebody needs to cover it! The neat thing about *U.F.O.* is, you get all this good stuff plus a new version of "It Ain't Easy"—and a very good one at that. It doesn't stray too far from the original—minus the bottleneck intro, with some keys added, harmonica, and perhaps the sacrifice of some of the primal bite for a rounder sound. Still damn good though. Why they re-recorded the song, we don't know. It's not like the new recording sounds like a radio-friendly hit, but apparently Ron wanted another crack at the song.

"Lay Down Your Burden" is a close cousin to "Long Hard Climb," a romantic piano ballad with sweeping strings, churchy organ parts, and soul-stirring backing vocals. "Shadows" is one of the most interesting songs in Ron's repertoire. There's the Leon Russell influence for sure in the vocal and piano comping, but then the strings and gospel shrieks commence, random shards of electric guitar rain down, and the song achieves a weird, evocative levitation—kind of like the aural equivalent of that round, rumpled brown hat hurtling through the desert dusk on the LP cover.

Although *U.F.O.* didn't burn up the charts, Davies had attained a modicum of success as a songwriter. By 1973, he was drinking and drugging excessively. Although Gail described him to me as "terminally shy and introverted" and "a complicated individual," Davies was also a serial ladies' man, always motivated by the conquest. Buckling under the pressure of show business, infidelity, and substance abuse, Ron and Vicki Lynn split after twelve years of marriage.

Gram Parsons and Davies wrote songs together that have never seen the light of day, according to Gail. "He and Ronny had a mutual admiration for the songwriting talents of Boudleaux and Felice Bryant," Gail recounts in her book, recalling that Gram taught Ronny the chords to "Sleepless Nights." The photo inside the gatefold LP of *U.F.O.* shows Ron leaning on a big rock out at Joshua Tree. The photographer is Jim McCrary (1939–2012), A&M Records' in-house photographer at the time, who also photographed Gram Parsons extensively. Were they all hanging out together in the desert during this shoot around 1972? Gram may have also provided the inspiration for Davies' *U.F.O.* album title, having starred in an unreleased lost movie about extra-terrestrials, *Saturation 70*, filmed at Giant Rock near Joshua Tree during a UFO convention in 1969.

Davies' demons did not prevent him from making some more good music in the '70s. *I Don't Believe It* was released on the First American label in 1978. Charting a similar formula as the first two albums, there are rollicking tunes like the title track and countrified laments such as "Good Old Song," co-written by Mentor Williams, composer of "Drift Away," which Dobie Gray turned into a hit. Gray would go on to cover "Good Old Song" as well.

There are also two co-writes with Barry Goldberg on the LP. Like many other independent records made in 1978, the production on *I Don't Believe It* is flat and unimaginative (the bass player was also the producer), but the material is solid and the vocals somewhat restrained, yet still affecting. The album does yield one stone classic, "Laughing Into Love," a plainspoken breakup song if there ever was one. Someone should have told Elton John about this one in 1978! Everyone would have made a lot of money. It's not too late, Elton!

> *Oh, it's such a drag*
>
> *All our foolish pride*
>
> *We go laughing into love*
>
> *Just to come crying out the other side*

By the mid '80s, Davies was done with LA. The money was gone, and he wasn't receiving steady publishing residuals like he should have. He was working odd construction jobs and drinking. It was time for a change, so Gail flew Ron out to Nashville.

Multi-instrumentalist Chris Scruggs was raised by Gail Davies after a paternity battle with Chris's father, Gary Scruggs, went nowhere. Gary Scruggs is the eldest son of bluegrass legend Earl Scruggs of Flatt & Scruggs fame. "On a daily basis, people say 'Scruggs!'" Chris told me. "They want to know all about that, but I had no connection to the Scruggs side." His uncle Ron lived in a funky apartment about five minutes away in Nashville's Hillsborough Village.

"Ron was a cool, bohemian songwriter, really deep, read a lot of poetry, a cosmic kind of guy. He was painfully shy, would self-medicate with alcohol," Chris said. One of Davies' local pals at the time was Townes Van Zandt. Chris fondly remembers going to lunch at Bogies in Lionhead with his Uncle Ron, Townes, and one of Townes' kids.

Davies would later write "So Long Old Friend" for Townes after his death from a heart attack at age 52 in Smyrna, Tennessee, on January 1, 1997. In that song, Davies expressed what a lot of folks were thinking at the time—they were surprised the great songwriter had lived as long as he had:

I close my eyes and hear your song
And I'm surprised you stayed so long
When your heart was so gone
Around the bend

Most telling is how Townes' death prompted Davies to lay bare his own mortality, knowing he was being sucked into the same self-destructive undertow:

I could see the other side when I would look into your eyes
And then I knew I would see you again

And then:

So for now, so long, old friend
Not for long, old friend

Gail brokered a publishing deal for Davies with Cedarwood in Nashville, so he began to focus on songwriting, with minimal returns. Chris explains, "Ron wrote beyond what country music wanted. He grew up on Everly Brothers melodies, not typical 1/4/5 country songs. He was always writing for himself, as an artist. He poured himself into everything he did." Chris also marvels at his uncle's guitar technique. "He would really incorporate guitar into the song. You know, so many singer/songwriters, it's goddamn boring, but Ron was the opposite. He was big into fingerstyle. When you heard him play guitar in the kitchen, it would be a full arrangement, you know, a descending E with this melodic thing rising up ..." The performances Chris alludes to are collected on *The Kitchen Tapes*, an album of demos from the '80s and early '90s so intimate that Chris says he can "smell the cigarettes and mouthwash on [Davies'] breath." The impossibly gorgeous "Up in the Canyon," with its delicate fingerpicking, is among Davies' best. Most of these tunes were written about Davies' girlfriend at the time, Kathy Lee.

Davies was struggling in Nashville and felt like a failure. His deal with Warner/Chappell had expired, and he was having trouble getting signed elsewhere. He was destitute and resorted to borrowing money from his mother. His six-year relationship with Kathy Lee was ending. In 1993, he wrote in a letter to her:

> More than anyone else, you know how hard I have worked writing, typing lyrics and labels, recording, and pitching my songs; making hundreds of tapes for publishers, producers, and A&R people; and all of the rejections I have incurred time after time. You have no idea how frustrating and confusing it is to arrive at this point in life, jobless, broke, and confidence shattered at forty-six.

Davies went on to marry Therese Holguin, who, according to his daughter Desiree, was the major love of his life after her mother, Vicki Lynn. He worked odd jobs as a house inspector and as manager of an airport car rental location. In 2001, word got around to Dolly Parton's sister that Ron was looking for work. Dolly needed some help with spring cleaning at her house, and Ron was asked to come out. While working on her house, he fell off a ladder, shattering his hip. Dolly offered to pay his hospital bill, but he was covered through his wife's insurance. Dolly insisted on getting him an insurance settlement, and he would use this money to record his final album, *Where Does the Time Go*, in 2003. After recovering from the accident, Gail took Davies on his first overseas trip ever to the UK for a tour in February 2002. He was taken aback by the warm response, and found that many folks knew his work. He signed CDs for fans: "It still ain't easy – Ron Davies."

With his health deteriorating, Davies refused to make the lifestyle changes necessary to extend his stay on the planet, and on October 30, 2003, Ron Davies passed away from a heart attack in Nashville at the age of 57. In her book, Gail describes her brother's death as a "long, slow suicide." After his death, a routine audit by his estate uncovered $78,000 in unclaimed royalties.

Gail produced an album in loving memory of her brother in 2013: *Unsung Hero: a Tribute to the Music of Ron Davies*, featuring Dolly Parton, John Prine, Vince Gill, Guy Clark, Shelby Lynne, and others.

Davies' songs may not be as iconic as those of his tragic contemporaries and pals Tim Hardin, Gram Parsons, and Townes Van Zandt. But he deserves a seat at the table next to them. He was a damn great songwriter, and I'll stand on Steve Earle's coffee table in my Blundstones and say that. Poetic, searching, and quirky—at turns muscular and confessional—Davies actually made different music than those guys. There was a hoodoo in the uptempo songs, a natural looseness. He was able to take a pithy line and turn it into something conceptually complex. Hank Williams was very, very good at this; so was Ron Davies. To wit, "Tie It in a Knot," from his final album:

> *When a wolf is at the door*
> *And the window's full of snow*
> *And you wonder what it's all for*
> *And you're weary in your soul*
>
> *In the end, out of hope*
> *At the end of your rope*
> *You tie it in a knot and take ahold*
> *Hold on and don't let go*

Tia Blake in Paris, 1970
(Photo courtesy Tia Blake)

Chapter 2:

Tia Blake

Tia Blake's lone album with her "folk group," *Folksongs & Ballads*, was released in 1971 on a tiny French label, Société Française De Productions Phonographiques (SFP), and reissued on CD by the Water label in 2011. I had never heard of her until I saw the album on Water's release schedule, and I had to wait many more months for the album to come out. Having heard some songs on YouTube, I got impatient and bought the original LP online for more money than I'm used to paying for a record. But of course, it was well worth it.

Despite the heroic efforts of producer Ian Hetzner to make the reissue a reality, the new version met with about as much fanfare as the original had decades earlier. Which is to say, none. A shame, because I believe it is absolutely one of the greatest folk albums of the '70s, or of any era.

Tia Blake was born Christiana Elizabeth Wallman in Georgia in 1952, one of six children. Her father worked for the federal government, and her mother, Joan, would later open the renowned Double Hook Bookstore in Montreal. Tia graduated from Smith College and spent most of her life as a writer, publishing a story about Saigon in a 2006 issue of *Granta* and co-writing a play with her mother, which was performed at the 2007 New York Fringe Festival.

Tia tells of her journey from New York to Paris in the liner notes of the 2011 Water reissue CD. Upon graduating from high school in 1970, she took a publishing job in New York City and befriended some actors who crowed about their recent trip to Paris and London. "Jack (one of the actors) told me to read Hemingway's *A Moveable Feast*, and so I got it in my head that I had to go. I quit my job at Farrar, Straus and Giroux with sixty dollars cash and a cheap Icelandic Air one-way fare to Paris in my pocket." A friend of Tia's called her contacts in Paris and told them Tia was en route. One of them was Sicilian folk singer Benito Merlino, who would produce Tia's album. The chance circumstances of the recording session, coupled with Tia's innocence and lack of performing or recording experience, make for a remarkable study. How many albums of this caliber result from someone largely untrained, inexperienced, and innocent at 18 walking into the studio to make such magnificent music?

First, there is the voice: a poised, distant cool that today's female neo-folk singers so often aspire to. Tia had it in spades. There are no shrill *Mighty Wind* pretenses in the vocals, so prevalent in the folk scene of her day. Her voice has about as much in common with Judy Collins or Joan Baez as it does with Ronnie James Dio. The closest comparison I can draw is Nico, who comes off as cold and distant, but whose voice also wields immense emotional power. Tia's is a quiet, controlled, stoic, defiant voice, and although she claims it was a voice filled with abject terror vis-à-vis the recording process, all I hear is strength. It is steely, feminine, and about as willful and defiant as Joan of Arc.

The accompaniment is spare, acoustic, gently countrified in places, and wholly supportive of Tia's voice, front and center. The choice of material is so well suited for her style—mostly songs she had sung from a very young age. The album features a few jauntier tunes, but its true highlights are the haunting songs of murder, heartbreak, betrayal, and war all deftly disguised as lullabies.

"Man of Constant Sorrow," a folk song of possibly Irish origin that's "two or three hundred years old," according to Ralph Stanley, was recorded by Emry Arthur in 1928, by the Stanley Brothers in 1951, by Bob Dylan in 1961, and by Tia Blake in 1970, long before it became a hip thing for Ralph Stanley to sing again on the *O Brother Where Art Thou* soundtrack.

"Hangman" is a traditional English song with many variants, including "Gallows Pole," popularized by Led Zeppelin. However, Tia's version sounds nothing like the scads of versions recorded during the period by Odetta, Jean Ritchie, or whomever.

"Rising of the Moon" is a political folk song dealing with the Irish Rebellion of 1798. A version appeared on Peter, Paul, and Mary's 1965 album *See What Tomorrow Brings*, which also contains "Betty and Dupree" and "Hangman," so perhaps that album was top of mind at the time of Tia's recording session.

Listening, you get the sense that Tia could sing anything in the traditional folk canon, and for a long time to come. Alas, this is her only album. Yet, as I told her, she didn't need to make another record. Her version of the English ballad "Turtle Dove," sometimes performed as "10,000 Miles," deserves its rightful place next to Sandy Denny's "Blackwaterside," Anne Briggs' "My Bonny Boy," or any classic you'd care to mention by your favorite female folk singer.

The following is an interview I conducted with Tia Blake on my radio show on KZSU at Stanford University in Stanford, California, on May 8, 2012. It was her second interview ever and her first in 43 years. You can listen to the interview on SoundCloud.

JR: You grew up in North Carolina with five brothers and sisters who sang together, but not professionally. In 1970, at age 18, with $60 in your pocket, you fly to Paris; meet Benito Merlino, who teaches you to play guitar, which you didn't know how to do; and he hooks you up with the SFP label. Is this a real story?

TB: It's a real story! The times were so different in many respects, and this could happen then. I don't know that it could happen now. It was very relaxed. When I first went to Paris, I had Benito's name because I had a friend in NYC who was the nanny of an Irish couple, and she had lived in Paris the previous year. Benito's name was the only one I had in Paris.

I flew to Paris for $100 and found a wonderful hotel on the West Bank that was $5 a night. I called Benito; it was his birthday. We fell in love. I don't think that happens very often—it was very quick! I remember leaving Paris—I was so poor and hungry, we didn't live together—and when I came back he said, "I want to try and keep you here; can you sing?"

He owned a record store. He was a Sicilian folksinger and had produced other people's records. I played a little guitar, not a lot. I sang for him, and he said, "That's beautiful; let me call this friend of mine." That's how it happened. "Maybe if she can make a record, she can do a concert and she can stay in Paris."

JR: Quiet, stark, and haunting. A lot of the songs that you chose in terms of repertoire are from the British Isles. To me, this is not folk with a capital "F," like a lot of music being made in this time period was—Peter, Paul, and Mary, for instance. This is more in the direction of the spare, darker sounds of Bert Jansch or Anne Briggs, more from that tradition. I'm curious to know what you were listening to and what inspired you to sing the way you sing.

TB: I was actually thinking about that, because I was trying to think about who I listened to, and you kind of described it. Do you remember the old film *A Tree Grows in Brooklyn*? Well, Paul Dunn sings "Annie Laurie" in a tenement apartment to his two children at the piano. It's absolutely beautiful. It's just bare piano. That and Isobel Baillie, an English soprano. Very light, clear voice. We used to listen to her sing parts of "Messiah." I know these things seem unconnected, but the one quality was there was something raw and authentic and, I should say, kind of sad.

JR: The material—there are lighthearted moments on the

record, but even when you're singing the lighthearted songs, you're still in the same zone. (Tia laughs.) There's something stoic about your delivery of a murder ballad, almost detached in a way, and that makes it more powerful.

TB: I hope I don't reveal too much, but in the studio for those two days, although I always sang that way, I never sang any differently. I remember waiting all day for some kind of sign. There were three or four of us in the studio. Nobody talked too much—very sweet guys, but we were all very shy. I remember the feeling of hoping it was OK; we were just sort of marching through these songs. The guy recording it said, "Come on, come on, we gotta get on to the next one."

I think I always sang like that. I always felt the songs were sad; that was the undercurrent.

JR: A lot of the songs that you chose for this album are in the folk tradition. Irish, Canadian ballads like "Betty and Dupree." Some of them have been covered, but they're not the most popular songs. Some of them are actually quite obscure, especially for the time. So how did you go about selecting the repertoire for the album?

TB: Francois [Brigot, who plays guitar and sings on the album] and I sat for hour after hour. I can't remember who came up with which, but most of these songs I remember singing as a very young child. I don't even know where I first heard the songs, to tell you the truth.

JR: When I was researching the songs, I was surprised to see that "Plastic Jesus" was co-written by George Cromarty. He made two incredible solo guitar records, one on his own label out of Morro Bay and one for George Winston's label. The song was originally on the Gold Coast Singers album in 1957. Do you remember how it came to you? (Paul Newman sings the song in the 1967 movie *Cool Hand Luke*.)

TB: I have no idea where it came from. My younger brother, who used to sing all the time—I think this is one of the songs he used to sing. I don't know where he got it. And "Yellow Gal" by Lead

Belly—my brother used to sing that all the time. They didn't know anything about "Plastic Jesus" in Paris. I just remember saying, "Oh, let's sing this one."

JR: In the notes, you talk about a concert you performed on March 29, 1972, shortly before you left Paris for the very last time. There's a flyer for the show inside the package. And you said you got a standing ovation for singing "Plastic Jesus." Can you tell me about your upbringing? What was the musical environment like?

TB: As kids, we all sang in the church choir. We weren't particularly religious, but we loved to sing in church in a small town in North Carolina. We assumed we would all be singers, but it didn't really turn out that way. We went in a talent show—we were really young—when I was about seven. We hoped to win a big scholarship to Juilliard, but of course it didn't happen. We used to scheme about how we were all gonna get money to go off to these great schools.

JR: At this point in your life, it must be interesting to you to see the album back in circulation. Have you ever been interviewed?

TB: Only once, when the album first came out. It's such an honor. I can't believe anyone's interested. I'm just amazed.

JR: As more people hear this record, I have a feeling you will be interviewed more, Tia. Is it a heady thing to revisit that part of your life?

TB: I had sort of put it aside when I left. I was living in Montreal at the time and just sort of put it away. I never heard the record when I was in Paris. It wasn't ready before I left, so the record was mailed to me. I think I listened to it once with all my friends, and then I put it away. I had not listened to it in years. The two songs I had recorded at the CBC in 1976, I had completely forgot about them.

JR: The 1976 CBC recordings—the story in the album notes is that you were living in Montreal and heard about an invitation from the CBC for songs?

TB: I think I heard about it through a friend. I did quietly sort of begin to write songs. I thought, "Oh great, I'll see if [the CBC programmer] wants to record them and play them in his broadcast over the radio." He let me record them but, he said, "You can have the tapes; I'm not interested."

JR: When you put out the record on SFP, did you have the notion that you would be a recording artist and make lots of records? Or that this was a one-off, and that's not what you wanted to do with your life?

TB: I didn't enjoy performing in front of the public. I guess I was very shy. But I loved music and I did want to write it, and thought I'd continue to write it. I didn't have much business sense. Like, how do you sell a song? So I just continued to play and sing, but only for my friends.

JR: Well, Tia, as far as I'm concerned, you never had to do another thing, because this album is a shining classic.

TB: Aww.

JR: So you're sitting at home and someone calls and says, "We wanna reissue your album." How did that all come together?

TB: I have to say, Ian Hetzner was so nice and so patient with me, because when he first called I said, "No, no, I really don't want to do this." I just sort of ran. And he persisted and persisted, and he was so nice, and now I'm just so happy that he did it, but I was very reluctant at first. It brought up a lot of memories that were ... Paris was ... I guess ... Paris is beautiful, and it was also difficult. And I just wanted to push everything aside, but I'm so glad he went ahead and ignored me and did it. Or persisted, I should say; he didn't ignore me, he kept on.

JR: I'm glad he did too. Thanks for doing your first interview in 43 years.

●　●　●　●　●

I reached out to Tia in November of 2014 requesting any unpublished photos from her Paris days to use in this book, which she graciously sent me, and you will find one along with this chapter.

She told me that she was very ill with cancer at the time.

Tia Blake died of breast cancer on June 17, 2015, in Pinehurst, North Carolina, age 63. She is buried next to her two brothers, Chris and Peter, in North Hatley, Quebec, Canada. Her recordings, photographs, and original compositions are stored at the Southern Folk Life Collection, UNC Chapel Hill.

As I told her in our last email exchange, her legacy is secure. People will continue to discover her album. I feel so fortunate to have had the chance to speak with her. And to share her music with my daughters, who love her too.

Chapter 3:

Raccoon Records

The drive from San Francisco to Inverness is among the most beautiful in all of the Bay Area. Hugging the shimmering Tomales Bay as you pass through Point Reyes Station heading north on Highway 1, you can feel the city melt away in your rearview mirror. In this age of rampant development, you also marvel at how untouched everything is.

Maybe I shouldn't be writing about this. Ah well, it's too late. A one-bedroom house in Inverness goes for about $800,000.

A former fishing village, Inverness became a popular outpost for UC Berkeley professors in the '60s and '70s. Today, locals estimate that half of the roughly 700 homes in Inverness are occupied year-round. The rest are summer homes or weekend retreats owned by wealthy folk who use them infrequently, which some say undermines the long-standing community spirit of the tiny town.

Inverness was home base for the Youngbloods, led by Jesse Colin Young and best known for their 1967 single "Get Together." Everyone associates that song with the Summer of Love, yet it peaked at only 62 on the Billboard chart when it was first released. It wasn't until it was used as a music bed for radio promos and commercials that it became a #5 smash in October 1969.

The song was written by Dino Valente (Quicksilver Messenger

Studio B – where it all went down

Service), and performed and recorded by a host of artists, including Judy Collins, Jefferson Airplane, and the Kingston Trio, before the Youngbloods got a hold of it. Valente sold his publishing rights to the song to Kingston Trio manager Frank Weber to raise money for his legal defense after a drug bust in 1966. Valente's self-titled 1968 Epic album, reissued on vinyl by Tompkins Square in 2012, remains a crowning example of abstract, cosmic, quintessentially Bay Area '60s psychedelic folk.

It's easy to romanticize the '60s, especially if you didn't experience them. Talk to folks who lived through that era in San Francisco and you'll hear horror stories about how the Summer of Love gave way to Altamont and hard drugs, turning the whole groovy scene into a chaotic mess. When I moved here in 2011 from New York City, I left my Television and Suicide records in storage and made sure all my Dead and Airplane LPs came with me.

I'm always seeking out the soul of the city, especially as it relates to its music history. That's why I reissued the Dino Valente record. It's also why I reissued mysterious Mendocino fiddler Smoke Dawson's only LP. It was a very personal and deliberate process, my way of connecting with my adoptive city, of tapping into a lost era that I try to conjure—yes, romanticize—and seek to commune with.

I sought out the church in San Anselmo pictured on the cover of Van Morrison's *Saint Dominic's Preview*, an album rife with Bay Area references. I stood outside the shuttered Record Plant in Sausalito where the Dead cut *Wake of the Flood*. I went to Sweetwater Music Hall, where Bob Weir was seated in sandals and shorts watching a basketball game on a large flat-screen television. I saw Phil Lesh play at his club, Terrapin Crossroads. Waiting for the restroom moments before show time, I turned around, and there was Phil, standing in line a couple of heads back. I let him cut me. I hung out at the Phoenix, formerly the Travelodge, where Duane Allman once jumped into the swimming pool from the second floor. I drove up Bear Gulch Road by Neil Young's ranch in La Honda, the same town where Ken Kesey lived and hung out with his Merry

Pranksters. I saw Phosphorescent at the Fillmore, wondering what it might have been like to see Moby Grape, the United States of America, and the Hour Glass there on May 4, 1968. I went to the Regency (formerly the Avalon) to see Beth Orton, imagining Captain Beefheart on that stage. I hung out with Dino Valente's son and a bunch of Dino's old friends. I went to a reading by original Beat poet and Serpent Power band member David Meltzer. I hung out with Jerry Garcia's daughter, Trixie, at Jerry Night at AT&T Park, and chatted with Mountain Girl backstage at Warren Haynes' Jerry Garcia Symphonic Celebration at Bill Graham Civic Auditorium. Waiting outside the dressing room at the Fillmore to meet Jorma Kaukonen, I found myself on a couch next to Wavy Gravy, who proudly showed me his Emergency Inflatable Rubber Chicken in a can.

In 1989 and 1990, I saw the Grateful Dead in Oakland a couple of times. I remember spotting Bill Graham at the side of the stage. There was still a living, breathing subculture: the parking lot scene, the ever-hopeful ticket seekers outside with one finger up—"I need a miracle!" These were authentic Deadheads, not yuppies or weekend Deadheads getting dressed up (or down) for the show. Those people were still living the culture. That's Dead. Yes, other bands have tried to fill the void for the remaining faithful, but it's not the same.

I guess one place where the old spirit still lives is Hardly Strictly Bluegrass, the annual free concert in Golden Gate Park. The city's great roots-music tradition is given the full-blown festival treatment. I've seen Ralph Stanley, the Flatlanders, Emmylou Harris, Kinky Friedman, Richard Thompson, Sharon Van Etten, Mavis Staples, Lucinda Williams. Hundreds of thousands of people come to the park and experience the festival. The crowd is almost uniformly mellow and civilized.

Even with the backdrop of gentrification and moneyed elite taking over the city, San Francisco still has a music tradition. It's fading, but it shows itself in certain ways. I listen for it on Miles Davis' *Live at the Blackhawk*; on Archie Shepp's *Live in San Francisco*; on the uncirculated 1973 Grunt label LP *Getting' Plenty*, by Kaukonen discovery Richmond "Steve" Talbott (featuring members of Grootna and Goose Creek Symphony); on any number of Arhoolie Records LPs recorded in the Bay Area; on a 1969 Columbia album by Gale Garnett and the Gentle Reign, *Sausalito Heliport* (which I acquired from Jello Biafra's personal record collection). The Heliport was a popular rehearsal space. The Dead used it and even played a public show there on October 15, 1966. Eric Clapton and Jerry Garcia were photographed there together by Jim Marshall on March 10, 1968.

From the Garnett liner notes:

> There isn't a musician, singer, or groupie in the San Francisco Bay area who doesn't know the Sausalito Heliport ... There are no egos at the Heliport—all the bands help each other. Mike Bloomfield gives guitar lessons to the Ace of Cups; the Buddy Miles Express borrows the Quicksilver's studio; Clapton, Dino Valente, Elvin Bishop, David Crosby, and Procol Harum will sit in and jam with every and anybody.

The Raccoon Records story is a Bay Area story, the kind I revel in, with a local backdrop and a small, obscure catalog of unheard music ripe for rediscovery. Residing 75 minutes north of San Francisco, the Youngbloods were geographically separated from the city's music scene, but also steadfastly and deliberately removed from its inner workings. The outlier music they created in Inverness reflects this.

Indeed, the band did not carouse with the Dead, nor hang out at 2400 Fulton Street with the Airplane. Incredibly, the Youngbloods' Banana (guitar, keys) had never even met Jorma Kaukonen until January 2015. If the band had a gig in SF, they'd arrive an hour before the show, play, then head north right after the show, navigating the dark, yet-to-be-paved roads leading back to their idyllic hideaways.

The Youngbloods were pioneers, carving out a hip scene in unpopulated West Marin. Drummer Joe Bauer's brother John lived in Olema, which led the other band members to rent and eventually buy homes in the area. Soon, other musicians followed them up north: the Airplane got a house in Bolinas, and the Dead holed up to rehearse for a time in Point Reyes in the early '70s. Ramblin' Jack Elliott still lives in the area. I was talking with Jack on the phone about various places in California. He said, "Well, you know—elevation minus population equals the speed limit." "Did you just make that up?" "Yeah." Typical quirky West Marin old-timer humor.

The Youngbloods came out of the West Village and Cambridge, Massachusetts, folk scenes of the mid '60s, signing with RCA Records and releasing several moderately successful albums. Around 1970, they used their massive hit single "Get Together" to leverage a new record deal with Warner Brothers. The deal was negotiated between the Youngbloods' business manager Stuart Kutchins, former road manager for the band who followed them out West, and Warner Brothers A&R chief Joe Smith.

The legacy of Mo Ostin and Joe Smith's Warner Brothers in the late '60s/early '70s is indelible in rock history, boasting a roster of Jimi Hendrix, Grateful Dead, Van Dyke Parks, Randy Newman, Ry Cooder, Neil Young, Gram Parsons, Frank Zappa, Captain Beefheart, and on and on. With a giant hit in his back pocket, Kutchins worked out a production deal for the Youngbloods that promised them a much higher royalty rate than the standard record deal of the day. It also gave them creative control over their own production and allowed for several albums per year of in-house projects on their own imprint, Raccoon. There were also two recording studios: Studio B behind Banana's house and Studio A on Jesse's property. Kutchins told me, "I was very up front with Smith that having huge popular success was not important. I think they didn't believe me. The deal was built on considerable naïveté on both sides." Warner Brothers would have no idea what they were in for.

I didn't know much about Raccoon when I first heard Jeffrey Cain in guitarist Daniel Bachman's car in 2013. I had seen those round "The Youngbloods Present" logo stickers on High Country and Michael Hurley LPs in used record shops. Dan and I were on a road trip together across the US, and he would play "Saw a Man" from Cain's first album, *For You,* over and over. I was really into the openhearted voice, the solid country-rock trappings, the sneaky bass line courtesy of Rick Turner (now a builder of guitars, basses, and ukuleles). If that bass line were a pitch, it would be a filthy slider. The song is mellow gold. I found Cain's first album in Boise, Idaho, on our trip, and then his second one, *Whispering Thunder,* in North Carolina.

There's very little information about Cain online, an artist for whom there is no *All Music Guide* bio, no Wikipedia page. So I endeavored to talk with people who knew, played, and lived with him.

Jeffrey Cain Stevens was from the DC area, one of three boys. Cain was his mother's maiden name. His father was a literature professor, and his mother died young from Huntington's Disease, the same hereditary disease that Woody Guthrie succumbed to. Hal Singer, a founding member of Asleep at the Wheel, knew Jeffrey's younger brother Ned growing up, then came to know Jeff. Hal played bass with guitarist and mutual friend Eddy Ottenstein in high school. When Cain invited Eddy out West to play on his debut album, Hal quit Asleep at the Wheel and followed Eddy out.

"I lived up the hill from Jeff in San Rafael," Hal told me from his home in Virginia. "It was the music scene in 1971. The guys in Southern Comfort were around, Steve Miller. Eddy hung out with Lee Charlton, a longtime associate of Mose Allison. Lee lived next door to Van Morrison in Fairfax." Charlton played drums on Van's "Almost Independence Day" from *Saint Dominic's Preview.* "That's how Eddy met Van, went on the road with Van for about a year and a half," Hal recalls. "Jeff was a sweet guy, sunshine and light. He wasn't a hard druggy. Perfect for California at the time."

Eddy is pictured on the back cover of *For You,* along with Cain's first wife, and plays guitar on both Cain LPs. He lived in Inverness for twenty years, and recorded and played live with Jesse Colin

Young in the early '70s. Ottenstein died in a car crash in Mendocino County in 2004 at the age of 55.

Stuart Kutchins handled the Youngbloods' business affairs and was also Cain's manager. "Jerry Corbitt [of the Youngbloods] introduced us," Stuart told me. "Jeffrey was a prodigy; he sprung full blossom out of the universe. He was an amazingly charming, sweet, friendly, warm-hearted guy."

Although the Raccoon deal was already in place, Kutchins attempted to have Jeff signed directly to Warner Brothers, thinking this might give Jeff his best opportunity. He arranged for Jeff to play a song for Joe Smith in his office at Warner Brothers HQ. "Jeff played him 'Not I the Seed' (from For You) and it sort of blew Joe out of his seat. He had to get up and move around. The song had this tremendous intensity. It wasn't unpleasant at all, and Joe was good-natured about it, but it was just too much. Joe was very grounded and poised, but the song blew him out of the room. Afterward, Joe told me 'He's your artist—sign him to Raccoon.'" Stuart surmised that Joe found him too folky or intense, but in the main, Stuart's impression was that Smith probably felt he couldn't do anything with Jeff.

Susan Deixler was new in town, working for a baker who baked bread to order. The Youngbloods' bookkeeper ordered some bread, and when Susan delivered it, she mentioned she was looking for full-time work. She interviewed and landed a job in the Youngbloods' Point Reyes Station headquarters around 1969.

Susan knew a little something about the music business, having been married briefly to her high school sweetheart, Barry Manilow, back in her hometown of Brooklyn, New York. Jeffrey Cain lived in her house for two years. Most of the songs for his second album were written on her piano. "It was a joyful time, there was a real feeling of independence. Most everyone was doing something, except for Jesse. LSD, mushrooms, exploring cosmic consciousness. They all decided together what they wanted to put out," she says, describing the holistic Raccoon label philosophy. "Jeff was brilliant, high-energy, deep thinking; he took social issues to heart."

These qualities are evident on Cain's debut, which addresses political injustice ("Mr. Governor"), racial inequality ("Color Blind"), and many lyrical paeans to nature. Deixler recalls an unrecorded Cain song, "Love Is Blind," that Janis Joplin heard at one of his gigs in 1969 or early 1970 and wanted to record. She wanted him to sign over the publishing rights for the song, but he refused. Susan describes a dark side of Jeff, who struggled with alcohol dependence. She remembers a song he wrote, "Double A"— also not recorded—which extolled the virtues of recovery.

For You, featuring the Youngbloods' Young, Bauer, and Banana, along with Eddy Ottenstein, Scott Lawrence, and album producer Rick Turner, was released in 1970 as Raccoon #2 (#1 was the Youngbloods' live album *Rock Festival*, released that same year). Earnest acoustic singer/songwriter fare like "Heavenly Blue" and the title track were Cain's wheelhouse, but he also had a penchant for playful, borderline novelty songs like "Houndog Turkey." Which helps explain why Raccoon label-mate and legendary folksinger Michael Hurley and Cain were such good buds. "I sold him a car, repaired the motor," Hurley recalls. "He was a very nice guy; we all liked his songs. In '72, when we were making my album *Hi Fi Snock Uptown*, we hung out a lot." Hurley learned an unrecorded song, "Long Lost Mind," by watching one of Cain's gigs in Point Reyes. He asked Cain what that song was and wrote down the lyrics. Hurley sang it to me over the phone, accompanying himself on guitar.

The structure of the Raccoon deal didn't require any promotion on the part of Warner Brothers, and Raccoon had no such in-house resources at its disposal. Jeff played dates with the Youngbloods and appeared on local bills with Boz Scaggs, Joy of Cooking, and Dan Hicks. But there was little recognition or any kind of traction for the album. Cain's second album, *Whispering Thunder* (Raccoon #12), released in 1972, takes a different tack. No spoken-word poems, no bizarre interludes like the thirty-second "Lost in Space" on the first album. Instead, Jesse Colin Young takes over the production chair and shapes a more conventional full-band country-rock sound. Banana and Bauer are absent this time, and the laid-back vibe of the first album is supplanted by meaty, uptempo numbers like "When I'm Thirsty" and "Bless My Soul." Eddy Ottenstein, whose presence is muted on the first album, is cut loose to solo. The more chill material shines too, with a cover of Richard Farina's "Pack Up Your Sorrows," possibly picked up from Jeff's time playing with Mimi Farina, and the killer Tony Joe White–sounding "Mockingbird." The end result is more cohesive, more convincing, and more confident than *For You*. It showed a promising new direction for Cain. It would be his last album.

On August 26, 1972, Cain played the Bitter End in New York City with Jesse Colin Young and JD Souther. He continued to gig, but there was little response again to his album. "It was horrible for Jeffrey," Stuart Kutchins remembers. The lack of acclaim for Jeff and the bitter disappointment that came with it was impetus for Stuart to eventually leave the music business. Cain split too, heading back east. From there, the trail goes cold. A second marriage, a possible breakup, some real estate job. According to Susan Deixler, Jeff settled in Colorado in the early '90s and developed the symptoms of the neurological disease that ran in his family. He's deceased, but no one could tell me exactly when he died.

While combing the little there is to find about Cain online, I found a song posted on SoundCloud by Hal Singer, "Much More Magic," recorded by Cain later in life in the DC area. The track is rough, made rougher as it's not directly uploaded, but rather is a recording of the playback in Hal's room, where you can hear some clunking around. The song, which does not appear on his albums, was in Jeff's repertoire as early as 1970. When I mentioned the title to Susan Deixler, she was not aware of the online post, but immediately started singing the song to me. It is a gorgeous tune with a unique chord progression, easily one of his best. As of this writing, only forty people have listened to it in the two years since it was posted.

Much more magic
Than a moonbeam
On the water in a shower of shooting stars

That's what I feel
When you're by me
And the warmth of your touch heals all my scars

Much more music
Than a morning
In the springtime
When the birds meet the rising sun

That's what I hear
When you tell me
In a whisper
That our lives have just begun

And though I'm giving up being so free
It looks like the joke is on me
Cuz my freedom comes when I'm locked behind the
    door with you

And if it's freedom I was hoping to find
Then I've left the eagle way behind
Cuz these chains of love give me freedom like I never knew

Much more color
Than a rainbow
Shining through the newborn sky on a rainy day
That's what I see when you kiss me
And the storm clouds of my life vanish away

Much more magic
Than a moonbeam
On the water in a shower of shooting stars
That's what I feel when you're by me
And the warmth of your touch heals all my scars
© Lyrics by Jeffrey Cain

• • • • •

Former Warner Brothers executive Stan Cornyn blogged about Raccoon from his perspective inside the company at the time:

> Album after album, Raccoon recorded in its isolated studio on the side of a California mountain ... Album after album, the music fancies of various Youngbloods—guys named Michael and Jeffrey and Banana, each doing his own thing, his own albums—were recorded. The album masters got mailed down to Warner Records and left the label's Burbank execs somewhat puzzled about "What's this one about?" Critics were left in the dark, as well. But what Warner Bros. Records (not Reprise) had done was just what Jesse Colin Young had dreamt a label should do: let him do his things, whether those things sold or didn't.

At least Jeffrey Cain's first album was in a language Warner Brothers and your average listener could understand: a guy tunefully singing songs. Raccoon #3, however—Joe Bauer's 1971 album *Moonset*—was an entirely different affair.

Joe Bauer was born September 26, 1941, in Memphis, Tennessee. Trained as a jazz drummer, Bauer was playing in concert bands when he met Banana in Cambridge in 1965 and auditioned for the Youngbloods. Michael Hurley was present at the audition. "I remember Jesse made some remarks to Joe, and Joe said, 'You can't expect the drummer to be the cure-all.'" Bauer got the job anyway.

Improvisation was Bauer's thing. Stuart Kutchins recalls, "Joe knew how to maintain the rhythm, but where his heart was, was spontaneity." *Moonset*, the only album under Bauer's name as a "leader," was recorded in June and October of 1970 in Studio B, the small recording studio built behind Banana's house. The two sides have different lineups, with Bauer, Banana, and Youngbloods bassist Michael Kane on Side One and Steve Swallow replacing

Kane on Side Two. The eight-and-a-half minute "Earthquake Blues" features the harmonica talents of a very tall dude named Earthquake (Richard Anderson), an imposing figure who entered the Youngbloods fold by accident.

As Banana tells it:

> Joe and I used to love looking for stuff in people's backyards. We were in this junkyard in Alaska and found these great hubcaps to go with Joe's 1953 Kaiser Manhattan. So we told our road manager, Falcon, to wrap them up and pack them so we could take them. He said, "No, I only deal with musical instruments." So we fired him. Went to Seattle, we had two guys who wanted the job—Straight John and Not-So-Straight John. Guess which one we hired? Back in Marin, Not-So-Straight John shows up with Earthquake. We said, "We didn't order an Earthquake, and how are we gonna feed him; he's huge. He also plays harmonica, and we didn't order a harmonica player either!"

Banana says that *Moonset* and *Crab Tunes/Noggins*, which I'll discuss shortly, were both created with no forethought on the part of Bauer, no tunes or musical ideas written down. Banana says that as a drummer, Joe "played the melody," and you can certainly hear him take the lead at times. *Moonset* is pure improvisation. Bauer is surrounded by session bassists who already had serious jazz credentials, and would go on to do much more. The album opens with "Explosion," twenty-one seconds of clattering drums, a bicycle bell, a bass playing Westminster Chimes, and a choppy Spanish guitar run. The rest of Side One contains some memorable riffs amidst the proto-jam-band jamming, blues workouts, and frog noises. The title track is notable for the appearance of bassist Jack Gregg, who toured in Claude Thornhill's big band in 1961 and went on to perform with greats like Jaki Byard, Marion Brown, and Horace Silver. The nine-minute "Pelicans" features Banana's rapturous electric piano, slowly unfolding to an expansive crescendo. Steve Swallow, who had played with Paul Bley, Art Farmer, and Gary Burton, sits in on Side Two.

The album package is so complimentary: a pastoral, starry folk-art cover painting by Joe's wife Mina Raff; gangly band photos; a shot of Joe with his daughter, Cricket, on the back cover. LP sleeves with artists pictured holding their small kids were everywhere in the early '70s. Also inside is a 10x10 insert: a big "Raccoon #3" on one side, and a cat sticking its paw through a hole on the other.

Banana and Bauer were close friends. You can hear that on *Moonset*. They used to go kayaking together on acid. Joe loved photography and the outdoors. Michael Kane told me Joe studied *How to Make & Fly Paper Airplanes*, the 1968 guide by Captain Ralph S. Barnaby, and enjoyed designing his own paper airplanes and flying them off of hotel rooftops and cliffs. After the Youngbloods dissolved, Joe built a beautiful home in Inverness, where he lived with his family until his tragic passing in September 1982 from a brain tumor at the age of forty.

● ● ● ● ●

Of the 15 Raccoon Records albums released from 1970 to 1972, five were Youngbloods records. Among the 10 others, we have a singer/songwriter (2), an eclectic folksinger (2), jazz (1), bluegrass (2), out/experimental (2), and the unclassifiable Banana and His Bunch (1).

The only straight-up jazz entry is *What Was, What Is, What Will Be*, the lone album by pianist Kenny Gill (Raccoon #5). Kenny Gill came to the band's attention through Jack Gregg. The brief liner notes state that Gill was born September 23, 1944, in Philadelphia, started playing piano at 19, studied at the Granoff School of Music in Philly, and moved to New York City in 1968. Produced by Joe Bauer and Banana, the album was recorded in New York City on May 19, 1970, except for a solo piano piece, "Virgo-Libra," recorded at Banana's mother's house in Santa Rosa. The players on the album are drummer Norman Connors (Archie Shepp, Pharoah Sanders), tenorman Carlos Garnett (Miles Davis, Art Blakey, Charles Mingus), tenorman Bob Berg (Miles, Cedar Walton, Horace Silver), and Stafford James on bass (Sanders, Sun Ra, Albert Ayler). Gill's approach smacks of McCoy Tyner or Cecil Taylor in the freer moments. But he also displays a very delicate, deft touch in others. *Billboard* reviewed the album on May 22, 1971: "There is a great tradition of John Coltrane heard here as Kenny Gill attempts to explain and/or create the universe."

Gill lived in Inverness for about a year. According to Stuart Kutchins and Banana, Gill was an unstable individual, possibly suffering from paranoid schizophrenia and drug problems. When it came time to record a promised second album, Raccoon's deal with Warner Brothers was winding down. When Stuart told Gill there would be no second album, it made him very angry. Nothing more seems to be known about Kenny Gill.

● ● ● ● ●

When I place *Crab Tunes/Noggins* (Raccoon #8) on the turntable, I get the sensation that, on a planet with 7 billion other people, I am very likely the only person listening to this particular record. Even Banana has not listened to it since its release in 1971. This album was recorded in Studio B in June and July 1970, and Banana believes Joe Bauer should have received producer credit, as there is none indicated on the jacket.

The cover features a woodcut of a crab carved by Joe's brother, John. No one could explain to me exactly what inspired the crab title, although there are theories. Stuart said perhaps it had something to do with the way a crab moves. The music does sound like the soundtrack to a crab moving around. Susan Deixler said that Banana and Joe used to enjoy kayaking, and that maybe they encountered crabs on their trips. Dungeness crabs don't make it into Tomales Bay though, from what I understand. Banana remembers that one of America's first free-form radio stations, KRAB Seattle, eventually programmed 30 stations in the South, Midwest, and West Coast under the umbrella name "Krab Nebula," with the slogan "24 hours a day of beautiful unfamiliar music."

The back cover features Banana with the first of his seven children, Lorenzo, in his arms; Bauer; and Michael Kane. The record mainly consists of a series of short, spastic variations on a warped theme. The track listing looks like this:

Side One	Side Two
Crab Tune #1	Cybelle
Noggin Attempt #1	Crab Tune #5
Crab Tune #2	Noggin Attempt #4
Noggin Attempt #2	Crab Tune #6
Crab Tune #3	Noggin
Noggin Attempt #3	
Crab Tune #4	
Old Jasper	

The all-instrumental album is at once seemingly inept and virtuosic, making for a fascinating and disorienting listening experience. It is the most delicious peanut-butter-and-crab sandwich you can imagine. Whether this album is an innovative stroke of genius or self-indulgent tripe, it's certainly one of the weirdest albums ever released by a major label. The "Crab Tunes" revolve around a repeating seven-note guitar figure, the aural equivalent of being poked a lot by an annoying fifth grader. Combined with Bauer's spasmodic jazz drumming, the overall effect reminds me of ... the Minutemen. George Hurley rocked his kit with a similarly jerky, jazz-inspired fervor, while D. Boon's angular guitar approach comes vaguely to mind in Banana's playing. The "Noggins" are built around a whimsical recurring piano theme not far removed from Vince Guaraldi. By "Crab Tunes" #3 and #4, the sound grows more complex, with wailing free-tenor solos by Bill Mitchell and harmonica bleats courtesy of Earthquake. "Crab Tune # 5" and the nine-and-a-half minute #6 on Side Two feature Kenny Gill comping on piano, laying down some nice modal chords and impressive free-jazz runs, as if to deviate from the maddening fun and lend some legitimacy to the proceedings. "Cybelle," on Side Two, was written by Michael Kane for his baby niece, and originally had words that Michael sang to me over the phone. Kane receives sole songwriting credit on seven of the album's tunes and shares credit on the rest, yet he can't remember anything specific about the recording session or songs, other than "Cybelle."

● ● ● ● ●

Michael Hurley and Jesse Colin Young grew up in Bucks County, Pennsylvania, at the same time (and so did Steve Weber of Holy Modal Rounders), but they actually first met while playing the West Village folk circuit in the mid '60s. Hurley had released only one now-classic Folkways album—1964's First Songs—when Jesse signed him to Raccoon. Armchair Boogie (Raccoon #6) was recorded by Young on reel-to-reel tape in the bedroom of Hurley's Cambridge apartment and released in 1971. Hurley drove out West to record the second album, Hi Fi Snock Uptown (Raccoon #14), cut in Studio B behind Banana's house and produced by Joe Bauer and Banana.

For someone as eccentric and outsider as Hurley, who hadn't had a record out in seven years, to suddenly find his LPs distributed by Warner Brothers was a big deal. "In those days, it wasn't that easy to have a record out. Today, anyone can have a record out," Hurley told me. "Being on Raccoon really helped my career. It improved my ability to get gigs." Hurley recalls a Raccoon Records tour consisting of about four dates in California featuring himself, the Youngbloods, and bluegrass outfit High Country. Hurley signed a three-album deal, but the unwinding of Raccoon prevented the third album from ever materializing. Original copies of his Raccoon LPs are highly sought-after by collectors and have been lovingly reissued by Light in the Attic Records. Their version of *Armchair Boogie* includes a 36-page reproduction of the comic book that came with the original LP.

High Country, the California-based bluegrass band, is still active today. Banana brought them on board, but can't remember where he first saw them—at a festival, at local club the Lion's Share, opening for the Dead? However it went down, Banana expresses a special pride in introducing California bluegrass to a wider audience via Raccoon. Mandolinist Butch Waller, the only remaining original member of High Country, was part of the same South Bay bluegrass scene that spawned the Dead. He started out in a duo with Herb Pedersen called the Westport Singers before forming one of Northern California's first bluegrass groups in the early '60s. The Pine Valley Boys featured David Nelson, later of New Riders of the Purple Sage; Richard Greene, who went on to play with Bill Monroe; and Herb Pedersen, who played with pretty much everybody. Jerry Garcia played banjo with High Country at the Matrix in San Francisco during the last week of February 1969. Tape of the show exists, and you can hear it on YouTube. It is supposedly Garcia's only bluegrass performance captured on tape between 1964 and 1973. High Country also opened for the Dead a few times at the Hollywood Palladium and Winterland.

Waller calls his signing to Raccoon "an absolute fluke," but a welcome one. "I talked to a lot of people who said it was the first bluegrass record they could find, " he told me. The band recorded two albums in Studio B, produced by Banana: the 1971 self-titled LP (Raccoon #7) and *Dreams* (Raccoon #11) in 1972. The Youngbloods were presenting West Coast bluegrass to many for the first time on a national scale. A lot of purists didn't exactly cotton to that notion. "We were always the poor stepchild," Waller explains. "It was hard to break out of that in the East. But Bill Monroe invited us to play his festival; he was very good to us."

So it was OK for country music to have big stars from California, like Merle Haggard and Buck Owens, but not for bluegrass. Maybe it was the long hair or the Dead association. Today, bands like High Country are remembered as part of a revisionist "hippie-grass" movement that drives high prices for private-press LPs by Monroe-inspired longhairs. Waller dismisses "hippie-grass" out of hand. "We were into traditional bluegrass: Bill Monroe, Ralph Stanley."

The Raccoon posse embraced traditional bluegrass just as it did outsiders like Hurley or a talented local weirdo like Jack Bonus (his real name). A bit player on the early '70s Bay Area scene, Bonus is best known (if he's known at all) for "The Hobo Song," covered by Old & In the Way and String Cheese Incident, among others. He released only one self-titled LP in 1972 on Jefferson Airplane's RCA-affiliated imprint, Grunt. Jorma told me he didn't know much about Jack, and that Marty Balin would know more. The album is bizarre. Campy songs, twisted lyrics, fucked-up string arrangements, Joe Cockeresque soul numbers, a jungle song with animal noises, an extended Spanish-flavored percussion jam, Bonus's wild sax playing—all delivered with an almost overbearing conviction.

The album cover shows a bemused Jack sitting at a diner counter with baseball cap askew, Hawaiian shirt, and red beard, staring blankly at the camera, looking like Jimmy Buffett's demented step-cousin. A waitress is pouring coffee. The back cover shows Jack diving over the counter on top of her, the waitress's legs straight up in the air.

Susan Deixler was there for the photo shoot. "That was John's Truck Stop in Point Reyes Station," she tells me. "Now it's the Pine Cone Diner." I need to go there. The LP came with a pink eight-page folio of Jack's handwritten lyrics and drawings, some with a strong *Yellow Submarine* influence.

According to Banana, Jack Bonus was a Jew from Brooklyn with an encyclopedic knowledge of music from around the world, probably influenced by his musician father. He lived a reclusive lifestyle in the woods of San Geronimo Valley—for decades in poverty—and rode his bike everywhere. He played in the Sky Blue Band in the Valley, and appears on a few early '70s recording sessions with Tom Paxton, Grootna, Peter Rowan, and Papa John Creach. Toward the end of his life, he got help from West Marin Senior Services, and some kind people took him in and let him live in their cabin for years. Susan Deixler said he was fine when he was playing music, but otherwise he was extremely shy and had trouble maintaining eye contact. Michael Kane recalls Bonus freaking out at a gig. "Jack said, 'They came in to my house and scratched all my records!'"

Banana gave me an unreleased live recording of Jack playing on stage with Banana and His Bunch (Banana, Michael Kane, and a couple of other guys) in a small local club in 1973. Bonus's sax playing is clear and sharp, a fluent musician ripping it up in many styles, and his vocals are soulful and daring, pushing the bluesy boundaries of his rasp. On one song, "Precious Gold," Bonus gives everything, darting around vocally like Van Morrison's majestic "Listen to the Lion," his sax solo busting out into worlds beyond the tiny club's walls. When it's over, you can hear about five people clapping.

Jack Bonus suffered a heart attack and died on April 20, 2013, in Forest Knolls, California. At the local memorial service, Banana said Jack's brother, who he supposedly hadn't been in contact with for decades, was piped in via Skype. There were family pictures all around. He was loved and supported by his community. A local newscaster reporting on his passing said, "We will miss our Hobo."

● ● ● ● ●

It's time to go, but before I do, I ask Banana to show me Studio B behind his house, where Raccoon records like *Moonset*, *Crab Tunes*, and *For You* were conceived. No longer a recording facility, the house, bought in 1970, is now the dwelling of Banana's son and his girlfriend. Banana sells vintage string instruments, studies Italian, and pursues a solo career as a singer/songwriter. His backyard looks out onto a mountain of California bay laurel trees—one of the oldest bay laurel forests in the world, so he says.

As I make my way east along Point Reyes–Petaluma Road, through some of the most beautiful terrain in Northern California, I can't help but feel a sad twinge. It's too expensive for creative people to come out here with a dream and lay down roots now like the Youngbloods did in 1969. No one around here is going kayaking on acid. There are no more paper airplanes being launched off Elephant Mountain. Jack Bonus is dead.

But Raccoon Records is a lesson in creative freedom. About doing whatever the fuck you want. Whatever that happens to be.

Producer Bob Johnston (l) and Bill Wilson at Johnston's
Nashville home, 1973 (Photo courtesy of Tamra Wilson)

Chapter 4:

Bill Wilson

One day in February 1973, Bob Johnston heard a knock at his kitchen door. Johnston, who had produced several Bob Dylan albums, Johnny Cash's *At Folsom Prison* and Leonard Cohen's *Songs from a Room*, wasn't expecting anyone.

"I'm Bill Wilson, and I want to make a record."

"Well, you came to the wrong house. You can't just show up and make a fucking record."

"Well, will you listen to one song I got?"

"I'll listen to one song ...."

"So I listened to twelve," Johnston remembers. "Called the musicians and made the record that night."

Johnston hastily summoned his crew, some of the best Nashville session players of the era. Several had played on Dylan's *Blonde on Blonde*: Mac Gayden on slide, Charlie Daniels on guitar, Bob Wilson on piano, Charlie McCoy on harmonica, Kenny Buttrey on drums, Jerry Reed on guitar, Pete Drake on steel guitar. Cissy Houston and two other singers sang backing vocals. We think. There's no personnel listed on the LP sleeve, in Columbia's archives, nor at the AFM office in Nashville. McCoy and Gayden don't recall the session. So we have to rely on Johnston's memory.

Bob Johnston never spoke to or saw Bill Wilson again after the session.

"The fucker could really write," Johnston told me. "Doesn't matter what place you put it there. It's one of those that didn't matter, like Dylan, but it was really wonderful what he had. I don't know what happened to him."

Bill Wilson was born in Lebanon, Indiana, on March 14, 1947. He grew up on a Hendricks County farm, heard rock and roll on the radio, bought a $25 guitar, and started playing with friends in junior high. His parents hated it. Wilson enlisted in the Army in 1966 and went off to Vietnam. He was discharged to Austin, Texas, in 1969, and recorded his first demo for the Sonobeat label. In 1970, he sang two songs on the Sonobeat LP *Perpetuum Mobile*, a psychedelic blues-rock album by Austin-based band Mariani, featuring a 16-year-old guitarist named Eric Johnson. A promo copy of that LP recently sold on eBay for $2276. Disenchanted with Austin, Bill returned to Indiana and played local gigs for a couple of years with the Pleasant Street Band, who hired him to play dobro.

It's unclear whether Bill hooked up with manager Bud Prager prior to or after his arrival at Johnston's doorstep. Prager ran Windfall Records, distributed by CBS, in partnership with Cream producer Felix Pappalardi. Prager was responsible for Mountain's early success, and would go on to manage Foreigner and Bad Company.

Columbia shipped *Ever Changing Minstrel*, released under the Windfall imprint, to record stores on November 16, 1973. Rita Reiswig, Wilson's wife at the time, remembers Bill scrounging around local record stores to pick up a copy for himself. He was lucky to find one. The record was not well distributed or promoted. Bill blamed the changing power structure at Columbia for the album's poor sales, since label president Clive Davis had departed just prior to the album's release. "If I had to just depend on that album I would have died years ago of starvation. I've received less than $100," Wilson lamented in a 1976 interview.

Wilson was a Dylan fan, and that may well have led him to Johnston. We can only guess how pleased he was to be recording with Dylan's crew, but that's where any similarities end. The writing and delivery are more rooted in a Southern direction. Did Bill soak up Guy Clark and Townes Van Zandt in Austin? There's an array of material: '60s hangover songs with social messages, a funky Allman-like workout, a coming-of-age song, a blues song, gospel songs, road songs, and a lovelorn ballad. The album was written and recorded under some pretty serious personal duress, according to Bill's daughter, Tamra Wilson, who explains that "Long Gone

Lady" is about the distance between her mom and dad at the time.

After the commercial failure of the album, Bill continued to perform and record in Indiana until his death from a massive heart attack on Thanksgiving Day, November 25, 1993, at age 46.

I worked at SONY Music for 15 years, and I know the catalog pretty well. Over years of record hunting, and through many hours spent digging in the catacombs of SONY Music's LP archive at 550 Madison Avenue, I never saw a copy of *Ever Changing Minstrel*. One day in January 2012, I found the LP for a quarter in a Berkeley, California, record store. I bought it because I'd never seen it, and because it was produced by Bob Johnston. After hearing it, I knew I needed to find Bob Johnston and get the whole backstory. The Tompkins Square reissue of *Ever Changing Minstrel* is about Bill Wilson's forgotten talents, but it's also about Bob Johnston, who took a shot on a young unknown stranger from Indiana who showed up at his doorstep.

I really love the spirit of this record. And now I'm pals with Bob Johnston.

Not bad for a quarter.

Notes from the 2012 Tompkins Square reissue of Ever Changing Minstrel *(TSQ 2684)*

●　●　●　●　●

A few months after the reissue of *Ever Changing Minstrel* in 2012, Bill Wilson's granddaughter, who was 15 years old at the time, sent me a thank-you card:

> Dear Mr. Rosenthal,
>
> I would like to thank you for sending me the CD and letting people hear his music again.
>
> I sadly never met my grandfather, but through his music I can know more about him. He seemed like an amazing person to know and be around. So thank you again. It's a joy to hear this CD. I'm proud of him very much!
>
> :) M

Harvey Mandel tapping his inner Snake in the
mid '70s (Photo courtesy of Harvey Mandel)

Chapter 5:

Harvey Mandel:
An Appreciation

On the Occasion of His 70th Birthday
March 11, 2015

There's a sound in Harvey Mandel's "Long Wait," the last song on Side One of his 1968 debut, *Cristo Redentor*. A minute and 43 seconds into a searing, grinding, winding guitar passage, there's a little "plink." It's a moment of subtle yet daring ingenuity, the kind Mandel has wielded in spades throughout his 50-year career.

Diggers know. Somewhere in the bin between Malo and Mandrill, you'll find the records: *Cristo Redentor*, *Righteous*, *Baby Batter*, *Shangrenade*. Maybe you're lucky enough to find a *Cristo* promo in mint condition, with the shiny gold Philips label instead of black. Long a favorite of in-the-know DJs, producers, and gearheads, Mandel has been sampled by Del the Funky Homosapien and Nas, and he's played in Canned Heat, with John Mayall, and on the Rolling Stones' *Black and Blue* LP.

Today is Harvey's seventieth birthday, but it is not a happy one. He was diagnosed with nasal cancer in 2013 and has undergone sixteen surgeries. The type of cancer he has requires very specialized surgery by a top doctor in Chicago who does not accept health insurance. This is all fully disclosed on a website run by his sister at helpharveymandel.com. Harvey has had to pawn his guitars and sell his publishing to stay afloat. He lost his only son and his mother in recent years. And Harvey faces several more surgeries. We all hear about musicians who fall on hard times late in their careers, yet his seems an especially cruel turn.

Mandel grew up in Chicago and started playing guitar at 16, learning the Ventures' *Walk Don't Run* LP note for note. He met Sammy Fender, a black blues musician, who took him down to Curley's Twist City, a crucible of Chicago blues innovation. After a few months jamming with the regulars and his own combo, he could hold his own with anybody. He played with them all: Howlin' Wolf, Muddy Waters, Buddy Guy. "You could name a list of a hundred well-known blues people," he says, "and I got to play with all of them at one time or another in Chicago." He ran alongside locals Steve Miller, Charlie Musselwhite, Mike Bloomfield, and Barry Goldberg, all part of the burgeoning scene.

Bill Graham invited Musselwhite and Mandel out to the Fillmore in San Francisco in August 1967 as the first of three on a bill with Electric Flag and Cream. In 2011, he recalled, "I came in from Chicago with this little Fender amplifier with one 12-inch speaker, and I look up onstage, and here's Eric Clapton with a wall of Marshalls. And he was so cool, I asked him, 'Think I could borrow one of those things during my set?' No problem."

Back in Chicago, Mandel had worked up a certain sound he had in his head—a heavy sustain—through trial and error with the equipment of the day. "We didn't have the array of pedals and electronics and all the little gadgets," he told KCTH in 2011. "The only way to get that sound was to have the magic guitar and be able to plug into a certain amplifier—certain ones that would give you that overdriven, sustaining sound. I was a maniac at trying to find the magic things, experimenting with different speakers. I used to punch holes in speakers."

Harvey settled in San Francisco, jamming with Jerry Garcia at the Matrix in 1968 and hooking up with Blue Cheer producer Abe "Voco" Kesh, who scored him a deal with Philips. *Cristo Redentor* was recorded in LA, Nashville, and San Francisco with crack players like Pete Drake, Kenny Buttrey, Pig Robbins, Goldberg, Musselwhite, and Miller. At once gritty and elegant, *Cristo Redentor* combines Nick De Caro's lithe string arrangements with Harvey's groundbreaking electric guitar technique to create something unearthly, far transcending the narrow blues conventions of many of his contemporaries.

Mandel's long, sinewy guitar lines earned him his nickname "The Snake," apt not only for his drawn-out sustain but also for his unpredictability; the listener is never sure where he's going. He doesn't follow predictable patterns for soloing within songs. He's in full slither on the epic "Wade on the Water," partially recorded onstage at the Avalon Ballroom. "I wanted the song to be a big production number with a wide, live feel and lots of natural reverb," he said in a 1995 interview. It takes a certain vision to record a live band performance in order to get that "big" sound and then blend it with orchestration in the studio to create a track that seamlessly matches the thread of the album. Who does that?

Mandel's second LP, *Righteous*, released in 1969, swaps out arranger De Caro for Shorty Rogers and features a new set of players. The result is brassier and busier, Mandel's guitar at times overwhelmed by Rogers' overly ambitious charts. Neither of the albums sold, and so by album number three, 1970's *Games People Play*, Mandel thought the addition of a singer might do the trick. But pedestrian vocalist Russell DaShiell is an unwelcome presence on three songs, and while there is some great playing, most notably the backwards tape experiment "Ridin' High," *Games People Play* sounds like a half-measure.

The skinny kid with the muttonchops, brown crushed-velvet slacks, and open-neck dark blue dress shirt on stage with Canned Heat at Woodstock—that's Harvey. It was his third show with the band since taking over for Henry Vestine, who had recently quit. Although the Heat's performance was sliced at the last minute from the original Woodstock movie, it appears in the Director's Cut released in 1994. During "A Change Is Gonna Come," lead singer Bob Hite is bum rushed onstage by some dipshit, but actually looks happy to see him. The kid takes a pack of cigarettes out of Bob's breast pocket and pulls one out; Bob is all too happy to light it for him, and they have a conversation. Classic. Then Mandel unleashes a torched solo, as he does in other clips such as "On the Road Again," which became a Woodstock anthem.

Harvey's high-octane playing at Woodstock and on Canned Heat's studio album *Future Blues* added an outer dimension to the band's meat, meat, and more meat-and-potatoes blues. Mandel would re-unite with a reconfigured Canned Heat in 2009.

From 1970 to 1975, Mandel released five albums on the Janus label, including the fantastic *Baby Batter* from 1971: a funky, blistering set featuring Canned Heat bassist Larry Taylor, Howard Wales on keyboards, and Big Black on congas, with some string arrangements by Shorty Rogers. "El Stinger" will set your hair on fire. It must have been a blast to be in the studio. From the album credits: "Special thanks to Harry Nilsson, Wine Consultant and Bearer." The album is described in liner notes by KSAN's Dusty Street as "a 'produced' jam. 'Produced' because it was done in a studio, but kept the spontaneity of the all-night session."

Mandel went on to join John Mayall for two albums, *USA Union* and *Back to the Roots*, followed by a stint in Pure Food and Drug Act, who released one album, *Choice Cuts*, on Epic in 1972. The next year saw the release of the double-LP *Free Creek*, a mysterious, forgotten 1969 super-session featuring Clapton (listed as "King Cool"), Jeff Beck (listed as "A.N. Other"), Dr. John, Todd Rundgren, Linda Ronstadt, and others. This is one of those "giant pile of coke in the studio" records with dozens of musicians that never happens anymore. Mandel also played on a Raymond Louis Kennedy LP released in 1970. Harvey's never heard of him.

Much has been said about Mandel's influence on other guitarists, certainly with regard to sustain but also because of "tapping," a technique used by Eddie Van Halen, Kaki King, and any number of heavy metal players. Harvey tells me the first guy he actually saw doing it was Randy Resnick, a member of Pure Food and Drug Act. Mandel's first recordings to heavily employ the method appear on his fusion-tinged 1973 Janus LP *Shangrenade*, although he was doing some form of it years before that. While Mandel didn't invent tapping (Roy Smeck did it in the '30s and George Van Eps did it in the '50s), at least one guitarist of note saw the Snake do it first.

Deep Purple/Rainbow axman Ritchie Blackmore recounted in a 1991 interview:

> The first person I saw doing that hammer-on stuff was Harvey Mandel, at the Whisky a Go Go in '68. I thought "What the hell is he doing?" It was so funny [laughs], Jim Morrison was carried out because he was shouting abuse at the band. Jimi Hendrix was there. We were all getting drunk. Then Harvey Mandel starts doing this stuff [mimes tapping]. "What's he doing?" everybody was saying. Even the audience stopped dancing. Obviously, Eddie Van Halen must have picked up a few of those things.

In 1976, the Rolling Stones auditioned Mandel as a possible replacement for outgoing guitarist Mick Taylor, and Harvey plays on two tracks from *Black and Blue*: "Memory Motel" and "Hot Stuff." Keith was kind enough to recently send a signed guitar for Harvey to auction off as a fundraiser to help cover some of his medical expenses. Gregg Allman did too.

After a dormant solo recording period between 1975 and the mid '90s, Harvey's first three Philips albums were reissued by PolyGram in 1995 on a long out-of-print two-CD set overseen by Bill Levenson. Numerous self-released solo albums followed through the '90s and '00s. Bob Dylan's camp asked Harvey to accompany Bob onstage during his Grammy performance in 2011.

I tried to interview Harvey recently, but when you're missing your nose, retracing the nuances of late '60s recording sessions tends to take a backseat. And there's also the rent. I'm not trying to make you sad, dear reader, or give you another sob story. But when one of your musical heroes is so besieged with suffering, it prompts you to act. We all see pleas online to help someone. They are easy to ignore. Harvey really needs help.

Let's see if we can help Harvey Mandel on his 70th. Let's try to make this a happier birthday for him. A musician of Harvey Mandel's stature deserves it.

Donate at helpharveymandel.com or directly using this PayPal address: harveysnake@comcast.net

Originally published by Aquarium Drunkard *on March 11, 2015.*

● ● ● ● ●

As of this writing (July 30, 2015), Harvey still needs your help. [JR]

Chapter 6:

Ernie Graham

How many bands could boast that Jimi Hendrix produced their album? Only two. Cat Mother and the All Night Newsboys, and Ireland's Eire Apparent, featuring Ernie Graham.

Ernest Harold Graham was born into poverty in Belfast on June 14, 1946. An aspiring auto mechanic, Graham ditched that and cut his musical chops in two bands, Tony & the Telstars in the early '60s, and the People, formed in 1965. His mates in these bands went on to careers with established artists: drummer Davy Lutton with Marc Bolan, Chris Stewart as bassist for Joe Cocker, and guitarist Henry McCullough with Paul McCartney. Henry can also famously be heard muttering at the end of "Money" on Pink Floyd's *The Dark Side of the Moon.* The People sounded very similar to other bands on the scene in Northern Ireland, especially Them with Van Morrison.

The People changed their name to Eire Apparent (Eire is Irish for "Ireland") at the behest of their new manager, Chas Chandler, who was also looking after Jimi Hendrix. The band toured the US with the Animals in 1968, and then appeared on a US bill with Hendrix and Soft Machine. They recorded a couple of songs with Jimi at the helm in New York City at the Record Plant, and then cut their own only album, *Sunrise,* in Los Angeles in October of 1968,

Cover of Ernie Graham's self-titled
debut album, 1971 Liberty Records

released on Buddah Records in 1969.

A pleasant enough example of the sunshine/baroque pop of the era with an acidic twist, lead vocalist Graham writes or co-writes six songs, and Hendrix plays on several tracks, including "Yes I Need Someone" and "The Clown." Soft Machine's Robert Wyatt, Noel Redding, and Mitch Mitchell guest on the album as well. After more touring that year with Hendrix, the band supposedly recorded a second album, produced by Robert Wyatt, which has never been released. They broke up in 1970.

Graham wasted no time sussing out a solo deal. Eventual Stiff Records founder and manager Dave Robinson struck a deal with Liberty Records in the UK and co-produced Ernie's debut. The session was recorded at Olympic Studios in 1971 with iconic British pub rockers Brinsley Schwarz, whose lineup featured Schwarz, Nick Lowe, Ian Gomm, Billy Rankin, and Bob Andrews, alongside members of the band Help Yourself. Olympic was the site of recording sessions by Hendrix, the Rolling Stones, the Who, Led Zeppelin, and many others.

After the release of his solo album in 1971, Ernie joined Help Yourself for a short time and played the Glastonbury Festival with them that year, followed by a stint in pub rock combo Clancy, which recorded two albums for Warner Brothers. From there he drifted, giving up his music career after very little commercial success. He became a security guard on the Orient Express, and toward the end of his life, was training to become a counselor. By various accounts a very heavy drinker, Graham's health deteriorated, and he passed away in London on April 27, 2001, at the age of 54.

Today, an original copy of Ernie's eponymous solo LP fetches $300 to $600. Hux Records in the UK reissued it on CD in 2002, adding on two songs from a 1978 Stiff Records single and illuminating liner notes by Nigel Cross. 4 Men With Beards released a 180-gram vinyl reissue of the album in 2014.

The press release for the album, dispatched by London publicity outfit Tony Brainsby Publicity Ltd., describes the album as "a gentle restrained account of what Ernie is all about. There's a lot of Ireland in it, a lot of chicks, and a lot of dope. Ernie stopped being a pop star when Eire Apparent failed; now he's a guy who sings his songs."

"Sea Fever" is the centerpiece of the album. The song has this evocative, soupy atmosphere—you can almost taste the marine layer in the air. What gives it such a cinematic lift, beside the opening seaside sound effects, is the piano over a swirling organ, and then an electric guitar over an acoustic guitar. Two keyboards. I can't recall a song that uses them together in a spare setting so effectively. You can see the sand, the birds. The overall sound is quiet, yet very intricate.

The song was written during a bout of depression. From a 1971 interview in *Beat Instrumental*: "That was at a time when I was contemplating suicide ... I read somewhere that drowning was a pleasant way to die. It's something to do with the water shutting off the air to the brain, and as a result the brain gets incredibly high." The repeating words "You get high" at song's end dissolve and fade upward over the lapping surf, evoking exactly what Ernie describes: a calm, surreal, pleasurable death.

The opening of the song sets the stage, with gentle wave sound effects, dirge-y piano, and strummed acoustic guitar. The organ swells.

> *Pull my velvet cloak around you*
> *Come and walk with me along the sand*
> *Where only happiness surrounds you*
> *You just come along and take my hand*

The song is a gorgeous meditation on escaping the chaos of the city with a loved one, just the two of you, heading out to a retreat by the sea.

> *When your friends all seem to doubt you*
> *And your life begins to get you down*

There's a place that I can show you

Where there's never anyone around

The album opener, "Sebastian," is reliant on Dylanesque phrasing, so much so that I used to skip it entirely and start my listening with track two. But I've grown to appreciate it within the context of the album. Graham defended his copping of Bob's style in *Beat Instrumental*: "When other people notice it's like Dylan, and they also know that *I* know it's like Dylan, there's a direct communication from myself and through the song into the audience."

"So Lonely" highlights Graham's cunning songwriting and arranging prowess: a mellow backbeat, then an urgent, funky break with insistent bass drum and scrappy electric guitar. The aforementioned epic "Sea Fever" sits at track three, oddly juxtaposed with the jaunty, accordion-laden track four, "The Girl Who Turns the Lever," wherein Ernie inhabits a character reminiscing about his days in "Detroit City." "For a Little While" is a sweet ode to lost love, vividly depicting a short-lived affair that leaves a sense of longing in its wake long after it's over. He darts around in his mind, as one is wont to do under the circumstances. Her hair. Her lips. Her in his bed. Her voice when she said "I love you." On the eve of the fifteenth of May, when she said, "I am glad you come my way." The spring of '69. There's a solid two-minute "la-la-la-la-la-la" mid-section between verses and at the end that sounds like an exorcism—like he's trying to sing himself into a happier place. The locomotive energy of "Blues to Snowy," written for Ernie's future blues-loving brother-in-law, is fuel-injected by Richard Treece's biting guitar solo.

The most surprising twist on the album is the closer, "Belfast," sung in a thick Irish brogue unlike any other voice that Graham employs on the album. Cross explains that the song was written on a trip back home for Christmas in 1970, a time of escalating violence in Northern Ireland, describing it as "one of the first songs to be written about the political situation there." Chris Cunningham contributes a nice traditional fiddle part throughout, and a gorgeous solo at the end. The whole thing rips, years before the Pogues. I considered this song out of context from the whole for a long time, but now, like "Sebastian," I've come to appreciate it as part of the whole—the whole of Ernie Graham's art, in all its many guises and voices, brilliantly displayed in a mere 41 minutes.

I interviewed the very gracious Ian Gomm on June 12, 2012, for my live radio show on KZSU Stanford University in Stanford, California, and asked him what it was like to know Ernie and to play in the studio on Ernie's only solo LP. Gomm played rhythm guitar for Brinsley Schwarz from 1970 to 1974, wrote "Cruel to Be Kind" with Nick Lowe, and had one big hit in the US in 1978, "Hold On."

JR: How did Brinsley Schwarz hook up with Ernie Graham, and when did you meet him?

IG: We actually met in 1970. There was a management company called Down Home Productions. They had about three groups and Ernie, and we all combined to become the Down Home Rhythm Kings. I think that's how it worked. Ernie decided he was gonna make a solo album, and I remember it was cut at Olympic Studios in Barnes, London, which is where Eric Clapton recorded *Layla*. It didn't take very long to do; I think we did it over a few nights. Our manager, and Ernie's as well, Dave Robinson, who was involved with Stiff Records over here, we had cheap studio time, which meant we worked through the night in one of the small studios, and it was two or three nights to do it all.

JR: Seemed like he had command of the material.

IG: We lived in a commune; we rented a very big house; we were a five-piece group, so we had five different areas for ourselves as well as rehearsal facilities, which is where we routined it all with Ernie, which cuts costs as well. Ernie had all the songs ready to go. I think he'd been working on it for a few months.

JR: So you knew Ernie prior to this, from being in other groups then?

IG: I wouldn't say I knew him that well; I mean, I knew about the Eire Apparent with Jimi Hendrix, because our manager, Dave Robinson, was the tour manager. He used to stand behind the amps onstage. Hendrix played so loud he used to pop valves during the set, and Dave had to push new valves in as they blew up.

JR: Do you have any recollection of being in the studio and playing with Ernie in the studio?

IG: I do remember. How can I put this? They were very long nights. I did dig out the CD the other day and listen to it again; I hadn't listened to it for ages—it's not bad! "The Girl Who Turned the Lever"—I can remember back then that was the one I thought, that's good.

JR: Ernie is in various vocal guises throughout, like, for instance, this Dylanesque thing on the first track; then he's got this very ethereal vocal on "Sea Fever"; then he gets into a very gritty vocal, and then "Belfast" in a full traditional Irish brogue.

IG: I think what we did was we shuffled everybody about with the instruments. The backing has a lot of variety too.

JR: "Sea Fever" is this heady, celestial tune with those swirling keyboards. So great.

IG: That would be Bob Andrews, who was the keyboardist in Brinsley Schwarz. He's still excellent. Did you say the album goes for $500? Well, I've got one. And I'll tell you another thing, I know the guy at Hux Records, and he's reissued some of the unreleased Brinsley Schwarz stuff. When he told me he was putting out the Ernie Graham, nobody could find the cover, so if you've got *that* CD, the actual cover of it. I supplied ... I sent my vinyl copy to Hux Records; he scanned it, and that's how they did the cover.

JR: What do you remember about the man?

IG: He was short. He had a bit of attitude. I'm half Irish; they were *very* Irish. The Eire Apparent, you know, they came over to Britain from Ireland. I'm sure the other guys went on to get involved in the Grease Band with Joe Cocker. Ernie though, he just knew what he wanted; he was very blunt. How can I put this? Well, I've met Van Morrison. Do you know the sort of Irish character I'm referring to?

JR: I see this photo of him here. He's got no shirt on and a feather boa around his neck.

IG: He did like a drink as well, I'll tell you that, Josh.

JR: Did you have any contact with him after the album? He died in 2001.

IG: I know he did. Well, I was going back through boxes of memorabilia and found publicity shots that were taken on old Kodachrome color slide sort of things, and I found a series of shots that had been done for the album cover—there must have been like 30 of them—and through Hux Records, I heard Ernie had died and managed to get them sent. They put me in touch with Ernie's daughter—I'm sure she was a ballet dancer or something like that. I asked her if she wanted the pictures of her dad and sent them to her.

JR: So she's still in the UK then?

IG: Yeah, she was. Have you heard of the Orient Express? It's a train that used to go from London right across Europe to the Orient, and Ernie, at one stage, was a guard on it (after his musical career). And then he went on to be in another band called Clancy. I was in groups with a guy called Colin Bass—he was our bass player—and I put him in touch with Ernie when he was forming Clancy. What an incestuous group we were!

JR: Thanks for sharing your story with me, Ian.

Chapter 7:

Syosset

For a nondescript suburban town, Syosset, Long Island, has some pretty substantial rock credentials. Joan Jett's *I Love Rock 'n Roll* was recorded at Kingdom Sound in Syosset. There's "135 Syosset" by Long Island punkers Giants at Large and "The Syosset Polka" by Blameshift, the only active band I know of that's actually from Syosset. George Drakoulias, producer of albums by the Black Crowes, the Jayhawks, and Tom Petty, attended Syosset High School. Bee Gee Robin Gibb reportedly frequented Village Hero (still there) on Jericho Turnpike in 1979 while living in Lloyd Harbor. That year, John Lennon purchased a whaling-era 19th-century mansion, Cannon Hill, in nearby Laurel Hollow, overlooking Cold Spring Harbor. Lennon was said to have enjoyed perusing the Huntington flea market on weekends, where my brother claims I once spotted "someone who looked like John Lennon." I don't recall the incident, but I wish I would've said hi.

In *Uptight: the Velvet Underground Story*, guitarist Sterling Morrison said of drummer Moe Tucker in the early days of the band's development, "Maureen had been playing with a band on the Island. She had recently quit when the guitar player in the other band on the bill was shot on stage at a gig in Syosset." Moe walked back the story in a 1997 interview: "Yeah, that was wrong. I played with this band for two weeks, and the only show that we ever did, as far as I remember, was at this little dive in Long Island. And the night after we played there, someone pulled out a gun during a fight or something. Bullets flew and the guitar player or drummer got shot."

On January 20, 1988, Mick Jagger inducted the Beatles into the Rock and Roll Hall of Fame. "We heard there was a group from Liverpool. Now, everyone talks about, y'know, Syosset, Levittown—but I can tell you, Liverpool, this is *really* ..." Mick said in mock disgust.

Hicksville, the next town over, is where Billy Joel was raised. Billy was a source of enormous hometown pride for my friends and I growing up on Long Island in the early '80s. Lou Reed would overtake that mantle a few years later, once we reached high school. The fact that they were both angst-ridden and had Jewish roots was a bonus. We thrilled at Billy name-checking "Oyster Bay, Long Island" on "The Ballad of Billy the Kid" from *Piano Man*. His parting words from the stage were always "Don't take any shit from anybody!" Pure blue-collar Hicksville.

Billy's debut album was titled *Cold Spring Harbor*, for chrissake! That's where I made out with my girlfriends on the decrepit dock next to the seafood place that burned down and, a short walk away, where I found an abandoned yellow Schwinn bike, with a banana seat, in the park later christened Billy Joel Park. Whether or not "Scenes From an Italian Restaurant" was actually written about Christiano's in downtown Syosset is a debate that still rages from Shinnecock to Wyandanch. We just deemed it so. My parents nicknamed their cars Brenda and Eddie.

The first recording I owned was given to me by my Uncle Joe: a cassette (with no box) of *How Great Thou Art* by Elvis Presley— an album that seeded my appreciation of gospel music. But *The Stranger* was my first album purchase, at Straub Music in the Plainview shopping center. Straub sold sheet music, "I'm with Stupid" iron-on T-shirts, posters, "Fuck Iran" and "Disco Sucks" buttons, LPs, and instruments, and they also gave music lessons downstairs. The guys who worked there would geek out over Steely Dan guitar solos while kids tilted pinball machines. It's where I first experienced the thrill of music discovery: the titillation of Pretenders and Blondie album covers; the obliqueness of the

Motors, Fabulous Poodles, and the B-52s; the futuristic freakishness of Gary Numan and Moon Martin; the cutout bin filled ten-deep with copies of Yes's *Tormato*. I wanted to hear it all.

The only way you could, unless your friend had the records, was to buy them: $5.99 for an LP, $6.41 with tax. This led to some truly terrible purchases. My friend Scott and I bought Toto's *Hydra*, smashed it to pieces, and threw it down the sewer in front of his house. Same goes for Jethro Tull's double-live *Burstin' Out*, which we defaced (or decrotched) with a dick and balls between Ian Anderson's wide open, white-tight clad legs before throwing it out the window and then down the sewer. I also hung out with Brad Bernstein, whose older sister was a Zappa freak. She had every album of his. She also had a copy of *Yessongs*, with its triple-disc fold-out jacket. I thought it was the fucking coolest thing I'd ever seen. And she had a waterbed.

In the pre-MTV era of the late '70s/early '80s, information on bands was limited to what you could read in *Rolling Stone*, *Circus*, *Hit Parader*, *Musician*, and *Creem*. There were unofficial fanzines with lots of black-and-white pictures dedicated to Led Zeppelin, the Doors, and the Who. I remember a Keith Moon memorial edition and one published shortly after the awful Cincinnati Who concert stampede in 1979. It had all these graphic pictures of kids with light blue jeans and bright white sneakers covered in blood, body bags, and quotes from family and local law enforcement. The rag smacked of exploitation, like an early iteration of TMZ, but it was the only way I could learn about what had really happened.

Bands had mystique back then; you had to make an effort to learn about them. Sad to say, but incidents like the Who concert stampede only added to the mythology. When Pink Floyd toured *The Wall* and played Nassau Coliseum in February 1980, some kids waiting in line outside smashed the glass doors and windows. I read about it the next day in *Newsday*. It just made the band seem cooler, more dangerous, and even huger.

My folks had a few pop records that I was weaned on. *Sgt. Pepper's Lonely Hearts Club Band* was released in the US the day after I was born, and mom bought it shortly thereafter. I still have that copy, with crayon marks in the gatefold where I traced each Beatles' face. She had Simon & Garfunkel's *Bookends*, Sammy Davis Jr.'s *Now*, Tom Jones *Live!* My dad was interested in classical, Arabic, and Indian music. Somehow he picked up *The Devil's Anvil: Hard Rock from the Middle East* from 1967, a very odd mix of Turkish, Greek, and rock instrumentation produced by Felix Pappalardi on Columbia Records. He also owned a 78 rpm 10" of "I Walk the Line" by Johnny Cash. He didn't understand jazz or rock music, and I never acquired a taste for classical, except for minimalist composers like Satie. With that said, I love it when strings are used tastefully in rock music. My brother was into prog-rock, while I was more into the Stones. I was OK with Yes, King Crimson, and the lot, until he started bringing home Rick Wakeman solo albums.

Around 1978 and '79, I was really into songs that today are considered one-hit wonders, although we had no knowledge of this terminology at the time. In his 2015 MusiCares Award acceptance speech, Bob Dylan said, referring to Billy Lee Riley's "Red Hot," "Sometimes, just sometimes, once in a while, a one-hit wonder can make a more powerful impact than a recording star who's got 20 or 30 hits behind him." These '70s soft-rock songs—mushy, overwrought—helped me locate my heart. I see the same thing in my daughters and their relationship to pop songs. Too young to know what romantic love is firsthand, they may see love in the adults around them, they may have crushes and get crushed, but they do not yet know the true essence of romantic love as depicted in songs.

And therein lies the power of the pop song. The artist gives a youngster not just a melody to sing, but also a window into her own future, for better or worse. "Give Your Heart a Break," "Jar of Hearts," "The Heart Wants What It Wants." These are all very profound songs for little girls to hear and profound words to hear your little daughters sing. At the height of Taylor Swift's *Red* album, I told T Bone Burnett that my daughters hung on her every word. He said, "These artists are raising our kids." Scary, but true in a way.

The songs that have really set me up to be the sentimental musical sap that I am today are: Robert John's "Sad Eyes," Randy VanWarmer's "Just When I Needed You Most," Eric Carmen's "All By Myself," Gino Vanelli's "I Just Wanna Stop," and Dan Hill's "Sometimes When We Touch." Most remarkable about this time in the music business was, in retrospect, that it seemed like any schmo could come out of nowhere and have a hit. Of course, Eric Carmen was in the Raspberries, and some of the others were accomplished songwriters, but I didn't know that at the time. There was a sense that anyone you might see walking around the Mid-Island Mall or in line at the post office could craft a sentimental song, score a few lucky breaks, and make it onto Casey Kasem's *American Top 40*. It was more or less true. And that could never, ever happen today.

Randy VanWarmer was repped by Bearsville Records chief and former Bob Dylan manager Albert Grossman, so he was connected. However, the success of "Just When I Needed You Most" was a fluke. Picked up randomly by a DJ as the B-side of the non-hit A-side, "Gotta Get Out of Here," the song then spread across the US and reached #4 on the Billboard chart in the fall of 1979. In one of the strangest follow-ups to a hit in recorded music history, VanWarmer then released *Terraform* in 1980. On the cover is a nauseous-looking Randy wearing a spacesuit, with the moon behind him and a motel sign reflecting off his helmet. The title track, 10 minutes and 16 seconds in length, opens with a choral vocal arrangement and synths, echo-ey guitar and falsetto over a funky soft-rock groove, a Devoesque section wherein he repeats "I'm so 21st Century!," then a reprise of the intro section, which leads to a final frenetic outro with Randy yelling, "I'm soooo! I'm soooo!" By the end, you cannot fathom that this is the same guy who sang the gentle "Just When I Needed You Most" one year earlier.

The breezy Jackson Browne–sounding pop of the opening

track, "Whatever You Decide," sounds like a hit, although it could have used an edit at 5:15. He sings the words "whatever you decide" 22 times. The song peaked at #77 on the Billboard chart, and the album tanked. VanWarmer died of leukemia at age 48 in 2007 and had his ashes sent into outer space.

Dan Hill's "Sometimes When We Touch" is just as deadly. At twelve, listening to this song, I wondered what exactly was in store for me in my life. What would have to happen to make me sound like Dan Hill, this broken down, wimpy man? At some point I'm going to have to see *South of Wawa*, a 1991 Canadian comedy with the following storyline: "The film stars Rebecca Jenkins as Lynette, a woman stuck in an unhappy marriage who organizes a road trip with her co-worker Cheryl Ann (Catherine Fitch) to see Dan Hill in concert."

Another song that really tore me apart inside was 10cc's "I'm Not in Love." That dizzy, spinning intro; the gauzy, layered production; the delusional protagonist; that dreamy mid-section with those spare, plinked piano notes; the ghostly repeating female whisper ("Be quiet, big boys don't cry ..."). All too much to bear. The money line: "I keep your picture upon the wall/It hides a messy stain that's lying there." This song, along with Queen's "Bohemian Rhapsody," gave me pause. "These people have real problems. I wonder just how fucked up my own life is gonna get."

In 1979, I was listening exclusively to AM pop radio. I would wait all day to hear a song that I wanted to tape, and I rigged up my blue Toot-A-Loop radio next to my cassette recorder. "That's it! Hit record! Hit record!" One day I was mowing the lawn in the backyard, listening to my radio through the earphone jack, when I accidentally heard "Whole Lotta Love" on an FM station. I couldn't believe what I heard at all. Listening to the song while mowing the lawn, with that big psychotic swirling break in the middle, was its own psychedelic experience, and that is precisely when I decided to start listening to FM rock radio.

I was developing a more discerning eye and ear when it came

to rock criticism. My bible was the *Rolling Stone Record Guide*, all dog-eared with pages falling out, which I spent hours poring over. I also read *Stranded*, edited by Greil Marcus, with great interest. These tomes were my search engines for music discovery. At the same time, I was becoming very wary of mainstream music press, especially *Rolling Stone's* reviews section, which I had always accepted as gospel. The tide turned for me when they gave a five-star review to the J. Geils Band's *Freeze Frame*. I went out and bought it, and thought it sucked. I felt burned and decided I was no longer going to listen to these people, or in the case of the informative *Rolling Stone Record Guide*, I would at least take everything they wrote with a grain of salt.

Syosset High School has a 10-watt student run radio station, WKWZ. A lot of things happened there in the mid '80s that would never, ever happen today. During Music Marathon, an annual weeklong 24/7 block of programming, we slept overnight at the radio station. Our beloved faculty advisor Jack DeMasi was known to jump on desks, screaming and playing heavy metal air guitar. He would vociferously diss community colleges ("Don't wind up at fucking Nassau!"), openly discuss sadomasochistic imagery in Velvet Underground lyrics, and smoke (tobacco) with his students. Today, he would be summarily dismissed. Instead, he was a towering inspiration to scores of outcasts, misfits, future media executives, and creative types throughout his 25 years overseeing the station.

My friend Sean Griffin, who also shaped my taste with his encyclopedic music knowledge, would demo records in the back studio all day. He spent an entire summer just listening to records in there. Of course, pre-internet, having access to such a vast collection of music was formative. What kid had that opportunity back then, unless someone in his or her household had a huge record collection? Have you spent any time lately with folks in their twenties who love music? The curious ones know *everything*. I've hung out with guys like Daniel Bachman and Ryley Walker. They know *so* much music.

l to r: Judd, me, and Scott Kertes outside WKWZ

I was Music Director at WKWZ, which involved talking to various record label reps and trade publications like *CMJ*. *CMJ* was located about thirty minutes away in Mineola, so I interned there, taking the train from Syosset a couple of days a week after school. In 1983, I attended the Intercollegiate Broadcasting Convention in Washington DC. R.E.M. sat at an IRS Records table, waiting for someone to talk to them. They signed a photo for me. The Bangles, Jason & the Scorchers, and Lou Miami & the Kozmetix were down there too. I attended and worked on the annual CMJ Convention in 1984, where I met Lou Reed and scored Andy Warhol's autograph. He was just wandering around the exhibition hall, alone. In 1983, I took an unpaid internship at PolyGram Records, working for Jack Isquith (now at *Slacker*) as a college radio promotion rep. Jack was Dennis Miller before Dennis Miller, prone to launching into long analytical diatribes about music peppered with rapid-fire far-flung references and analogies. The sheer breadth of stuff that came out between 1983 to '85, when I worked there, was staggering: three Van Morrison records, Bananarama, a breaking Bon Jovi, Tears for Fears, Richard Thompson, Mellencamp's *Scarecrow*, Green on Red, Mark Knopfler's *Cal* soundtrack, all the Immediate catalog reissues, New York Dolls reissues, Trio, all the Velvet Underground records reissued for the first time. The executives who roamed the halls were giants to me—like Bill Levenson, often credited with refining the concept of the CD box-set in the earliest days of the configuration. Bill would tell me what he was doing with the Velvets reissues and what he had planned for *VU* and *Another View*, both brand new albums of previously unheard Velvets material.

I was taking the Long Island Rail Road back and forth to the city, learning the business. But I also made time to hang out with my friends. How many kids in Syosset (or anywhere) have Victor Hugo's autograph hanging on their wall? Judd Apatow did. He got it as a gift from his grandpa, record producer Bob Shad. I didn't know who Victor Hugo was, but the aged sepia photo and handwritten letter were so cool.

I would go over to Judd's house in the Gates, a wealthy enclave in Woodbury. There would usually be a heated screaming match between Judd upstairs and his dad downstairs. I never saw them yell at each other face to face—it was always level-to-level yelling. I think they both got more out of the argument that way; it made it less scary and confrontational. After their volley, Judd would cry a little.

His parents had divorced when he was 12, his mom decamping for Los Angeles with his sister and brother while Judd stayed on Long Island with his dad. Judd's maternal grandfather, Bob Shad, owned Mainstream and Time Records, labels that churned out titles in every conceivable genre from the '50s until Bob's passing in 1985. He signed Janis Joplin and Ted Nugent to their first record deals, produced Ray Charles and Charlie Parker in the '40s, and released LPs by Lightnin' Hopkins, Sarah Vaughan, John Cage, and scores of others.

Judd's mom, Tami Shad, and his Grandma Molly shared a house in LA, and I used to love looking through Bob's incredible record collection of vintage jazz LPs. Tami took over her dad's business after he died, and we used to talk about all the great records on Mainstream and different ways to market the label. I had steady contact with her until she passed in 2008. Judd definitely got his hustle from her. She was always optimistic, hyper, and excited, even toward the end of her life.

Judd ran with the popular crowd in school, but he was well liked among all the different cliques. I encouraged him to come down to WKWZ and do a comedy show, as that was his main interest. So he started cold-calling people like Jerry Seinfeld, Henny Youngman, Paul Reiser, and Jay Leno, and got them to talk about their craft on tape for his radio show, *Club Comedy*. Judd still has all the tapes, and some of the interviews have recently been compiled in his book *Sick in the Head*. I went with him to interview Steve Allen in his hotel room at the St. Regis in New York City and covered for him when he couldn't make a date with Shirley Hemphill (*What's Happening!!*).

Judd worked as a busboy at East Side Comedy Club. Soon he was doing his own stand-up routine there and at other Long Island clubs like Governor's. Although he tried to emulate his heroes, his own act didn't go over too well. So he started plotting how he'd write jokes for other people instead. It's nice to see him get some vindication, thirty years on, having resumed his stand-up performance career of late.

Judd and I would watch *Barney Miller* or *Gilligan's Island* or a game show, eat SpaghettiOs and Jello Pudding, and talk about comedians, music, and autographs. It was always a bit unclear what parents in the Gates did for a living and I couldn't figure out exactly what Judd's dad did. Something with real estate? But Judd had money, because he always held down a restaurant job. He was a busboy at El Torito on Jericho Turnpike for a while, and he also worked at a place called Raisins in the Woodbury Commons that his dad was involved with. He blew his cash playing cards, placing sports bets with other kids, and buying autographs. We would go to autograph shows at the Pierre Hotel in New York City, and Judd would blow a few hundred dollars on Beatles and movie star signatures. Although I didn't spend like that, collecting signatures was a passion we shared. We spent hours on the phone at night negotiating trades for our autographs. I had an aunt in Los Angeles who worked with B-level celebrities. She would send me signed 8x10s: Jack Carter, Norm Crosby, Shields & Yarnell, Rip Taylor, Charlie Callas. Jack Albertson of *Chico and the Man* fame wrote "Congratulations on your Bar Mitzvah, Jack Albertson." Judd and I were big fans of that show. In fact, Judd unloaded his very annoying pet cockatiel on me, named ... Chico.

Things got serious when I bought an autograph price guide. James Cagney was one of the most expensive signatures in there, so after he sent me a signed photo, I wrote to him again for another, which he again sent. I wrote to Roald Dahl and Charles Schultz. They wrote back. I asked George Burns to sign an 8x10 and burn his cigar into the photo. He did it. I cut out a *Sport Magazine* Blue Bonnet Butter ad with Mickey Mantle and Willie Mays wearing bonnets and eating large steaks. The caption read, "Playing For High Steaks." I had something called the Baseball Address Book, which was basically a computer printout of every living baseball player's home address—and those of the deceased ones' widows too. I cut out the picture and sent it to Willie at the address listed in the book. "Dear Willie, Please sign this, send it to Mickey, have him sign it, and send it back to me." They both did it, and I still have it. Pete Townshend wrote me back on Twickenham letterhead. I interviewed Jann Wenner for the school newspaper. He wrote back, "Good luch [sic] with your career in journalism."

My obsession with autographs culminated with a "rock auction," staged as a fundraiser for WKWZ, which took place in the Syosset High School auditorium. I wrote to loads of musicians and labels to send us autographed stuff like instruments and photos. A lot of that shit would be worth a fortune today, but it all sold for peanuts. I remember Elton John was nice enough to send a personalized signed photo. "To WKWZ, Best Wishes, Elton John."

In order to draw kids, we decided to stage a concert before the auction. Derek Simon, now a Nashville-based music executive, suggested we book a Kiss knock-off band called Alien. Derek was the resident metalhead (long hair, tight pants, Frye boots) and, God bless him, he took so much shit from everyone, especially Jack DeMasi (in a good-natured way, most of the time). The band showed up in colorful jumpsuits, leather, spandex, capes. The lead singer, Frank Starr, had a really, really high voice. Derek recalls watching them snort coke off the WKWZ news desk. I introduced the band on stage—"Ladies and Gentlemen, Alien!!!"—and couldn't find my way offstage with all the dry ice. Frank Starr died in a motorcycle accident in 1999 after a series of prison stays and other motorcycle accidents. Bassist Damien "the Beast" Bardot went on to appear in an episode of *Miami Vice* before a 1987 murder conviction sent him to Florida's death row, where he died in 2013, having maintained his innocence for 26 years.

At 16, I wrote a "biography" of Judd entitled *You Don't Toy with the 'Tow* as a class assignment. "This is a kid with dreams and ambitions far beyond that of the common teenager," I wrote. "Judd Apatow plans to make it." The summer after college, we hung out at Judd's mom's house in LA, got stoned, consumed large amounts of Doritos, sang Loudon Wainwright songs in the swimming pool, and rode around Laurel Canyon with a video camera, filming and acting silly. He entered USC's Film Program that fall and wrote me a letter.

> So, now I've found my WKWZ at USC. It's the Program Board. The people who set up all the speakers and concerts on campus.... We offered Jay Leno 3000 bucks plus 80 percent after our expenses are paid ...

It may sound corny, but honestly, I don't know what would have happened to either one of us if we didn't have the radio station as a catalyst and Jack DeMasi as our mentor. I do know that both of our careers would have been different. (Trust me, I'm not comparing the size of our careers.) Maybe the same results would have been realized, but the trajectories would've been different. It's hard to say. Judd wrote in *Sick in the Head*, "In your life you come across people who encourage your voice and originality. For me, that person is Jack DeMasi."

Judd's works contain subtle and not-so-subtle nods to Syosset, which make them extra fun for me to watch. Certainly *Freaks and Geeks* is loaded with Syosset references. The male lead played by Paul Rudd in *This Is 40* is a former SONY Music executive who starts his own independent record label, has two daughters, and is in a complicated marriage. Sound like someone you know? Because I've watched the whole ride—seen him struggle, fail, and battle adversity both internal and external to get to a very successful place—I admire how Judd has stayed true to himself and how he can't stop creating. Just like his grandfather Bob Shad, who never stopped making a record, he's restlessly creating something new all the time.

Judd and I were running along parallel lines back then, obsessed with celebrity culture. With WKWZ as our incubator, we were able to forge identities for ourselves, interacting with a whole world outside Syosset.

Chapter 8:

Robert Lester Folsom

My favorite album of 2014 consisted of songs recorded between 1972 and 1975. Shocking, right?

Robert Lester Folsom's private-press album from 1976, *Music and Dreams*, is one of those rediscovered artifacts that music journalists and reissue fiends devour. A thousand LPs and a hundred 8-tracks were pressed up upon release. The album languished in obscurity until 1996, when it was reissued by the Keystone label in Japan. Yoga Records reissued the album in 2008, Riverman in South Korea and Mexican Summer in the US both re-released it in 2010, and Anthology Recordings reissued it for a fifth time in 2014. Full of chorus pedals, flangey guitars, synths, and breezy mid '70s soft-rock tunes, the album sounds like a homemade version of things that were happening on the pop scene at the time, like Todd Rundgren or Bread. "We were trying to get a sound like Eric Clapton's *Badge*," Folsom told me.

Today's renaissance in vinyl consumption is partly fueled by labels that uncarth lost gems like *Music and Dreams*. Some of these releases get so lathered up in hipster media hyperbole, you wonder if the writer actually listened to the record. There is a forced cool assigned to some of these releases, and the original intent of

Folsom Afraid of Fame

By CHARLES POSTELL
Herald State Editor

TIFTON, Ga. — "When all my friends were getting high, I was writing songs, playing my guitar and feeling inferior," Robert Lester Folsom said.

Now, at 22, Folsom, like a lot of other struggling artists, still feels inferior.

But, the small audiences who hear his music love it. Now many have heard it. His lone album, "Music and Dreams", is considered top-notch. He writes everything he sings.

So if Folsom is so good, why is he worried about the grocery bill?

"He's afraid he's going to make it, and he's afraid he can't handle it," said a young clerk who worked a while with Folsom in a clothing shop.

So he moved from one dark cavern to another, from Valdosta to Tifton to Albany, often playing one-night stands.

His music and lyrics are distinctly Lester Folsom. It is a king of soft white-man blues, simple and smooth.

"I'm a bad business manager," Folsom said. The five-foot-eleven-inch singer-composer believes his biggest problem is not knowing how to take advantage of an opportunity when it comes along.

The biggest single influence on him has been the Beatles. He continues to idolize them, even though they've split and gone their separate ways.

"The Beatles got into my blood," he said. "They were the one thing that made me want to get out and do something. They were getting all that attention, and I'm the type

FOLSOM PLAYS HIS MUSIC TO SMALL, LOYAL AUDIENCES
Singer Says Business His Problem, Lets Opportunities Slip Away
(Herald Staff Photo by Charles Postell)

that likes attention. I mean, here I was, a skinny little kid who couldn't do much of anything but play a guitar and sing.

"I like George Harrison because his music is so pure, his slide playing so clean," he said, speaking in a soft authoritative tone. "Like right now he's playing what he wants to, even though he ain't sounding like the Beatles. It's his own style, with a little spiritual influence, like Indian religion — but still it's his.

"I love John Lennon because he's so open-minded about everything. He's a genius. A lot of his stuff is almost avant-garde and a lot of people don't

understand it.

"Paul McCartney — well, he's very commercial. He's the one who's making all the money, but I sort of appreciate that, because he probably sounds more like the Beatles than anything else.

"And Ringo, well — you just can't hate Ringo."

The Beatles and all the other things that influence Folsom come out of the 1960s. He regrets not coming up during that decade. When he talks of the times, it is with a kind of reverence.

"A lot of bad things happened in the 60s" he said, "but a lot of good things came out of it too. The 1970s have been dull.

Nothing is happening."

Except that his band, Abacus, has dissolved, and Folsom is miserable.

He muses aloud what went wrong.

I think a few of the guys in the band became envious, jealous, possibly. There were a few hassles, but nothing serious. Then they started thinking about things they shouldn't have been even thinking about.

"The drummer wanted to start writing songs. That would be about like me saying that I wanted to start playing drums," Folsom said. "I could no more play drums than he could write songs, but that's the way it went. It spoiled everything."

Herald State newspaper article, Tifton, Georgia, 1977 (Courtesy of Robert Lester Folsom) their creators gets distorted beyond recognition. You can decide for yourself whether *Music and Dreams* is one of those. The chasm that often exists between the draw of these rediscoveries and their quality is a topic few music journalists have tackled. In his January 2015 *Las Vegas Weekly* piece "Is the Lure of Rediscovered Artists Better than Their Music?," Smith Galtney seizes upon the question with an audacious frisson, calling out recent reissues by Rodriguez, William Onyeabor, and Lewis. Folsom seems uncomfortable being associated with reissue culture or any hipster scene. "I sort of think I don't belong to it," he told me. "People who have accepted *Music and Dreams* are on to it. I don't want to be a novelty—I want to be accepted for who I am." Mexican Summer asked him to play a CMJ bill in 2010 alongside the label's indie bands. He showed up at the Knitting Factory in Brooklyn, which was mobbed with young hipsters. "How are we going to fit in here?" Folsom wondered. His set was extremely well received, but one blogger's account illustrates the generational mismatch that can occur in such a setting:

11:00 – Robert Lester Folsom's band comes on stage and I'm sort of confused. First of all, they're old. Maybe in their 50s or 60s? Which is fine, I love them for that, but they don't necessarily fit Mexican Summer's vibe. Come to think of it, none of these bands (minus No Joy) fit MS's vibe. I'm so confused and depressed and drunk.

11:15 – Robert Lester Folsom sounds like that band Chicago.

11:20 – The lead singer explains the meaning of each song. So far, they've been about burning Thanksgiving dinner and Dora the Explorer.

11:30 – Oh my God. They just told the audience that they were "big in the '70s" and Mexican Summer has reunited them. This makes so much sense. Now, I'm slightly less confused and a little more drunk.

Folsom may or may not have been out of place on the Mexican Summer bill, but he isn't the first artist from the early '70s to get re-contextualized for a new generation, and any lo-fi indie rocker can find something to love about *Ode to a Rainy Day: Archives 1972–75*. Panda Bear is a fan. "See You Later, I'm Gone" sounds like a Dinosaur Jr. demo. The sensibility isn't that far removed from Guided by Voices, Kurt Vile, or Beat Happening. Hopefully enough youngsters will get their hands on the LP and start covering these songs.

Framed next to *Ode to a Rainy Day: Archives 1972–75*, also released by Anthology in 2014 and originally recorded on 2-track reel-to-reel, *Music and Dreams* sounds more like a lost opportunity than a lost classic. Folsom's fine songwriting gets sucked beneath an undertow of contemporary production. It's no one's fault. Those were the sounds of the time, utilized by independent musicians with limited resources. That said, it's still better than 90 percent of the '70s singer/songwriter private-press records I have heard, and I have heard many. "Show Me to the Window" appears on both *Ode* and *Music and Dreams*. The 2-track version on *Ode* has that winning melancholic ache, intensified by the ghostly, crude recording dynamics. The version on *Music and Dreams* is mired in phasey vocals and synths. This was subtraction by addition, and Folsom seems to know it. "I am very proud of *Music and Dreams*," he states in the liner notes to *Ode*, "but it's the early reel-to-reel archives that truly bare the soul of my music and life."

Robert Lester Folsom was born January 3, 1955, at Moody Air Force Base, Lowndes County, Georgia, and raised in Adel, Georgia. A railroad track ran straight through the town. Adel's other famous residents include Ray McKinnon, who played Reverend Smith in the HBO series *Deadwood*, and Tom Smith, a member of experimental rock units Pussy Galore and To Live and Shave in LA. Robert grew up across the street from Don Fleming, who went on to play in Velvet Monkeys, B.A.L.L., and Gumball, and now works for the Alan Lomax Archive. Don was present for some of the sessions Robert recorded throughout their high school years, at times manning the tape deck. Fleming produced the recent *Ode* reissue LP, combing through about ten reels of old tape. Although he was present for some of the sessions, Don had never heard most of the material until about five years ago, when Robert hauled out the tapes. *Ode* only represents a small fraction of Folsom's recordings from 1972 to 1975. The sessions were conceived as full albums, and could be broken out as such. "I used to sit in my room making sequences, coming up with titles, drawing the album covers," he says. The prospect of hearing so many more Folsom "albums" elicits great levels of excitement in me.

I hung out with Don a bit in the early '90s when Gumball was signed to Columbia Records. I was working as a promotion guy at the label at the time. The band was picked up at the height of a major-label feeding frenzy around "Alternative Music," which only intensified with the explosion of Nirvana. Don moved in the same circles as Dinosaur Jr., Sonic Youth, and Jad Fair. But years earlier, he was getting a master class in songwriting, producing, and DIY recording from his friend Lester.

"He wrote so many original songs. There was no precedent for that where we were from," Don told me. "People were playing in cover bands." As Folsom's tape library bears out, he was a prolific songwriter and recording artist. There are country songs performed with Folsom's dad, loads of instrumentals, and yet more original songs in the vault. "I always guessed that he would be the one to go on, get famous," Don reflects. "He really influenced me to produce and be a musician. He was influenced by the Beatles; he's a bit in the Gram Parsons camp, but he wasn't into the Southern Rock thing."

Folsom sure sounds like an outsider. "We weren't the guys playing football," he says, "We were in our own little world, making music in our amateur, simplistic way." You can hear adolescent confusion in "Situations," a song about being misunderstood by friends, getting nailed by cops for speeding, and feeling alienated at parties, all whimsically accented at the end with a Jew's harp.

Friends they say I'm crazy
And they put me on the spot
By calling me a redneck
Just because I don't smoke pot

Folsom's parents belonged to all the record clubs and ordered up albums by Johnny Cash and the Platters. Folsom sang four-part harmony in church, and listened to Fats Domino, Chubby Checker, and Elvis. "Then the Beatles came along and that was it," he says. "Don was a member of the Beatles Fanclub. You had to write your own songs at that point, because we saw Lennon/McCartney, we thought, OK, that's what made you a celebrity."

He and his friend Roger Sumner headed to a rural farmhouse outside Adel and borrowed a family's reel-to-reel tape recorder. Once they mastered some recording techniques, they ordered their own 2-track machine from Sears and started taking it everywhere as a mobile recording unit, duplicating 8-track tapes of their songs to pass around to their friends. "We'd ride around the Dairy Queen and the hot dog stand and we'd hear people playing our songs out of their cars," Robert marvels. With assistance from his close friend Hans Van Brackle, the recordings became more elaborate, adding elements like Farfisa and Wurlitzer organ and overdubbed vocal parts. The songs were recorded in bedrooms, porches, living rooms, and barns with a rotating collective of friends. Folsom became adept at manipulating his 2-track to act like a multi-track recorder, layering harmonies and instrumental parts. The crude nature of the recordings, the innocence of the whole enterprise, the simple yet sophisticated writing, like Brian Wilson's—these elements make for an engrossing listen.

In 1973, Folsom formed the band Abacus at South Georgia College, playing primarily original tunes, which was very unusual for their time and place. Most local bands played covers. They chose the name *Abacus* because Abba was red hot at the time, and they figured they could get in front of Abba alphabetically in the record store bins with that name. Clever! Some of the earlier recordings were used to work up a demo that Folsom sent to Capricorn, Dark Horse, and other labels. He still has the rejection letters. Folsom had a knack for sneaking backstage at shows and ingratiating himself with engineers at Capricorn studios in nearby Macon, where he'd sit in on sessions in the control room, soaking it in.

In 1976, Abacus's bass player's mom offered the band some money to record a demo, and they laid down seven songs. Folsom shared it with me. The highlight is "Lunar Pie," a nine-and-a-half minute opus that begins as an uptempo blues workout, then bleeds into a woozy, dark jam about asteroids and spaceships, then goes full-tilt Blue Oyster Cult boogie. The engineer at LeFevre Studios in Atlanta became very interested, and at that point they decided to record *Music and Dreams*. Don Fleming marvels at how Folsom adopted a DIY approach to record-making as well as purveying via his own label, Abacus, releasing *Music and Dreams* in 1976, followed by *Green and Yellow* by the Stroke Band, which featured Fleming, Hans, Folsom, and others, in 1978. *Green and Yellow* was reissued by Anthology Recordings in 2014.

In the late '70s, Folsom worked for a short time at Cal's Records in Jacksonville. Mike Campbell's grandmother would come in to find out how Tom Petty's records were selling. Around 1979, Robert settled into professional house painting, got married, and raised kids. He continues to make music, and enjoys all the acclaim and attention his music has inspired. He wonders if "fear of success" played a part in derailing his music career. He sent me a local article written when he was 22 that alludes to this.

"He's afraid he's going to make it, and he's afraid he can't handle it," said a young clerk who worked a while with Folsom in a clothing shop.

Being re-discovered decades later is its own sweet success. I can't wait to hear the rest of Folsom's archival "albums." Meanwhile, I asked him to offer up an exclusive song-by-song rundown of *Ode to a Rainy Day: Archives 1972–75,* and he was kind enough to oblige. Fire up Spotify and follow along!

Ode to a Rainy Day

An instrumental for one of those rainy South Georgia summer days when we could at least stay indoors and record music. Me on 12-string acoustic and electric guitar through a Fender Vibratone Leslie cabinet. Bob Jones on percussion. Recorded on my Sears reel-to-reel in the music suite at South Georgia College, where I basically set up residence. The rain is from a sound effects record from the college library. In the key of E minor. A favorite key for guitar doodling.

Written in Your Hair

My bass player from Abacus, Sparky Smith, had a cool old organ in his parents' home with funky programmed sounds. I found a sound that I liked, so I got Sparky to hit certain high notes on this song to give it an outer-space folky vibe. I had already recorded the drums and guitar at the college music suite. Sparky is not a keyboard player but he was always happy to follow my wacky instructions on what to play. Me on guitars, Bob Jones on drums, and Sparky on bass and space sounds. This song was written about how people can be so judgmental. In those days, about the length of your hair. No matter how good or bad you are, they can always judge your character by your hair! Ha! Ha! Ha!

Love Is

High school love song. Perfect song for a flute solo. Silly but sincere lyrics and a powerful chorus.

Heaven (On the Beach with You)

Hans Van Brackle and I put together a medley of some of our individual instrumentals called "Warm Horizons Suite." This segment is one of mine about being at the beach, probably in

Mexico, if you imagine that from the ending segment. Being only a few hours from the Atlantic Ocean, Hans and I would take road trips with our guitars and play them to strangers and ourselves on the beach.

See You Later, I'm Gone

A combination of longing for home and a summer romance coming to an end. Going home could be a metaphor for summer ending and going back to school. In this case, the girl with the "summer smile" did not return to school; instead she moved away. A seriously sentimental song for me.

On and On

A song I wrote when my band Abacus was living and rehearsing in Auburn, Alabama. I wrote it to express that, despite all the crazy things that happen in this world, life goes on and on. I think this is a great heavy song both in music and in lyrics. The lyrics are also unique in that I probably was pretending to be a little more intelligent than I truly am. I was probably trying to impress my critics. After all these years I am somewhat impressed with the song and the performance by my band.

Another Sunday Morning

I grew up in a home where everyone was expected to be in church on Sunday morning. When I got to a point where I had a choice, I would more likely take nature walks by myself on Sunday mornings. Somehow in my Sunday morning meditations I think I imagined what it would be like to be with someone on the weekend, and realizing on Sunday morning that the weekend was not gonna last forever. I liked the pairing of Kris Kristofferson and Rita Coolidge, and I chose to find a young lady at school that could do this song as a duet with me. Today I simply think it is a very catchy song, and I am very proud of it.

Situations

A song about being myself and dealing with the situations I would come across. I was a hippy wanna-be, but I didn't want to do drugs. I thought you could be cool by not following the crowd. I caught a lot of flack for being that way, but I maintained my non-conformity.

Oblivion

On a rainy summer day, I invited my friend Hans Van Brackle to come over my house and play guitars. We recorded this tune, and I liked the title "Oblivion." I imagined this instrumental being used in a Western music soundtrack. That's me on guitar and organ and Hans on guitar and bass.

Can't You See (the Light in Me)

This is just me and my guitar wishing everyone could just understand what I was all about. Probably just a typical teenage sentiment, but I was able to express it through music. I think I really thought I had something to share with the world, or was it just wishful thinking? I have gotten a lot of good compliments on this simple, quiet tune.

She (Ode to a Rainbow)

Just another song from my imagination about someone who is lonely. Might be a little bit about myself. I couldn't let my friends think it was about me, so I made it about some lonely girl.

Blue Velvet at Low Ebb

Not a happy time in college. This song is like a soundtrack to my days in school between winter semester and spring. Written after I also wrote "See You Later, I'm Gone." Just a weird time when nothing was going my way. On one hand, I didn't see how losing someone could seem like the end of the world, and on the other hand I couldn't see how this person could just walk away, and I didn't understand how any of it could truly bother me except for the simple fact that I wanted to be loved. Whatever!

Show Me to the Window

Probably one of my best songs. Don't really remember writing it, but I was thinking about friends who gave up their dreams. And friends who were running from their dreams. The "show me to the window" harmony is haunting to me, and I think it is beautiful. It is a true musical reflection of my spirit. It is a sincere expression of my originality (in music). I thought about writing a follow-up song with the lyrics "Show me to the window / Let me jump through the pain." This song is beautiful, and it haunts me a little.

I follow my dreams and die a poor man. My friends discard their dreams, follow reality, and die wealthy. (Some died early). I don't know what to say. I'm still here!

Robert Lester Folsom
2015

Chapter 9:

Obscure Giants of Acoustic Guitar

Fans of Tompkins Square know that a major focus for the label over the years has centered on American Primitive Guitar. This school is descended from players of the '20s and '30s like Riley Puckett, Sam McGee, Sylvester Weaver, and Lemuel Turner. Only a handful of solo acoustic performances exist from this era, but they provided the blueprint for much of what was to follow. In the '60s, John Fahey and his contemporaries would search Southern back roads for 78 rpm discs, rediscovering blues and old-time country records, and if they were really lucky, the players themselves. Many of these solo guitar selections are compiled by producer Chris King on the Tompkins Square album *Imaginational Anthem Vol. 6: Origins of American Primitive Guitar.*

My interest in guitar music started with Jimmy Page. His version of "Black Mountain Side" on *Led Zeppelin I* eventually led me to Bert Jansch, one of my favorite singer/songwriters. Zeppelin was also my conduit to blues masters like Elmore James, Blind Lemon Jefferson, and Memphis Minnie. Whether or not the band "plagiarized" some of this old material is pretty irrelevant, considering their versions are classics in their own right, and heavily re-engineered ones at that. Zeppelin weren't reaching very far back at all to gather their influences. Perhaps because of how raw the blues and early string-band recordings sound to our ears, we think of them as ancient. When Led Zeppelin covered Memphis Minnie and Kansas Joe McCoy's 1929 version of "When the Levee Breaks" in 1971, the recording was only 42 years old. *Led Zeppelin IV* is now

44 years old, yet we don't view it, or other records from 1971, as some arcane artifact from another world entirely. The music that John Fahey and Led Zeppelin were channeling in the '60s wasn't old. Maybe some of it was obscure and hard to locate. But it was relatively recent popular music, much of it released on major labels.

By the late '60s, independent labels like Yazoo, Rounder, and Folkways were starting to reissue 78 compilations, making many of the rarest sides available again. This had a major impact on musicians, especially in the UK, where so much of the music had never been available. Artists like Big Bill Broonzy and Reverend Gary Davis had an incalculable influence on British rock musicians.

Much has been written over the past few years about John Fahey and his towering influence, with new books and research surfacing. We are now a couple of generations down the line from Fahey, Basho, and the influential players of the '60s. When I talk to young players, they certainly revere Fahey, but my sense is they also feel eager to get out from underneath his shadow. Modern-day baseball players generally don't sit around talking about Sandy Koufax and Ted Williams; they just play the game. There's a restless sense that in order to move acoustic guitar music forward, there needs to be a marked departure from Fahey's style, whether it's his signature syncopated picking, his enigmatic song titles, or even his adherence to blues structure. A major step forward in this regard was William Tyler's *Behold the Spirit*, released on Tompkins Square in 2010. Tyler came to my attention via an unsolicited email sent to me in December, 2009, from someone named Sharon Van Etten. I didn't know who she was, but she wrote, "I hope you don't mind me writing out of the blue like this, but a friend of mine recently sent me his new album, and I think you would really enjoy it."

I didn't know it at the time, but William had already appeared as a sideman on *Charlie Louvin Sings Murder Ballads & Disaster Songs*, released on Tompkins Square. I signed him, and then he turned me on to Michael Taylor/Hiss Golden Messenger, and then Michael hooked me up with Alice Gerrard and produced her album

Follow the Music, which gave Alice her first Grammy nomination at age 80. So, read your unsolicited email!

On *Behold the Spirit*, Tyler takes a lot of acoustic guitar pastiches and blows them up onto a panoramic canvas. The guitar is central, but there are grand, sweeping arrangements and a Southern flavor, given Will's Nashville roots. Upon release, *Pitchfork's* Grayson Currin spotted the evolution straight away:

> You either fully embrace Fahey—like, say, the late Jack Rose—or you run the other way, like Ben Chasny with his work as Six Organs of Admittance. A middle ground exists, certainly, but it's rarely been claimed with the grace and elocution of *Behold the Spirit*, the debut from young Nashville guitarist William Tyler. Arguably the most vital, energized album by an American solo guitarist in a decade or more, it accepts Fahey's legacy while escaping its shadow.

My exploration of acoustic guitar music has resulted in seven volumes of the *Imaginational Anthem* series, as well as lots of solo guitar albums in the Tompkins Square catalog. After the first four volumes, I decided to let others curate the compilations. This is more fun for me, as I get turned on to new players just as any listener might. *Volume 5*, compiled by guitarist Sam Moss, featured Daniel Bachman, who I subsequently signed for two albums, and who turned me on to Ryley Walker, who I signed. *Volume 7* was compiled by 20-year-old guitarist Hayden Pedigo. His work compiling *Volume 7* illustrates the state of the art, as the series has always sought to do, at a critical juncture for the genre. There has been some fatigue setting in, but his compilation shows a vibrant new generation coming forward once again.

I created a Trading Card set, "Obscure Giants of Acoustic Guitar," just for fun a couple of years ago. Here are some of the entries, with my synopses from the backs of the cards, for those who would like to delve deeper into the solo acoustic world. These are some of my very favorite players from today and days gone by.

George Cromarty

How many obscure solo guitar giants have had their songs covered by Paul Newman? If you watch *Cool Hand Luke*, you'll see a tearful Newman plucking a banjo and singing "Plastic Jesus," a tune George Cromarty co-wrote in the late '50s when he performed as half of a duo called the Gold Coast Singers. Drafted into the Army in 1963, he settled in Morro Bay upon his return, releasing two LPs on his tiny Thistle label in 1973: the solo Grassroots Guitar and a children's album, *The Only Ones*. Performed on an 1896 Washburn, Cromarty's delicate, melodic playing reflected his Northern California surroundings—playful splashes of cascading notes against quiet, contemplative passages. His final album, the gorgeous *Wind in the Heather*, was produced by George Winston, released in 1984 on Winston's Dancing Cat label, and distributed by Windham Hill. All three of Cromarty's records have been out of print for decades. He took his own life on February 12,1992, at age 50. Although his body of work is small, his music will deeply affect anyone who endeavors to seek it out.

Max Ochs

A boyhood friend of John Fahey and Robbie Basho, Maryland's Max Ochs recorded two influential guitar ragas on the long-out-of-print Takoma compilation *Contemporary Guitar Spring '67* alongside Fahey, Basho, Bukka White, and Harry Taussig. He befriended Mississippi John Hurt and Skip James during the '60s folk revival. Max's composition "Imaginational Anthem," originally recorded for Joe Bussard's Fonotone label in 1969, inspired the guitar series of the same name on Tompkins Square. His 2008 album, *Hooray for Another Day*, includes a new take on Fahey's arrangement of "In Christ There Is No East or West," a few heady ragas, and several spoken-word poems, one entitled "Phil," dedicated to Max's cousin, the late folk legend Phil Ochs.

Harry Taussig

Released as a short-run private-press LP in 1965, *Fate Is Only Once* has long been a coveted collectible among American Primitive Guitar enthusiasts. The album presages the broader movement. Acoustic musicians were still largely stuck in a rigid "folk" mindset in 1965, and there are just not that many other examples of the exploratory guitar sounds found on *Fate* during this time period. Alternating between haunting originals and jaunty blues-based traditional numbers, this absurdly rare LP was reissued by Tompkins Square in 2006. Taussig's only other early recorded works appear on the long-out-of-print Takoma compilation *Contemporary Guitar Spring '67* alongside John Fahey, Robbie Basho, Max Ochs, and Bukka White. Taussig spent years as an educator, published instructional guitar books, and traveled extensively to photograph weird museums. Amazingly, he resurfaced in 2012 with his first album in 47 years, appropriately titled *Fate Is Only Twice*. The same stark, smoldering playing is evident, with all the cleverness and inventiveness intact.

Bob Hadley

Born in Alabama and raised in Fairfax County, Virginia, Bob Hadley recorded three excellent solo guitar albums on Kicking Mule: *The Raven* (1975), *Tunes from the Well* (1976), and *On the Trail of the Questing Beast* (1980). Hadley is featured on a 1979 John Fahey tribute album, and Takoma Records co-owner Ed Denson wrote liner notes for his first two albums. Largely self-taught, his open tunings and improvisation were inspired by Fahey and Leo Kottke, but he referred to himself as a "Romantic" composer/guitarist—deriving inspiration from nature. Hadley settled in Canada in the mid '70s and spent many years as Professor of Computing Science at Simon Fraser University. Tompkins Square hunted him down to record a tune for *Imaginational Anthem Vol. 1* in 2005, his first new recording in 25 years.

Suni McGrath

Harry "Suni" McGrath recorded three rare and masterful 6- and 12-string guitar records from 1969 to 1973 on the Adelphi label: *Cornflower Suite, The Call of the Mourning Dove,* and *Childgrove.* A student of Mississippi John Hurt and Reverend Gary Davis, Suni played with a style that featured old-time finger-picking; strong Appalachian, Bulgarian, and Celtic influences; and "the long lost seven mysterious flavors of feeling and beauty of the Western musical heritage." Tompkins Square tracked him down in rural Indiana in 2005. Suni was playing a lot of violin and piano locally, but not much guitar. I coaxed him to record his first new tracks in 33 years: "Train Z," which appears on *Imaginational Anthem Vol. 1,* and a 7" single consisting of two new songs, "Seven Stars" and "Fantasia."

Richard Crandell

Eugene, Oregon-based guitarist and mbira player Richard Crandell released several albums in the '80s—most notably his 1980 private-press debut album, *In the Flower of Our Youth,* reissued on vinyl by Tompkins Square in 2008. An indispensable "rainy day" or driving record, it is a stone classic. Crandell's composition "Rebecca" was recorded by Leo Kottke on his LP *Chewing Pine.* Echoes of John Renbourn, Fahey, and the topography of the Pacific Northwest inhabit his playing, but a closer listen unearths a deft and unique melodic touch. An NPR *All Things Considered* piece in 2009 brought attention to Richard's music and his struggle with essential tremor, a movement disorder that causes uncontrollable shaking. In recent years, Crandell has immersed himself in the mbira, a Zimbabwean thumb piano, recording two albums for the Tzadik label.

Mark Fosson

If you're talking 12-string guitar, you have to talk about Kentucky native Mark Fosson. But because he's an obscure giant, few ever do. Tompkins Square released *Digging in the Dust: Home Recordings 1976* in 2012. Fosson sent a tape to John Fahey's Takoma label in 1977. Upon hearing it, Fahey wrote, "Best demo tape I've heard since Kottke." But Fahey sold Takoma to Chrysalis, and the album languished for decades before it was finally reissued in 2006. Some years later, Mark found the earliest home demos for that album in his house—gorgeous, complex arrangements (plus a Gene Autry cover) exquisitely recorded in his living room. Pitchfork aptly noted, "Fosson is a purely American-sounding player. The raga, drone, and concrete that almost inevitably make their way into solo players' repertoires are largely absent in Fosson's playing."

George Stavis

Although George Stavis is a banjo player, not a guitar player, he truly belongs alongside his obscure acoustic guitar brethren. Stavis formed the psychedelic band Federal Duck, who released one self-titled album on the Musicor label in 1968. Stavis then recorded a solo album for Vanguard in 1969, *Labyrinths*, subtitled *Occult Improvisational Compositions for 5-string Banjo and Percussion*. This essential LP is the oddest and best psych-banjo record of the period, rivaled only by fellow obscure banjo giant Billy Faier's 1973 Takoma LP, *Banjo*. *Labyrinths* is a wonderful devil's brew of ethnic, old-timey, and psychedelics, and you gotta love his medieval getup on the cover. George resurfaced in 2006 by contributing a new track on *Imaginational Anthem Vol. 3*, and even played some live shows in the US with Cian Nugent and Ben Reynolds, only to then mysteriously fade back into banjo obscurity.

Wilburn Burchette

Some of Wilburn Burchette's album titles: *Music of the Godhead for Supernatural Meditation, Opens the Seven Gates of Transcendental Consciousness, Psychic Meditation Music.* Equal parts psychedelic, mystical, occult, and American gothic, Burchette occupies his own unique hemisphere in guitar lore. Releasing seven albums in the '70s, some under the name Master Wilburn Burchette, the records are instructional, as if there is a specific purpose for them beyond passive listening or mere enjoyment. Some of them came with extensive booklets outlining his philosophies and musical approach. He used a variety of stringed instruments, as well as electric guitar and synthesizer. We believe he is still alive, and have tried to track him down by mail. He has not released anything in decades, and all his albums are out of print.

Michael Chapman

Born January 24, 1941, in Yorkshire, England, singer/songwriter/guitarist Michael Chapman absorbed influences ranging from Blind Blake and Jimmie Rodgers to Iberian flamenco during his formative years on the UK folk-club circuit. The English journalist Charles Shaar Murray described Chapman's songwriting as imbued with "a kind of aggressive stoicism"—a commitment to emotional truth-telling, free of sticky sentimentality and sometimes leavened with a streak of sardonic Northern humor.

On his 1969 debut *Rainmaker* and other early LPs, Chapman and producer Gus Dudgeon alternated full-band tracks with the artist's own electric and acoustic guitar accompaniments in which he deployed finger-picking, expressive bottleneck playing, and an assortment of open tunings. Chapman has been "re-discovered" in recent years by way of Thurston Moore's Ecstatic Peace label; a reissue campaign by the Light in the Attic label; an acclaimed two-disc anthology, *Trainsong: Guitar Compositions 1967–2010*; and US tours with the late Jack Rose, Bill Callahan, and Kurt Vile.

Robbie Basho

The five albums he released on Takoma Records established Robbie Basho as one of the most distinctive and gifted acoustic guitarists of his generation. Born in 1940 and adopted by a family in Baltimore, Daniel Robinson Jr. developed his passion for guitar and Asian culture while studying at the University of Maryland. (He took his surname from the 17th-century Japanese poet Matsuo Basho.) Basho's music incorporated a world of influences: Arabic, Himalayan, and Indian themes; Japanese and Chinese scales; and classical and European folk strains. In Berkeley, the guitarist studied North Indian music with Ali Akbar Kahn. In 1986, while undergoing routine chiropractic treatment, the vertebral artery in his neck suddenly ruptured; Basho fell into a coma and died at age 45.

"He felt and played and sang like someone possessed, and many were bewildered by him," wrote Will Ackerman in the liner notes for the Tompkins Square reissue of Basho's 1969 album *Venus in Cancer*. "And many of us will remember him as a true visionary who offered the world a remarkable body of work before he left us."

Fred Gerlach

In the folk music revival of the early '60s, 12-string guitarist and vocalist Fred Gerlach was a respected peer of such performers as Pete Seeger and Cisco Houston. His debut album, *Gallows Pole and Other Folk Songs* on the tiny Audio-Video Productions label, featured songs the artist had learned firsthand from Lead Belly and Reverend Gary Davis. The album was reissued in 1962 on Folkways as *Folk Songs and Blues Sung and Played by Fred Gerlach*, a showcase for his spirited finger-picking and roughly authentic singing. The album included a new version of Lead Belly's "Gallows Pole" that became the basis for Jimmy Page's arrangement of the song on *Led Zeppelin III*. Leo Kottke's Capitol debut, *Mudlark* (1971), was recorded on a 12-string he borrowed from Gerlach, who eked out a living as a dealer in rare woods (and ivory, when it was still legal). His 1970 LP *Songs My Mother Never Sang* on Takoma is a 12-string gem. Fred Gerlach died in San Diego at age 84 on December 31, 2009.

Peter Walker

In the liner notes to his 2008 album *Echo of My Soul*, Peter Walker called flamenco "the missing link between Eastern and Western music." This singular guitarist has dedicated his long career to exploring and extending the intertwined traditions of Spanish flamenco and Indian raga. Born in 1937 to a musical family in Boston, Massachusetts, Walker began playing guitar as a teenager. His earliest public appearances took place in 1959 in San Francisco, where he heard Ravi Shankar perform for the first time; the guitarist later studied with Shankar in Los Angeles and with Ali Akbar Khan in Berkeley. In 1965, Walker became musical director for the LSD "celebrations" hosted at Dr. Timothy Leary's estate. His classic Vanguard debut album, *Rainy Day Raga*, appeared the following year. After his 1968 Vanguard release, *Second Poem to Karmela or, Gypsies Are Important* (on which he played sarod and sitar as well as guitar), Walker faded from public view but remained dedicated to the study of flamenco. In 2008, Walker released *Echo of My Soul*, his first new album in four decades.

Sandy Bull

Alexander "Sandy" Bull was a true world musician long before the term was common parlance. Born February 25, 1941, Bull played guitar from the age of eight and took banjo lessons from the Weavers' Erik Darling. In the late '50s, he heard North African music during a trip to Paris and began to study Ravi Shankar's albums, which led to his mastery of the oud and the sarod. In 1963, Bull released his Vanguard debut, *Fantasias for Guitar and Banjo*, an album years ahead of its time. Side One was devoted to the 22-minute track "Blend," with Bull's hypnotic open-tuned guitar paced by jazz drummer Billy Higgins. On Bull's second LP, *Inventions*, he overdubbed blended electric bass, guitar, banjo, oud, and pedal steel on interpretations of works by J.S. Bach, Chuck Berry, Brazil's Luiz Bonfa, and the medieval French composer Guillaume de Machaut.

Following two further LPs for Vanguard, Bull's career was derailed by drug addiction. He moved to Nashville, raised a family, built a studio, and released new music on his own label. He died of lung cancer on April 11, 2001. His *Los Angeles Times* obituary quoted him thusly: "I like to think of my music as a dog whistle—only certain types respond."

Steve Mann

Born May 3, 1943, and raised in the San Fernando Valley, Steve Mann took guitar lessons from Bess Lomax Hawes and Dick Rosmini. During Mann's sophomore year at UCLA, Hoyt Axton turned him on to the music of Robert Johnson—a life-changing event. In San Francisco in 1963, Mann briefly but memorably accompanied aspiring folk-blues singer Janis Joplin. In Los Angeles, he worked with Taj Mahal and Ry Cooder, and played the 12-string acoustic part on "I Got You Babe," Sonny & Cher's No. 1 hit of 1965. Dick Rosmini produced Mann's studio album, *Straight Life*, released in 1967 on the Custom Fidelity label.

Soon after this auspicious start, Mann developed symptoms of mental illness. He was diagnosed as schizophrenic and disappeared into a maze of mental hospitals, halfway houses, and homelessness for nearly forty years. Friends and admirers in the Bay Area came to the guitarist's aid, and in 2003 he began performing occasionally and overseeing reissues of *Straight Life*; the historic *Live at the Ash Grove*, recorded in 1967; and *Alive and Pickin'*, a collection of informal recordings that included three tracks with Janis Joplin.

Steve Mann passed away after a series of falls on September 9, 2009, in San Pablo, California.

Scott Witte

Born in Milwaukee, Wisconsin, in 1958, Scott Witte began studying guitar at age eight. After playing electric guitar for several years, Scott fell under the spell of the Takoma Records stable of guitarists in the late '70s. Witte studied flamenco at the Milwaukee Conservatory of Music, and then applied all he'd learned to his self-released 1980 debut album, *Sailor's Dream*, recorded in the same Minneapolis studio as his heroes, Peter Lang and Leo Kottke. In 2006, worlds collided when DJ Shadow sampled Witte's track "Grow" from *Sailor's Dream* on his album *The Outsider*. After a 28-year hiatus, Witte released *Sound Shadows* in 2008, fusing modern and traditional approaches within his virtuosic 12- and 6-string guitar compositions. The album features some of Witte's unique hammering and odd time signatures.

William Eaton

William Eaton is one of the most extraordinary instrument builders in the world, having established the Roberto-Venn School of Luthiery in Phoenix in 1975, where he still creates new instruments. Originally from Lincoln, Nebraska, Eaton received a ukulele from his uncle at age seven. Upon moving to Tempe to attend Arizona State University, Eaton became enchanted by his new desert surroundings. After a two-year stint at Stanford, he returned to Arizona, this time to deep mountain areas outside of Phoenix, where he began building instruments while using the surrounding canyons and endless skies as his sonic canvas. Recorded in the guesthouse of a mansion near Camelback Mountain, *Music by William Eaton* was released as a limited private-press of 1000 copies in 1978. Three instruments were used on the eleven untitled, completely improvised compositions: a 6-string dreadnaught acoustic, a 12-string dreadnaught, and a 26-string guitar (Elesion Harmoniom). The album was reissued on CD with new photos, bonus tracks, and notes in Japan in 2006. Eaton continues his work as a luthier, performer, and recording artist in Arizona.

Richard Osborn

Richard Osborn was born in 1947 in Pasadena, California. His musical roots are in both East and West: Western classical music (as well as folk and jazz) and an early passion for world music, especially Hindustani classical music and the incomparable Ali Akbar Khan. As a folk guitarist, his earliest influences were Mississippi John Hurt and John Fahey. His own approach to the guitar was transformed after hearing Robbie Basho in concert. He studied with Basho in 1968 and opened on a couple of Robbie's concerts in the early '70s. A serious injury to his left hand in 1980 left him unable to play the guitar for over 15 years. During that time, he turned to painting. Discovering that he had regained enough strength to play the guitar again enabled him to "return home." For the last seven years, he has focused on developing what he prefers to call the "free raga style" of improvisation. He was included on the Tompkins Square album *Beyond Berkeley Guitar* and released his very first solo CD in 2012, *Giving Voice: Guitar Explorations.*

Linda Cohen

That giant sucking sound you hear is folks buying Linda Cohen's long-deleted albums on eBay and out of the indie-store folk bins after they've read this. As it should be. *Leda* (1972), *Lake of Light* (1973), and *Angel Alley* (1982) are fine testaments to her extreme talent. Based in Philadelphia, Cohen was mostly self-taught, although she did study classical guitar briefly. She opened for Ramblin' Jack Elliott, Dave Van Ronk, and John Fahey at the Second Fret in the late '60s, and played folk clubs like the Bitter End in New York City. Her main gig for 35 years was teaching out of the Classical Guitar Store on Sansom Street in Philly. Cohen's debut album, *Leda*, released on the Poppy label, includes gorgeous compositions for classical guitar with assorted electronic sounds, tape collage, and other instrumentation. The mainly solo *Angel Alley* featured Cohen on steel-string guitar as well as classical, presented in her singular style: mannered yet loose, dark yet whimsical at times.

Linda Cohen died from lung cancer on January 23, 2009, at age 61.

Billy Faier

Banjo and guitar player Billy Faier was born on December 21, 1930, in Brooklyn, New York. He first encountered folk music after moving with his family to Woodstock in 1945. At 17, Faier moved into a cold-water flat on Avenue D and began playing banjo and guitar at the Washington Square "hootenannies." In 1954, he traveled cross-country with Woody Guthrie and Ramblin' Jack Elliott. In 1957, following a ten-minute audition for Riverside Records, Faier recorded his debut album, *The Art of the Five String Banjo*, followed by a second LP, *Travelin' Man*. While living in the Bay Area, he hosted a weekly KPFA radio show, and famously interviewed Bob Dylan in New York on WBAI in 1962 as host of his radio show *Midnight Special*.

In 1964, now resettled in Woodstock, Faier self-released his third album, *The Beast of Billy Faier*, with John Sebastian on guitar and harmonica. *Banjo* (1973) was recorded with a budget of $200 and became the artist's lone Takoma Records release. Faier contributed "New World Coming" to the 2006 Tompkins Square anthology *Imaginational Anthem Vol. II* and performed at South by Southwest. Now residing in Marathon, Texas, and still playing banjo and piano, Billy Faier sells music and memorabilia through his website, including "a handwritten letter from Big Bill Broonzy to my wife trying to get her to leave me and come live with him in Europe." (Price: $5,000)

T. Damien

Can you be a Giant if you only recorded four songs and no one knows your full name or what you looked like? Sure, if your name is T. Damien. This mystery man showed up at Fonotone label owner Joe Bussard's door on April 9, 1969, asking to make a record. Joe obliged, and recorded two songs: "Creamsicle" and "Drunk Song

No. 2." The former appeared on a cassette that Joe used to circulate, while the latter can be heard on an out-of-print 2005 Fonotone CD box set. Joe doesn't recall much about Damien, except that T. was "very, very nervous" during the session, and he thinks he was from New York.

Damien returned to Bussard's house in 1970 and cut two more sides: "Lovely Linda" and "Red Branch South," which became the very last Fonotone 78 rpm record ever, catalog number 7000.

Jack Rose

Jack Rose was born February 16, 1971, in Virginia and died of a heart attack at age 38 on December 4, 2009, in Philadelphia. Rose amassed a large and eclectic discography and became one of the most influential and admired guitarists of his generation.

Rose started out playing electric guitar with drone-rock trio Pelt, with whom he released more than a dozen albums. As the group moved in a more folk-influenced direction, he began to concentrate on acoustic playing. Following a pair of self-released CDRs, *Red Horse, White Mule*—the first proper Jack Rose solo album—was issued on vinyl in 2002. Rose went on to release albums, EPs, and compilation tracks on ten different labels. *Raag Manifestos* and *Kensington Blues* were masterful sets of ragtime, ragas, and country blues featuring Rose on lap steel, 12-string, and 6-string guitars. Collectors promptly snatched up such limited-edition releases as the EP *Ragged and Right* (500 copies) and the LP *The Black Dirt Sessions* (2,021 copies).

Jack's influence continues to resonate far and wide.

Ian Buchanan

Ian Buchanan was born November 10, 1939, in Ontario, Canada, and raised by adoptive parents in Forest Hills, Queens. He took up guitar in his early teens, amassed a large collection of pre-war blues 78s, and studied for several years with Bronx resident Reverend Gary Davis. At Antioch College in Ohio, Buchanan gave guitar lessons to fellow students John Hammond, Jr. and Jorma Kaukonen. In 1959, he dropped out to play the Greenwich Village club circuit.

Buchanan dabbled in classical and jazz guitar studies but invariably returned to his first love, the country blues. In 1964, he recorded Jelly Roll Morton's "Winding Boy" ("Whinin' Boy") for the Elektra anthology *The Blues Project*. "Many of us who knew him thought that after his first release, he would zoom to prominence in an era when blues appreciation was growing greatly," guitarist Suni McGrath later recalled. "He certainly deserved it for his innate talent, his diligence and time in study and pursuing it, and what could only be described as his 'authenticity.'" However, the guitarist cared little for self-promotion and failed to capitalize on the 1967 album *Whatever Happened to Ian Buchanan?*, recorded for GRT with the Pigmeat Blues Band. In 1970, Ian Buchanan suffered the first in a series of psychotic episodes. He jumped out a window and was left a paraplegic confined to a wheelchair. But he continued to play and teach guitar, occasionally performing in public until his death in 1982.

Don Bikoff

Don Bikoff released one lone, rare solo album, *Celestial Explosion*, on Keyboard Records in 1968. It's now reissued on LP/CD/DL by Tompkins Square. Watch the YouTube video of Bikoff playing on the *Ted Mack Amateur Hour*, taped May 12, 1968. You'll see the sheepish, long-haired, mustachioed musician spinning gold in a style (still?) so foreign to the mainstream listener. After Don's performance, the befuddled host concludes, "That's unusual, to say the least." A kid from Oyster Bay, Long Island, Bikoff got his start in Greenwich Village annoying Dave Van Ronk and playing the folk/blues circuit, where he met Sonny Terry and Brownie McGhee, Jesse Fuller, and Mississippi John Hurt. The comparisons to John Fahey and Robbie Basho stated in the LP liner notes touched a nerve with Fahey himself at the time. Today, those comparisons are still inevitable; however they are for lazy ears. Bikoff has his own approach. He's only 67 years old, and he's still playing strong.

John Hulburt

Guitarist and singer-songwriter Ryley Walker discovered John Hulburt's 1972 private press LP *Opus III* in a Chicago record store, loved what he heard, and teamed with Tompkins Square to produce a reissue of the album. Hulburt (1947–2012) was a member of legendary mid '60s Chicago garage rock band the Knaves, whose records were recently reissued by Sundazed. *Opus III* showcases Hulburt's exceptional talent on the acoustic guitar, proving somewhat of an anomaly in a city not known for its solo guitar recordings during this era. Walker writes in his liner notes, "Solo acoustic guitar music was adopted by several in the Berkeley school and the ever expansive roots fanatics in the South, but here in the middle of the country, with harsh winters and the landlocked prison of corn fields, it was almost destiny that the amplifier assault of electric blues and controlled chaos of dance music came from the South Side." *Opus III* has another notable Chicago connection: It's one of the earliest studio credits for Styx and Ohio Players engineer/producer Barry Mraz. Styx's debut album would also be released in 1972.

Gimmer Nicholson

This Memphis-based fingerstyle guitarist recorded one solo instrumental album, *Christopher Idylls*, at Ardent Studios in the late '60s with Terry Manning at the helm, and he also appears on albums by Lynyrd Skynyrd and Jim Dickinson. Chris Bell and Alex Chilton were reportedly influenced by Gimmer's clean, lyrical, orchestral-sounding guitar tone, similar to the signature sound heard on Big Star's *3rd: Sister Lovers*. Not much info about Larry "Gimmer" Nicholson is available online. He apparently died in 2001. *Christopher Idylls* was reissued on CD by Manning in 1994, and I hear another label is threatening to reissue it at some point. Although Gimmer's playing is luminous, and the album is beautifully recorded, he isn't compositionally that strong, and the album sort of wears thin after about 30 minutes. Still, no one was recording solo guitar music like this in the '60s in Memphis, and for that alone it's a worthwhile curio.

Chapter 10:

Alex Chilton

I interviewed Alex Chilton on September 17, 1987, in Albany, New York, before his appearance that evening at a club called QE2 on Washington Avenue. I was Music Director of the Albany State University radio station, WCDB. It was the peak of my Big Star fandom, and I was in awe of my polite if somewhat cranky hero. Maybe it was just that he was in Albany. The interview appeared in the December 1987 issue of local rag *Buzz Magazine*. I recorded it, but I don't have the tape anymore. I was lucky enough to save the magazine, though, and my three signed Big Star LPs. Here is the piece in its entirety:

● ● ● ● ●

Alex Chilton ordered the stuffed quail at Quintessence. When it arrived, he offered me a piece, but I refused. The salad was the best salad Alex Chilton said he'd ever eaten. There was a slab of cheese that looked like feta, but Alex insisted it was parmesan. It was feta. But Alex is from Memphis. There can't be much feta cheese in Memphis.

He didn't want to be interviewed in the restaurant, so we sat— Alex, his two band members, and I—and stared out the window. He didn't want to be interviewed at all. The following conversation took place in his Isuzu while driving around Washington Park:

JR: Do you understand the "pop god" billing you've received?
AC: Not really but ... (pause)
JR: How do you feel about the Replacements song?
AC: Uh well, I didn't feel any way about it. I mean I'm so used

WIK 53

#1 Record

Bell's and Jody Stephens (drums). They played the grab bag of English and American pub rock. Chris also had a cache of his own songs, some o which he demoed at Ardent, songs which would form a basis of interes when Chilton returned to Memphis in 1971.

Alex had moved to New York when the Box Tops disintegrated, attemptin a folkie-type career with acoustic guitar and original material. He ha even attempted to lure Chris Bell into a duo, but Chris preferred to stay a home and so, with this solo gig making little impression, Alex decided t return to Memphis. He too could be found at Ardent studio, piecin to having, uh, you know, these kind of fawning, imbecilic fans, you know. To have it take on some coherence is refreshing.

JR: It seems that Big Star means more now with a modern perspective than it did when it was actually happening.

AC: It's hard for me, you know, to understand what a young person, or a person younger than myself, must perceive of that stuff. I know how *nowhere* it was for us at the time. You know, we just made this record and worked for about a year on it, 'cause we had time in the studio. We could do anything we wanted at the studio, and the people at this place were pretty sharp technically, so we did it. So we just made this record like we wanted it to sound. You know, we just made the best record we could and put it out, and there was some critical response and stuff like that, and then we couldn't sell it. AM I IN YOUR WAY??!! *(Yells at blocking vehicle)*

JR: Do you like touring?

AC: Yeah.

JR: What about interviews?

AC: Yeah, I don't particularly like doing interviews, but I guess getting press is a helpful thing.

JR: In your solo work, particularly *No Fun* and *Feudalist Tarts* and the new LP *High Priest*, there's a sharp leaning towards the blues, and less so funk. Where does all that stem from?

AC: I don't know. I guess that I'm not a real fluent sort of musician; you know I'm not like Charlie Parker or somebody, and so I can do some primitive sorts of blues sometimes better than a lot of other things ... When I was playing with that group Big Star in the '70s, they were anti-blues, the rest of the members of the group, you know, so I didn't want to rock the boat.

JR: How do you feel about your experience with Big Star now?

AC: You know Chris Bell, that was kinda the other leader of the band or somethin' like that, was somebody whose music I dug, and I feel like I learned a lot from playing with him and learned a lot about recording. It was a time in my life when I made progress.

JR: Do you feel like you're making progress now?

AC: Yeah.

JR: You really like the new album?

AC: Yeah. I worked hard on it.

JR: What about the title *High Priest*? Is that sort of a double entendre that you like?

AC: Maybe more like triple or quadruple. There are two songs on the record that are sort of gospel tunes, and one about the Dalai Lama, who if there was ever a high priest, he's gotta be the highest one, I mean 19,000 feet or something, you know. And then you know this whole Jim and Tammy (Baker) thing that's been shaking up, you know, that's why there's a picture of a church on the front and me in front of a motel on the back, and then Ray Charles called himself "the High Priest," and I've always been a Ray Charles fan.

JR: You just finished up a reunion tour with the Box Tops, right?

AC: *(pissed)* I wasn't saying that, no. Each summer there's a guy who gets together a revue of '60s groups and that comes in the summer.

JR: Let's get back to the so-called Alex Chilton pop-god phenomenon. How do you perceive that thing? Who are your fans?

AC: I see the people who come to my dates. They seem to be college students who don't look like Ramones fans, they don't look like Cramps fans, you know, they're not all dressed in black. You know, they wear colorful clothing. They just seem like normal college students.

JR: Do you enjoy listening to old Box Tops and Big Star records?

AC: I don't listen to my own records too often, although I guess I've been listening to some of the more recent stuff lately and getting a kick out of that. Big Star has five or six songs I dig listening to, and the Box Tops—I guess there are a few things I enjoy. It's a kick to hear old Box Tops songs on the radio.

JR: When was the last time you were in Albany?

AC: The '60s.

Chapter 11:

Eric Clapton

According to Jewish tradition, I became a man on my bar mitzvah on May 31, 1980. But something else happened several weeks prior that had much more to do with my passage to manhood: I bought Eric Clapton's double live album *Just One Night*.

Ah, the double live album. The opening paragraph of Rick Johnson's 1980 *Eagles Live* review in *Creem Magazine*:

> *Double live album* is one of those red-flag phrases anyone sensible doesn't want to hear. Those little words carry a Nuisance Potential comparable to such winners as *consecutive life sentences, minimal brain damage,* and *"was that red car yours?"* and rival the infamous *Dear Tenant* for provoking a fear of upcoming events so anxiety-filled that many sufferers are forced to medicate themselves with alcohol and illegal drugs.

Funny, and sometimes true. But wait. What if the live album is the purest distillation of an artist, and the studio is actually the canned version? Maybe a live recording is the more faithful one. Can you get closer to Tim Buckley's essence than *Dream Letter: Live in London 1968*? What about *It's Too Late to Stop Now* by Van Morrison? Can you get more intimate with Townes Van Zandt than via *Live at the Old Quarter, Houston Texas*? How about the Allman Brothers' *At Fillmore East*? Or Hendrix, *Band of Gypsies*?

Just One Night, released April 16, 1980, is embedded in my soul. It's not just the music on the record, but the sound and ambience of the recording that resonates. The mere sound of the record is

My room in Syosset around the time I bought *Just One Night*

my lifelong friend. It's bone-dry, brittle, airy, kind of hollow. The energy is contained. This is not Ted Nugent's *Intensities in Ten Cities*. Like the Who's *Live at Leeds*, the polite Japanese audience inside Budokan Theatre is barely audible. There is nothing between you and the music. There's no sensation of sound being projected or amplified. It's more like you are onstage with the band. Or, if you're a musician, you might feel like you're *in* the band.

The peculiar circumstances of the recording may explain the feel. Producer Jon Astley describes his process of recording back in December 1979:

> The main challenge on *Just One Night* was that Eric wasn't supposed to know that I was doing it. I put up all these mics, and the manager came running in saying, "No, no, no! If Eric sees that, he's going to know it's being recorded!" So I had to hide the audience mics, and I had to duck backstage at the Budokan and keep out of everybody's way. I built a studio in one of the dressing rooms and just had all the cables coming in. And I sat there all afternoon and daren't venture out in case any of the band saw me. I got no sound check—I just had a roadie go round the drums and I just guessed levels. I thought I'd lose two or three songs sorting it out, but we'd got two nights recording. And that's how it went down. It was all the first night, which is why we called it *Just One Night*. That first night was just brilliant.

Just One Night was recorded during a transitional time for EC, personally and professionally. Although he was newly married to Pattie Boyd after a long pursuit to win her hand from husband George Harrison, he was already messing around with other women and drinking heavily. "However much I might have thought I loved Pattie at the time, the truth is that the only thing that I couldn't live without was alcohol," he reveals in his 2007 autobiography.

In 1979, Clapton swapped out the American band he'd been touring and recording with for five years for an all-British ensemble featuring guitarist Albert Lee, who he'd known from his days playing with John Mayall. Clapton was drinking beyond excess and wracked with guilt over firing bassist Carl Radle, who would die from drug and alcohol abuse on May 30, 1980, age 37. The new lineup toured in support of Clapton's *Backless* throughout Europe and Asia, and also recorded the album *Turn Up Down* in the spring of 1980—produced by Glyn Johns, supposedly rejected by his label and to this day unreleased. Some of the songs that made it onto 1981's *Another Ticket* sound better in their previous incarnations: the gritty, Cale-esque "Rita Mae," with its understated yet intricate solos on *Turn Up Down*, is neutered as a coked-up, polished blues workout on the official album.

An artist saddled with the "god" tag early on is bound to have some issues, but Clapton's human frailties are borne out page after page in his autobiography in admirably excruciating detail. In 1985, he convinces his drunken self that his estranged wife Pattie still wants him. Meanwhile he's all ready to leave his mistress when she suddenly announces she's pregnant. So he drives to Pattie's house—his old house—to find her cooking dinner with her boyfriend. "Suddenly my world was absolutely in tatters. I was disenchanted with my now-pregnant mistress, and I'd lost my wife."

Ugh, Eric ...

I didn't know anything about these messy personal details when I first heard *Just One Night*. All I saw was a bad-ass rocker on the cover. The photograph exudes masculinity and authenticity—the rolled up jeans, trimmed beard, workmanlike button-down shirt rolled up above the elbow, waistcoat, cross-sword kilt pin, big belt buckle, boots. Although his band now consisted of British musicians, the Southern roots of previous American collaborators Duane Allman, Bobby Whitlock, Carl Radle, Delaney & Bonnie, and JJ Cale carried forth in his sound, if only fleetingly. You can hear it on subsequent albums *Another Ticket* and *Money and Cigarettes*, but that was the end of the line.

Awash with synths and other unnatural sounds, 1985's unforgivable *Behind the Sun*, produced by Phil Collins, began a spectacular creative descent few rock icons have rivaled. Not entirely his fault, as so many '60s rockers found themselves adrift in a post-punk/new-wave world, adopting all manner of ill-conceived production techniques and hairstyles. Of course, this coincided with EC's sobriety and immense commercial success. I say this with no disrespect, and I'm certainly not the first to express this opinion, but I just have a hard time listening to anything he's done post-1983. These days, Clapton seems like a punching bag for music journalists, a go-to example of an artist who betrayed his own gifts. In a recent *New York Observer* piece entitled "In the Beginning, There Was My Hatred of Eric Clapton," writer Tim Sommer describes his horror at hearing Santana and Clapton's "The Calling" piped in overhead at a retail store:

> It was music that would move no one, even the people who desperately pretended to be moved by it. It was tasteless music, both insomuch as it left no taste and it had no point of view, nor was there any evident source for its creation—no emotional source, no evocative source, and no inspiration, be it envy, energy, lust, or a desire to recreate a dream or nightmare.

But that twenty-year run—from joining the Yardbirds in 1963 to Mayall's Bluesbreakers to Cream to Blind Faith to Derek & the Dominoes to Delaney & Bonnie, Harrison's *All Things Must Pass*, followed by the first six solo albums—reveals a restlessness, a resilience, a striving for reinvention, and, yes, a reckoning with dreams and nightmares. While on tour with Blind Faith in 1969, Clapton was spending more time with opener Delaney Bramlett offstage than with his own band, eventually quitting to become ... a humble sideman on tour with Delaney & Bonnie & Friends.

Which was something of a problem in the UK, where audiences screamed for Eric to step out and solo. Working with Delaney would change the course of Clapton's career in profound ways. Bramlett encouraged him to find his own voice, for one, producing EC's debut solo album. Delaney also turned him on to the music of JJ Cale, whose style irrevocably altered Clapton's entire musical direction. Clapton's decades-long stumping for Cale is just as important to his legacy as his championing of Robert Johnson and Freddie King. All have had far-reaching effects. Delaney's influence on Clapton is similar to the impact Gram Parsons had on Keith Richards, guiding him deep into the backwaters of American music.

Just One Night feels like a career culmination, a greatest-hits of sorts with spirited versions of "Tulsa Time," "Cocaine," and "After Midnight," but there's nothing cheap or flung out—seven of the fourteen songs are over seven minutes long. EC whips everything out of his old guitar kit bag, with solos ranging from keening to languid to majestic. The musicianship is wonderfully devoid of any hint of contemporary or trendy sounds, hovering in its own timeless void. Had the band even heard the Sex Pistols or the Clash?

I've heard some folks diss "Wonderful Tonight." It does have a clunky structure. There's something endearingly off-key about the vocal, kind of like Led Zeppelin's "All of My Love." But it is one of the most intimate (some might say, cringe-worthy) songs ever. You're right there in the bedroom with this couple. If you've been in a relationship, you know this moment. You're getting ready to go out, you're both getting dressed, it's kind of harried, but there's an intimacy to it. All your little quirks, habits, vanities, fashion foibles, and insecurities are on display. You get back home, the night was OK, you feel like shit, but you're there for each other. You turn out the light, maybe you make love, maybe you don't. It sounds like Eric just wants to go to sleep. It's incredibly open and honest, much like his book. It's this song on *Just One Night* that shows his vulnerability amidst the pain of revenge rockers like "Further Up the Road" or the bitterness of "Worried Life Blues."

Now that I know about what EC was going through around the time of *Just One Night*, it makes it all the more potent a listen. How did he harness the strength to get on stage and play with such conviction in the face of it all? I'm reminded of a Bob Dylan quote from a recent interview, responding to a question about critics: "They don't have any idea what it takes to be on a public stage and couldn't do what you do not even for one single second." Not just on stage, but on stage with all the burdens of fame, envy, addiction, brutishness, callousness, emotional weakness, insecurity, and endless self-sabotage.

Clapton was God to me at 13. Now he's 70. And I'm twelve years older than he was when he recorded *Just One Night*. The way he's overcome so much trauma throughout his life and persevered to do his work—it's inspiring.

Smoke Dawson
(Photo by Joe Alper. Courtesy of Joe Alper Photo Collection LLC)

Chapter 12:

Smoke Dawson

I was doing some research for a box set of music recorded at Caffè Lena, the hallowed folk music venue located in Saratoga Springs, New York, when I came upon a photograph of a musician I didn't recognize. He looked like a sixth member of the Band—a handsome fiddler with wax moustache, goatee, and dark Western hat. There was a traditional air to him, a seriousness, but there was also something wild there. I needed to know who he was, and everything about him.

The producers told me his name was Smoke Dawson, and they had tape on him. One listen to the tape and it didn't take much coaxing to get a track placed on the box set. Then I started digging. I found a 1996 blog post from someone named Oliver Seeler, who claimed to have recorded a solo album by Dawson in 1971. I called the number on the site, not expecting much from an 18-year-old blog post. But he picked up. He gave me background on the record. And, he gave me Smoke Dawson's phone number.

George Dawson was born June 5, 1935, in the Greenpoint section of Brooklyn, New York. His father was an Irish immigrant blacksmith who worked for years on the Brooklyn Bridge. He was a choral tenor singer, and his wife, a Philadelphia native of Irish descent, sang as well. Around 1955, George picked up the banjo and started meeting fellow musicians. In March of 1960, George joined a trio, MacGrundy's Old-Timey Wool Thumpers, with Rob Hunter on guitar (not of Grateful Dead fame) and Peter Stampfel (of the Holy Modal Rounders) on fiddle and mandolin. That was Peter's first band, too. As Peter recalls:

> Wool Thumpers was a euphemism for fucking. George played banjo. He was an extremely good player, and a wrestler and a weightlifter. There was a halfway house for bad Jewish girls who had been sent to a mental facility called Hillside. There were periodic reunions of the bad girls, and they hired our group to play. Paying gigs were extremely rare at the time. The woman who ran the show hated us. We had a choreographed stunt that we had planned. We're playing "Dallas Rag," Rob has a pipe in his mouth, and Dawson swings his banjo into Rob's face, and the pipe goes flying right into the boss lady matron's forehead, and there's a big loud gasp. Rob and Dawson fell down on the floor laughing.

And so it began. According to George, it was actually Peter's proficiency on banjo that turned him into a fiddle player. "Peter was such a good banjo player. I said, 'Why don't I learn the fiddle and you can play the banjo?'" Or as Peter tells it, "George took a fuck-ton of speed and came back in a couple of weeks playing fiddle better than I did."

Around 1962, George was a new father to a boy named Wade (named after old-time banjo player Wade Ward). But he left his family behind, and ran off with Peter's wife.

George began frequenting Caffe Lena in 1960, playing there October 14th and 15th of that year with Rob Hunter. George would live at the cafe on and off for eight years. "It was the nicest place I knew of in the whole country. I helped cook, painted, I had romances there. It was the place I came of age," Smoke told me. He also immersed himself in the West Village folk scene, hanging out at

Izzy Young's Folklore Center, seeing Dave Van Ronk, Tom Paxton, Jack Elliott. "There was no one playing fiddle, and suddenly I was in demand. I watched Dylan slowly sink into the scene. I ran a Sunday afternoon show at the Gaslight for (owner) John Mitchell."

Eager to discover the influences of so many folk artists during the period, George took an extensive southern road trip. "I looked up people who Alan Lomax recorded. I lived in North Carolina and Virginia and spent a week with Doc Watson and Wade Ward. Eventually I moved to Florida, playing on the bar circuit, on the street. Then I drifted to California, chasing a girl. Went back and forth to Saratoga but stayed in California from 1968 on."

Dawson played bagpipes at the California Renaissance Pleasure Faires and busked on the streets of San Francisco. He fell in with a collective called Golden Toad, a rotating troupe of folk musicians led by Robert Donovan Thomas, a charismatic bagpipe player who designed the Grateful Dead's skull-and-lightning-bolt logo. Their first gig took place at Grace Cathedral in San Francisco, and although original member Mickey Zeckley claims it was recorded, there's no evidence of this, and sadly, no other recordings of the group are known to exist. Golden Toad would open for the Dead on occasion (never with George). Zeckley remembers, "George was a crazy, wacky guy who could play a hell of a fiddle. He was with Suzy Marceau, who had a green-card marriage to Marcel Marceau's son."

On the afternoon of October 20, 1968, George joined his girlfriend Ruth Denny Decker Sennepf and another couple on the Mendocino Headlands, a rugged stretch of coastline, while "experiencing enhanced consciousness," as George recalls, out on the rocks, watching the waves. A sneaker wave came and swept them out. George and the other couple were caught between some rocks down below and escaped, but Denny, as George called her, was swept away and drowned. The *Ukiah Daily Journal* reported the story on October 21, 1968: "A 27-year-old Mendocino woman drowned Sunday at 1:30 p.m. when she was swept from a rock by a towering wave. Victim was Ruth Denny Decker Sennepf, formerly of Mill Valley, who was sitting on the rock when she was swept away. Her companions, two men and a woman, escaped." Fellow Mendocino resident Ramblin' Jack Elliott knew George in the early '70s and recalls the tragedy. Folk musician Bob Gibson describes a lonely bagpipe player who can be heard in the Mendocino night in his tune "Smoke Dawson," which recounts the incident. "George went home and burned his fiddle and swore he would never play again," says Mickey Zeckley.

Oliver Seeler, a bagpipe player inspired by Golden Toad and Robert Thomas, recorded fellow busker Dawson in 1971 in Sea Ranch, California. Seeler would go on to build bagpipes and run a worldwide bagpipe website. The studio was situated near an airport, which made recording difficult. Oliver describes George as restless and uncomfortable in the studio, but George remembers a kid coming in with very good hash.

Either way, what we hear is remarkable. "My whole training came from Mozart's father's book about violin technique (*Versuch einer gründlichen Violinschule: A Treatise on the Fundamental Principles of Violin Playing*). A tune like "The Minotaur," however, sounds like a swarm of bees violently shaken from their hive. Where did he come up with that technique? "I made it up. But my influence is from baroque violin, and on bagpipes I know Dutch, German, Spanish, Welsh, tunes from a couple of hundred years ago," he says. These are traditional tunes leavened with a touch of sorcery (note the Merlin on the cover) and a bit of Mendocino hippie. Only 750 copies of the album were manufactured.

In 1972, Dawson took the stage at the Ash Grove in West Hollywood with the White Brothers—Clarence, Roland, and Eric— along with their father (Eric White, Sr.), LeRoy Mack, and Pat Cloud. One photo exists from the show. A fiddle player was needed, and George somehow got the call. Roland recalls George as a fine player, although a somewhat awkward fit. He played in a very traditional old-timey style maybe not best suited for a bluegrass group. It would be one last moment in the limelight for Smoke Dawson, at least in terms of playing with nationally recognized musicians. "I've been a computer programmer for IBM, a commercial fisherman, blacksmith, aerial photographer, gold-mining engineer, wrestler, entertainer," Dawson says. "I've played music for three to eight hours a day for thirty, forty years."

In 1992, George was diagnosed with cancer at the base of his tongue, was given six months to live, and went through an experimental treatment protocol. The treatment was devastating, and it took five years for him to recover. Around this time, on his way from Eugene to Spokane, his car broke down, and he has remained in that same small town in Washington State ever since. Although he was left with essential tremor and other debilitating effects from radiation, he continued to play bagpipes. His town bought him a beautiful set so he could play weddings, funerals, and town events. He is in touch with his four sons from four different relationships.

"I row a boat, smoke dope; my girlfriend of twenty years is in the advanced stages of Parkinson's disease. I talk to fish, deer, birds." George turns reflective. "I was cuckoo, couldn't get along in the world. The music always saved me. It got me friends, it got me shelter."

"I could go into my own dream world."

Notes from the 2013 Tompkins Square reissue of Smoke Dawson's Fiddle (TSQ 5036)

Chapter 13:

Jazz

On August 12, 1949, my Uncle Moe turned 18. His girlfriend got him the best present ever: a table right up front at New York's renowned jazz club, Birdland, to see Dizzy Gillespie. Dizzy bounded off the bandstand between sets, took a seat randomly at their table, ordered a drink, and told them about his upcoming trip to Puerto Rico.

It was one of many magical nights my uncle spent at the feet of jazz giants: Miles, Monk, Coltrane, Charlie Parker. He witnessed not only the burgeoning New York jazz scene of the late '40s, but also the one breaking out of Los Angeles in the '50s, where he spent three years after returning home from military service in Korea in 1953. He describes LA as a veritable paradise during that era—dirt-cheap rent, women everywhere, jazz everywhere, no smog, no traffic. He hung out with his buddy, actor Robert Vaughn, landed a studio job baking cakes for movie sets, and lived in the St. Francis Hotel on Hollywood Boulevard, steps from Jazz City, Peacock Alley, and the Tiffany Club. "Gee, who should we go see tonight—Chet Baker or Barney Kessel, Stan Getz or Clifford Brown?" Pianist Joe Albany lived one floor above him.

Returning to New York in 1957, Moe hung out at the Five Spot at 5 Cooper Square in the Village and Birdland at 52nd and Broadway, catching sets by every now-legendary artist in the jazz canon in their prime.

In 1951, a drummer friend of Moe's invited him along to a Manhattan loft at 317 East 32nd Street, where he was taking lessons from the blind pianist Lennie Tristano. Tristano is credited in some circles with inventing free jazz with his sextet in 1949, anticipating the wider movement to be ushered in by Ornette Coleman ten years later. The studio, a former furniture showroom above a garage, was located on East 32nd Street between First and Second Avenues. It was intended as a place for Tristano to teach, but also to hold jam sessions and record. Famed producer Rudy Van Gelder assisted in setting up the place, soundproofing walls and bringing in recording equipment. The idea was for Tristano to record there and start his own label, Jazz Records, but this resulted in the release of only one 45-rpm single, "Pastime" b/w "Ju-Ju," in 1952.

Tristano explained, "I can't be a musician and run a record company at the same time." The imprint was reactivated after his death via the Lennie Tristano Jazz Foundation. Charlie Parker frequented the studio, and at one point had designs on collaborating with Tristano on his label venture. An impromptu session with Tristano, Bird, and Kenny Clarke was supposedly recorded there. Max Roach, Charles Mingus, and Roy Haynes were frequent visitors. Stan Getz sat in. Leonard Bernstein dropped in to listen. You can too, if you pick up Tristano's *New York Improvisations*, an album of trio recordings made in his loft in 1955 and '56 featuring Tristano, Peter Ind, and Tom Weyburn. There's also a tune called "317 East 32nd," which can be heard on the double-live album *The Lennie Tristano Quartet*, recorded June 11, 1955, in the Sing Sing Room of Confucius Chinese Restaurant, and a version recorded live in Toronto in 1952 with his quintet as well. There's even an interesting Norwegian documentary about Tristano's space from 1983 on YouTube, *Lennie Tristano—Manhattan Studio*.

Financing Tristano's project was Phyllis Pinkerton, a young pianist from Chicago and a descendant of Civil War-era detective and spy Allen Pinkerton. A student of Tristano, she used some $10,000 of her inheritance to help him build his studio. Moe, 19, met Phyllis, a few years his senior, at the studio, and they carried on an affair for about six months.

Moe would spend weekends at Phyllis's basement apartment in Woodside, Queens, seated side by side at her grand piano, learning harmony and musical theory from her. Moe remembers her as rather flaky and eccentric. She had an "Orgone box" in her house, which he describes as a "phone booth lined with lead." Orgone, I've learned, was a popular junk-science fad in the '50s, with several Beat writers like William S. Burroughs citing it as a source of spiritual and sexual energy. Phyllis would go on to record with Charles Mingus and married tenor man and fellow Tristano student Ted Brown a few years after she and Moe split up.

My uncle used to bang around on the piano at our house when I was a kid, years before I started listening to jazz records. "All the Things You Are," "Laura," "How High the Moon." He was not a gifted or fluid musician, but his playing shaped how I now hear jazz. Similar to Tristano, and perhaps under his indirect influence via Phyllis, Moe had a percussive piano attack, a counter-melodic one where the notes were constantly engaged in their own call and response. Rooted in bebop, there were dissonant clusters of notes, ear-bending runs, and weird colors in Moe's playing—as well as endless "mistakes."

Those same qualities, sans the mistakes, can also be heard in Tristano's brilliantly unorthodox stylings. His hyper-intellectual approach, plus an abrasive personality, might explain why Tristano never quite clicked with critics or a wide audience, despite having two studio albums released on Atlantic Records. Listening to Moe trained my ear to gravitate toward piano jazz of the dark and complex variety. I'm talking about Herbie Nichols, Bill Evans, Monk, Mal Waldron, Elmo Hope, Ran Blake, Cecil Taylor, Andrew Hill, Horace Parlan. My Uncle Joe, Moe's brother, used to tease him at the piano: "Moe, you never end a song! How about 'Dah dah dah dah … the end!'"

It was funny, but true. Moe disregarded convention, and I've always demanded the same from my jazz. Just like the Joe

Henderson album title *In 'n Out*, there has to be something "out" for me to connect to it, even if it's "in" a traditional vein. Not to be overly dismissive, but I have no use for any era's commercial or mainstream jazz. I don't want to hear Benny Goodman, unless he's playing with Charlie Christian. And I don't care if something "swings" or not.

I saw pianist and composer Mal Waldron at the Blue Note in New York City on August 22, 2001, with Reggie Workman on bass and Andrew Cyrille on drums—Waldron's only appearance ever at the club. He is best known as Billie Holiday's accompanist in her final years and as the house pianist for Prestige in the late '50s, sitting in on many classic sessions by Eric Dolphy, John Coltrane, and a long list of others. He went on to release over a hundred records as a leader.

I was so excited to see Mal's show listed in the *Village Voice*, as I knew he had expatriated to Belgium in the late '80s, and I'd never seen an NYC listing for him. Pianist Benny Green opened both sets, and I recall the crowd was very thin for the second. Mal sat at the piano, perfectly quiet and still, without a word between tunes. A woman in the audience was so moved by Mal's playing, she moaned "Ohhh ..." over the sustain as each tune ended. It drove me insane. I later discovered the offending moaner was a certain well-known bassist's wife. Unforgivable! Anyway, I don't remember the selections played that night, but luckily, *All About Jazz* reviewed the show, and the write-up is online with mention of songs "Hooray for Herbie" (dedicated to Herbie Nichols and Hancock), his signature tune "Soul Eyes," and Miles Davis's "Jean Pierre."

Mal was certainly influenced by Miles, despite this anecdote from a 2001 interview:

> When Miles first met me, he said, "You know, you look just like my brother." I said, "Oh yeah, Miles?" He said, "Yeah, and I hate my brother because he's a faggot!" [LAUGHS] So me and Miles were never close after that.

Uncle Moe in Korea, 195?

The concert was riveting. Mal had arrived at a place where he was effortlessly fusing elegant traditional bop with the more avant-garde exploration he pursued after a heroin overdose sidelined him in 1963. Suffering a nervous breakdown, Waldron basically had to re-learn his technique, which resulted in a darker, freer palette. He opened up to Ted Panken in 2002.

> I was out for about six or seven months, in East Elmhurst Hospital, and they gave me shock treatments and spinal taps and all kinds of things to relieve the pressure on my mind, to get my memory back, because I couldn't remember where I was, I couldn't remember anything about the piano or anything.

Albums like *Free at Last* (1969), *Tokyo Bound* (1970), *Black Glory* (1971), and *Up Popped the Devil* (1973) reveal a new direction that relies heavily on repetition and drone. If you are looking for true innovation in jazz, it can be found here. Listen to Side Two of his 1977 solo LP *Signals*, recorded in 1971, featuring the original compositions "Zapata" and "Touch of the Blues." All of Mal's influences come into play—R&B, classical, post-modern jazz—cloaked in an otherworldly element.

After the show, as the sparse crowd filed out, I approached him to sign my copy of his landmark 1961 LP, *The Quest*. "How come you never play here?" I asked. He told me, "They won't let me smoke in the clubs in New York City." Waldron died about a year later, December 2, 2002, age 77, of complications from lung cancer. I attended his memorial service at St. Peter's Church on January 13, 2003. It was a very moving service, with several of his children singing. Abbey Lincoln, Max Roach, and Steve Lacy performed. Prestige Records released *Soul Eyes: the Mal Waldron Memorial Album* in 2003. But since then, there hasn't been any reappraisal of Waldron's vast body of work, or his contribution to jazz.

Andrew Hill got something Mal didn't in his final years: a victory lap. Like Mal, Hill honed his skills playing with giants like Bird, Miles, and Dinah Washington before launching an uncompromising solo career as a leader, releasing a string of classic albums on Blue Note from 1963 to 1970. Hill's late-career renaissance was highlighted by *DownBeat* "Album of the Year" honors for the 2000 album *Dusk*; acclaim for his final 2006 solo album on Blue Note, *Time Lines*; and a rigorous reissue campaign staged by Blue Note. They released handsome CD versions of mid '60s sessions *Pax* (first released on the double LP *One on One* in 1975); *Change* (first released under Sam Rivers' name on the double LP *Involution* in 1976); *Dance with Death* (sextet recordings from 1968); and, most significantly, *Passing Ships*, a mind-blowing previously unreleased 1969 nonet session with Dizzy Reece, Woody Shaw, and Ron Carter, released in 2003.

I saw Andrew Hill live only once, performing solo at the Jazz Bakery in Los Angeles in April 2001, a few years before he was "rediscovered" by the small coterie of musically enlightened folks who care about such things. There were about twenty people in attendance for the early show, and then the club invited everyone to stay for the late show, because no one had bought a ticket. Five people stayed. His solo playing was absolutely brilliant. We exchanged some words after the set, and he signed my Japanese CD copy of his awesome 1975 solo set *Hommage*.

When I started Tompkins Square, I didn't have any plans to record jazz musicians. But jazz was part of my environment. I lived on Avenue B (aka Charlie Parker Place) and 9th Street in the Christadora House from 1994 to 2011. Iggy Pop lived there for some years, and George Gershwin gave his first public recital in the building, back when it was a community center. If you looked out my window facing north toward the uptown skyline, and then looked straight down, there was a garden with a little koi pond. That was Charlie Parker's backyard. He lived in a brownstone a couple of doors down, and most certainly spent time back there. I always felt his presence, played his music for our babies, and listened religiously to Phil Schaap's beyond-obsessive WKCR Charlie Parker radio show, *Bird Flight*. You'd hear eight takes in a row of "Romance Without Finance" (they all sounded the same to me), or he'd wade into an extended discussion about some recording date minutiae for a full hour. I found Schaap's dry, incessant drone as New York–iconic as the Empire State Building or an H&H bagel. There was a cozy vibe in the apartment on snowy mornings, listening to Schaap bloviate about some musical peccadillo that only he gave a shit about.

The neighborhood was home to jazz players who I would run into frequently in Tompkins Square Park, like Bern Nix, who played with Ornette Coleman; Giuseppi Logan, who recorded for ESP in the '60s; and Charles Gayle, who lived a few blocks south. I was familiar with Gayle's saxophone playing, and had seen him play a few times. But one day I caught him playing a solo piano set at the Tompkins Square branch public library on East 10th Street, and it completely floored me. It had all the ingredients—stride, New Orleans, Art Tatum, Cecil Taylor—and I knew I wanted to capture it. So I set up a date at the now-defunct SONY Music Studios in mid-town where they had a Steinway. Charles, unaccustomed to high-end recording facilities, was pretty happy to be in such a fancy environment. Toward the end of the session, I felt like we needed a ballad as a closer, so I said, half-joking, "Make me cry." And he proceeded to play "That Memory," which I hope you will seek out and listen to. There's a theme there ready to bust out, and he teases at it from all angles, dancing around it, until 1:57, when he plays two notes, followed by those same two notes higher up on the keyboard. "Da-da. *Da-da.*" It didn't make me cry exactly, but the effect of those four notes ... It still hits me every time I hear it. It was great to bring out this under-appreciated dimension of Charles' talent, and bring him back full circle to the piano, his first instrument as a child.

I used to hear Giuseppi Logan play "Somewhere Over the Rainbow" over and over again, sometimes all day, in Tompkins

Square Park. The composer of that tune, Yip Harburg, attended P.S. 64 on 9th Street between Avenues B and C, now an abandoned building steps away from the park. I didn't know Giuseppi's history until someone forwarded me an amazing YouTube video of him hanging around the park with his young son in the '60s. As I got to know him, he told me about his years of addiction, his estrangement from his wife and kids in the late '60s, and his extremely impoverished state. So I cut him a check, called his old collaborator, pianist Dave Burrell, and we made a record—his first in decades.

The jazz record-making was more about forging a sense of community around my neighborhood than it was about setting sights on building a jazz catalog. I've never been entirely comfortable with the insular jazz press corps, and some genres are just better left to labels that specialize. With that said, I will always treasure the times I spent with Charles Gayle, and with Ran Blake, with whom I made several albums.

I associate jazz with wintertime, which is when I'd listen to it the most back in New York. Jazz doesn't organically connect with my surroundings here in San Francisco. It doesn't sound quite right here. I guess it was the snow, the Empire State Building, Phil Schaap's voice, living on Charlie Parker Place, the proximity of the Village Vanguard and the Stone—maybe the proximity to my Uncle Moe in Brooklyn, too. We have the new SF JAZZ Center here, but it's sad how the once-vibrant Fillmore district has been dark for decades, and there is no defined "scene." The SF JAZZ Center should be supported, and it's a wonderful place, but it's an institutional, somewhat sanitized and pricey environment. There's room for "concerts," and that's great, but jazz also belongs out in clubs. The SF JAZZ Center now rules the roost in terms of major shows in the city, especially since Yoshi's folded. The last of the great jazz clubs, like Kimball's, shuttered some twenty years ago.

There is a lot more going on in the East Bay, and it's chronicled daily by writer Andrew Gilbert, pretty much the only full-time journalist left surveying the Bay Area jazz circuit. Andrew is the opposite of the many snarky jazz journalists I've encountered. He takes a populist approach to his coverage, and genuinely strives to expand the audience for artists he's passionate about. Along with writing liner notes and essays for jazz festival program guides, covering Bay Area jazz is his main source of income. Whereas he used to go to shows and see three or four fellow writers, he's pretty much solo now.

I'm in this vestigial position in the media. I've ended up the last man standing. There are a lot of contradictory things going on. There's so much interesting music, young and old. There are a reasonable number of places to play, although you might be working for the door. But the scene is very underground and self-contained. About a third of the audience at a given show is other musicians. The weeklies stopped covering it years ago. The vast majority of younger musicians are coming out of music programs, like from Mills, Berklee, Oberlin.

Gilbert points to a fragmented jazz audience, where mainstream artists like Kendrick Lamar are tapping seasoned jazz artists to round out their sound. Jazz has permeated popular music forever, of course, and even if Lamar's fans aren't exactly jazz aficionados, they are still hearing and appreciating the music. It's baked into Lamar's presentation. So the masses are still getting their jazz; it's just being served up discretely, like a hash brownie.

Jazz has taken some major press hits over the past couple of years. "Sonny Rollins: In His Own Words," a parody published in the July 2014 New Yorker, pointedly called out various jazz stereotypes, sparking an online uproar, including a lengthy YouTube response from Rollins himself. The piece was full of cute zingers like this:

Jazz might be the stupidest thing anyone ever came up with. The band starts a song, but then everything falls apart and the musicians just play whatever they want for as long they can stand it.

It reminded me of Joe Queenan's 1994 *Spy Magazine* spoof, "Admit It! It Sucks! Part I: Jazz":

Jazz sucks. Admit it and you'll feel a whole lot better. You've never had the slightest interest in an art form dominated by guys named Toots and Dizzy and Philly Joe Something-or-Other. From the first time you heard Art Tatum playing "Tea for Two," you've always felt that jazz is a dip-shit idiom that chomps the big one.

Justin Wm. Moyer quickly followed the *New Yorker*/Rollins fracas with a non-satirical *Washington Post* piece, "All That Jazz Isn't All That Great," fanning the flames by debunking the supposed wonders of improvisation and claiming the genre has suffered from stunted growth since the '60s. "For the most part, jazz is being kept alive by nostalgic Americans, such as Coltrane associate Bill Cosby, unwilling to embrace the music of a more alien, more controversial 21st-century African American underground," he wrote.

Then, in early 2015, RIAA statistics for 2014 revealed that jazz accounted for only 1.4 percent of all music consumption, and even though streaming had grown, jazz only represented 0.3 percent of all music streamed between 2013 and 2014. One thing that's contributed to this dismal performance is a lack of star power and the marketing machinery that fuels it. Miles, Monk, and Coltrane were true innovators, but they also undeniably had help from major record labels in building their cults of personality. There are many brilliant young musicians on the scene today, but there is no machinery in place to bring them to prominence. Sonny Rollins noted in an interview amidst the fallout from the *New Yorker* piece,

"From when I started playing jazz and when I started reading jazz magazines, every five or ten years there would be a big article, 'Jazz is Dead' ... They've been trying to kill jazz ... But you can't kill a spirit."

Ultimately, all the recent controversy has been productive because it has sparked discourse and debate. The jazz establishment has never been known for its sense of humor, so it has been fun to watch them squirm. Maybe the purists needed a nice funny kick in the ass. Hardcore fans and the "industry" around jazz have always been exclusionary and rather snobbish, so perhaps they have invited derision, and are finally receiving their comeuppance for alienating a wider potential audience over the years.

Rather than focus on the debate over whether jazz is "dead," or whether the music has any relevance in the broader culture, I prefer to avoid the *J* word entirely, and instead listen for a sound. My jazz records are mixed in with everything else in my collection. I listen for anything with interesting texture, like the funky flotation of Miles' *In a Silent Way*, or "He Loved Him Madly" from *Get Up With It*; the Brazilian sizzle of Dom Um Romao's self-titled Muse LP; Dolo Coker's forgotten Xanadu recordings; the stripped-down sax, bass, and drums of Lee Konitz's *Motion*; the pristine elegance of Stan Getz's *Focus*; the super locked-in Roy Haynes Quartet's *Out of the Afternoon*; the sweet bombast of Elvin Jones and Richard Davis's *Heavy Sounds*; Freddie Roach's precocious *Good Move!*; and Marion Brown's deep Southern trilogy: *Geechee Recollections*, *Afternoon of a Georgia Faun*, and *Sweet Earth Flying*.

These are just a few of my favorite things!

●　●　●　●　●

Every kid needs an Uncle Moe, someone to enlighten him about music. Moe tried to teach me theory, but I was too thick. One day a couple of years ago, he told me over the phone that he'd made a list of his favorite tunes. It was rather out of character, not really something I thought he would do, so I quickly grabbed a pen and wrote them down:

LISTEN! MOE LIVES!

"Just Friends" Charlie Parker With Strings – 1949

"Ginza Samba" Cal Tjader and Stan Getz – 1958

"Wow" Lennie Tristano Sextet – 1949

"The Eternal Triangle" Sonny Stitt, Dizzy Gillespie, Sonny Rollins – 1958

"On Green Dolphin Street" Miles Davis – 1958

"Nica's Dream" Horace Silver – 1960

"I'll Keep Loving You" Bud Powell – 1949

"Mr. A.T." Art Taylor – 1992

"Giant Steps" John Coltrane – 1960

"Wise One" John Coltrane – 1964

"Strike Up the Band" Tal Farlow – 1954

"Blue in Green" Miles Davis – 1959

"Ruby, My Dear" Thelonious Monk/John Coltrane – 1957

"Pannonica" Thelonious Monk – 1964

Chapter 14:

Charlie Louvin

In 2003, I attended a college reunion at my alma mater, the State University of New York at Albany. I was looking in the local paper for something to do with my old buddies and saw an ad for a Charlie Louvin show a short distance from campus. I was pretty excited, but everyone just wanted to hang out, so I broke off and went by myself. I was a huge Louvin Brothers fan, but had never had the opportunity to see Charlie live. He was playing with the Hackensaw Boys, and they were making a holy racket in this little club. There was so much raucous energy; I was kind of taken aback. A rock band was playing very loud downstairs, bleeding through the floorboards, but Charlie and the band seemed unfazed. He was 76 at the time, yet had no trouble keeping up with his much younger backing band. I met him after the show, we chatted, and I bought a CD for him to sign.

The Louvin Brothers were experiencing renewed interest around this time behind a 2003 tribute album, *Livin', Lovin', Losin': Songs of the Louvin Brothers*, which won a Grammy for Best Country Album. Charlie was asked to join Cake on tour with Cheap Trick that year. He had a lot of fun on that tour, and it put him in front of large unsuspecting audiences.

Still, by the time I started up Tompkins Square and decided to contact him in 2005, I felt Charlie could use more recognition, considering his staggering contribution to music. It bothered me. He was half of one of the most influential duos in country music history, a Country Music Hall of Fame legend. Taking cues from early harmonizers like the Blue Sky Boys and the Delmore Brothers, the Louvins influenced countless artists, from Johnny Cash to Jack White. Louvins songs like "Cash on the Barrelhead" and "The Christian Life" were covered by Gram Parsons and the Byrds and handed on down the line. Parsons introduced Emmylou Harris to the Louvin Brothers, and her first hit in 1975 was "If I Could Only Win Your Love," a Louvins song. In 2010 she told *the Observer*, "I'd always loved the Everly Brothers, but there was something scary and washed-in-the-blood about the sound of the Louvin Brothers."

The duo presented secular and sacred material, chilling murder ballads, innocent songs of unrequited love, songs about making tough choices in life. Ira's thoughtful lyricism often carried weighty moral authority without sounding preachy, much like his contemporary, Hank Williams. It's the contrast of light and dark that still draws people under the Louvins' spell, especially musicians and songwriters.

Charlie had a successful solo career on Capitol Records after the Louvin Brothers split up, releasing ten albums on the label, including two duet records with Melba Montgomery, and scoring three Top Ten country singles. Ira released one solo album on Capitol before dying in a tragic car crash in 1965, age 41. Over the 32 years spanning 1975 until Charlie's self-titled Tompkins Square debut in 2007, he did not release a widely distributed studio album under his own name. There were live albums, compilations, and private label releases, but nothing beyond that. He worked steadily, appearing on the Grand Ole Opry and playing live during those years. At the time we got together, he was cutting albums for well-intentioned benefactors who would give him some money to make a record and then "release" it, with little consequence. Although the songs and performances on these records were OK, the production and instrumentation lacked dynamics and, it seemed, a sense of purpose.

I wrote to him in late 2005, and on January 29th, 2006, he emailed back:

Dear Josh;
sorry it took me
this long to get back to U.
I would love to talk to you about the recording.
I'll call next week.
charlie louvin

I told Charlie I would come down and meet him in person with a recording contract and, if everything felt right, he could show it to a lawyer. He said he only wanted the deal to be one page long, like the old Capitol contracts, so I tried to accommodate him. It was two pages. I rang up producer Mark Nevers, a recording engineer for top stars in Nashville, but more recently the go-to producer for folks like Lambchop and Will Oldham. I wanted someone who understood who Charlie was and could pair him with old friends and younger acolytes.

Mark and I went to the house Charlie shared with his wife, Betty, in Manchester, Tennessee, right near the Bonnaroo festival site. The small house was built into a hillside, which Charlie said protected them from tornadoes. We sat down in his front room, and Charlie placed a CD into a portable player. He played us a new spoken-word piece he had recently recorded, "The Silence of Aging." He referred to it as a *recitation:*

THE SILENCE OF AGING

There was a time when this man was young.
I had a quick smile and a joker's quick tongue.
Now those days are gone and I don't like the way I'm
   changing.
Now I'm learning about the silence of aging.

Folks thought I was funny when I was a kid.
They laughed at my jokes and all that I did.
But suddenly it seems that those good times are fading.
There's not much to laugh at in the silence of aging.

I was so loud then I had a flame.
We'd all sit and talk about all kinds of things.
Now I know something but nobody cares.
If I say too much they give me cold stares.

So I'll sit right here and silently swing.
I'll keep my mouth shut. I won't say a thing.
Though I might know the answer to the question they're
raising, I must hold my peace in the silence of aging.

Some silver-haired folks have wisdom worth gold.
But they can't always share the wisdom they hold.
Young folks think we're foolish when we're tired and old.
They don't want the truth if the plain truth is told.

Now don't get me wrong. I'm not down on kids.
I look back and laugh at all the childish things I did.
Once, old folks and wisdom were widely respected.
Now wisdom's forgotten and the old folks neglected.

All my grandchildren used to come around.
They'd laugh and play then we'd all go to town.
Now the swing set is empty 'cause they're all grown.
And they're all busy with kids of their own.

Now I pick up my guitar. My fingers won't work.
The notes don't sound clear ... and Lord, how that hurts.

The sweet sound of life is so quickly fading.

Still I strain to hear through the silence of aging.

My life's about over, the end must be near.

But one day from Heaven, the call will come clear.

Just leave that old body for a new life amazing

Where we'll all sing forever.

And there'll be no silence of aging.

© *Charlie Louvin and Jim Vest,* reprinted with permission
JMV MUSIC PUBLISHING, INC (ASCAP) & JLV MUSIC PUBLISHING, INC
(BMI)

We listened, and Charlie started to cry. Although the subject matter was dark and serious, it was marvelous to hear this powerful new original song.

Although they shared writing credit, Ira was the principle songwriter in the Louvin Brothers. Charlie would come up with a concept, a line, or a title sometimes, but Ira was the main lyricist. Charlie told the Associated Press in 2007, "My job was to listen to people, and if they said something that caught your ear that would make a good title I would write it down and I'd give it to Ira. A complete song would come to him like, God, like he was reading it off of another piece of paper. He was nice enough to put my name on the songs also."

The three of us discussed a possible framework for an album, a series of duets with guests performing Louvin Brothers material and some country standards. He seemed game. He smiled approvingly when I told him my middle name was Ira.

Charlie's self-titled album, which featured duets with Elvis Costello, Marty Stuart, Will Oldham, George Jones, Tift Merritt, Jeff Tweedy, and others, was released February 20, 2007. Charlie sang one song alone: "Ira," a tribute to his brother. We shot a video based around a live performance outside Shangri-La Records in Memphis, and Charlie found some unseen home-movie footage of Ira that was included in the clip. Charlie picked up all kinds of renewed press interest off the album, which tied in nicely to his 80th birthday on July 7, 2007. A huge party took place at the Louvin Brothers Museum, at that time located near the Ernest Tubb Record Shop. Of course there was a huge strawberry shortcake in his honor—his favorite. The museum has since moved out to the Smoke House in Monteagle, Tennessee—also the hometown of notorious folksinger Hamper McBee. You can pick up all sorts of McBee oddities there and visit the Louvins' museum. The original museum had this incredible hand-carved church that Ira created as a boy, with great attention to detail, down to a miniature pulpit and choir inside.

Charlie's Tompkins Square debut earned a Grammy nomination—his first, at age 80—for Best Traditional Folk Album. I got him a booking agent, and Charlie started touring all over the US, including festival dates like Bonnaroo. He loved being on the road and performing. It was truly in his blood from his days rambling with his brother. The road was always tough for him financially, and it was very challenging for me as his de facto manager. I always had outsized ideas about who Charlie was that didn't match reality in terms of selling tickets.

Equally frustrating was all the lip service so many stars would give Charlie—yet they would never invite him out on the road or ask him to record. There were many folks who were exceptionally kind to him though, like Alison Krauss, Brad Paisley, Marty Stuart, and Vince Gill. Charlie was very upset with the Opry, who were giving him fewer and fewer spots. He really felt snake-bit by that organization, having served as one of its longest standing members since 1955.

Only one major artist took Charlie on the road and into the studio while we worked together. Lucinda Williams.

I met Lucinda through her husband Tom Overby, who worked

at Best Buy during my SONY days and would later score me a distribution deal for Tompkins Square during his short tenure at Fontana Distribution. Lucinda invited Charlie out on tour. The first time they met on Lucinda's tour bus, the connection was instant— two Southerners sharing musical stories—and before long they were harmonizing together. It was really beautiful to watch that happen. Charlie opened for her on tour, and they duetted on a couple of songs at the end of her set each night. To see them sing and dance together during Lu's "Get Right with God" was just electric. Lucinda invited Charlie to sing on "Well Well Well," which appears on her 2008 album, Little Honey.

On February 18, 2009, Charlie was booked at Spaceland, an indie rock club in the Silver Lake section of Los Angeles. We invited Lu to come down as a special guest. Toward the end of Charlie's set, the power went out, and the whole club went dark except for the floodlights. Something went haywire in the neighborhood. But Charlie and his band played on without power as the backup generator kicked in. Charlie said, "Where is that blonde witch?" Lucinda came up and they sang "When I Stop Dreaming," with the floodlights beaming out from behind the stage. It's all there on YouTube.

Throughout my time working with Charlie, my goals were to facilitate whatever it was that he wanted to do, to find opportunities along the way, and to help him add to his incredible legacy. At that point in his career, he had more than earned the right to do whatever he pleased. He told me his dream was to record with a black gospel choir, so we set about making that happen.

Mark Nevers booked pianist Derrick Lee, who had played on dozens of gospel recordings by Angela Spivey, TD Jakes, the Mighty Clouds of Joy, and Shirley Caesar. Mark also signed up the McCrary Sisters—Alfreda, Regina, and Ann. Their father, Reverend Sam McCrary, was a founding member of the seminal a cappella gospel group Fairfield Four. Regina McCrary collaborated with Bob Dylan during his Slow Train Coming period, and even co-wrote and recorded an unreleased song with the bard. In recent years the sisters have worked with Buddy Miller, the Black Keys, and Eric Church.

Charlie appreciated gospel and blues music. Many of the early country artists that Charlie grew up listening to were influenced by black artists. We tend to make demarcations along racial lines with music from the '20s and '30s, when in fact black and white artists were influencing each other in powerful ways during that time. From Patrick Huber's essay "Black Hillbillies: African American Musicians on Old-Time Records, 1924–1932" from the book *Hidden in the Mix: the African American Presence in Country Music*:

> When US talking-machine companies began to record and market blues and old-time music during the early to mid 1920s, they effectively began the process of transforming southern vernacular music, heard for decades at fiddle contests, dances, house parties, tent shows, and other social gatherings, into immensely popular commercial products. This music, the product of more than three centuries of vibrant cross-racial exchange and adaptation, was profoundly and inextricably multiracial, but talking-machine companies, in an effort to streamline their marketing efforts, separated the music of black and white southerners into special categories of "race" and "hillbilly" records.

Steps to Heaven was probably not the first collaboration between a black gospel choir and a country artist. But it is a significant one, especially in light of stories that have circulated about Ira's use of the "N" word around Elvis Presley. The Louvin Brothers toured with Elvis in the mid '50s. Charlie tells the story in his autobiography, *Satan Is Real: the Ballad of the Louvin Brothers*. Elvis is sitting at a piano backstage singing a gospel song. Ira is drunk and goes off on him:

"Well, you damn white nigger," he said to Elvis. "Why don't you play that crap on the stage if that's what you love?"

Elvis just grinned at him. It wasn't the first time he'd been called a white nigger, I'm sure. A lot of people in Nashville felt the same way.

Unfortunately, because of this story, which made the rounds years before the publication of Charlie's book in 2012, I used to hear people tag Charlie as a racist. Charlie loved to flirt with women in a playful way. He never meant anything by it; it was all in fun, but some people took offense to it. The agent of a young, very hot duo asked me if Charlie would open for them. I said, "Sure." Then he called back with questions about Charlie's take on race and women, because the duo had "heard stuff." I told him to get bent. It was ridiculous. But stories circulate, and reputations are hard to break. I was around Charlie in all kinds of situations with all kinds of people, and he always treated everyone with warmth and kindness.

Steps to Heaven was a bold artistic move, and the experience was very satisfying for Charlie. "I did things on the gospel record I had no idea I could do," he told *PopMatters*. "I'd be thinking along the way, 'How can I do things I've never done before?' And I did it." The album is not only an important collaboration between an old-school country giant and a black gospel choir; it is also a very stark personal meditation on death and the afterlife. Songs like "Where We'll Never Grow Old," "If We Never Meet Again This Side of Heaven," and "Precious Lord, Take My Hand" are sung with such deep conviction, it's difficult for me to listen to them now.

Steps to Heaven earned Charlie a second Grammy nomination for Best Southern, Country, or Bluegrass Gospel Album. I attended the Grammys for a second time with Charlie in 2009. Before his award category was announced, a black gospel group performed at the ceremony. I looked over, and Charlie was crying. He was so moved by their performance. He didn't take home the trophy, and it wouldn't be until 2015 when the Recording Academy recognized the Louvin Brothers with a Lifetime Achievement Award that Charlie finally got his prize—posthumously. *Steps to Heaven* came out one month before its companion album, *Charlie Louvin Sings Murder Ballads & Disaster Songs*. My idea was to release the two albums back to back, representing Heaven and Hell, if you will. The concept was great, but the execution wasn't—I should have released both albums on the same day instead of waiting a month between them. While the albums were both well received, the separate release dates split the media attention and confused the marketplace. *Steps to Heaven* is Charlie's best album on Tompkins Square—and the worst selling one—so I think I'll reissue it soon and try to redeem myself.

On February 22, 1956, the Louvin Brothers opened two shows for Elvis Presley at the City Auditorium in Waycross, Georgia. A nine-year-old Gram Parsons was in attendance, and the show would influence him greatly. In September of 2009, Charlie was invited to co-headline the annual Gram Parsons Festival in Waycross with Leon Russell, so we stopped into the Civic Auditorium, where Charlie had played 53 years earlier. Someone from the city had to let us in because the place was completely dilapidated and out of commission. There were windows in disrepair, peeling paint, original flags inside, everything as it was in 1956. We walked across the stage and checked out the corroded commode backstage. We mused that Elvis had likely pissed in there. The whole thing was pretty eerie. How many perfectly intact venues are there in the US where Elvis performed?

We recorded a live album at the festival, which features Charlie singing a cover of Gram's "Hickory Wind." I suggested he work up that song for the festival and our live album. He respected Gram for turning so many people on to the Louvin Brothers and was eternally grateful to him for that, but he was not a huge fan of Gram's music. He complained to me about the opening line, "In South Carolina / There's many tall pines." "I been to South Carolina and there ain't no tall pines."

Charlie was diagnosed with pancreatic cancer in 2010. We stayed in touch. I had talked to him at least once a week from 2007 on, and when we had a record and a tour going we would talk pretty much every day. I'd often stop and tell myself, "I'm actually talking to Charlie Louvin on the phone." It was like talking to a ghost. The Louvin Brothers were from a bygone era. You could count Charlie's contemporaries on two hands. Around Christmas 2010, he called me. In a low voice, he said, "Josh, the preacher came today. He healed me. The cancer's all gone." I could hear that he believed that, so I just said, "Wow, that's great to hear, Charlie."

Meanwhile, I had signed a young guitar protégé of Charlie's, Ben Hall, who I'd first seen perform at Charlie's birthday party back in 2007. I made a record with him in New York City with producer Eric Ambel in 2010. I thought it would be a nice way to carry on Charlie's legacy, having this 22-year-old kid influenced by Charlie, Chet Atkins, and Merle Travis join the stable. In mid-January 2011, I went to Nashville to see Ben perform and invited Charlie down. It was freezing cold, and the roads were very icy, but he showed up with his teenaged grandson. He was frail but always smiling, conversing with fans who spotted him in the club. It was probably one of his last times out in public. William Tyler, who had played on Charlie's *Murder Ballads* record, was also in the room. There's a photo of us together from the show. I look really sad, but Charlie is smiling ear to ear. That's just who he was.

Charlie died two weeks later on January 26, 2011. I was packing up that week to move from New York to San Francisco. My lease was to start February 1st, so I sent all my stuff ahead and flew to Nashville for the funeral. I couldn't help but feel a symbolic tug, given the timing of Charlie's passing—I was closing a chapter and starting new ones a couple of times over. His band members and family were at the funeral, of course, but I didn't recognize anyone else except Vince Gill, who sang "Go Rest High on That Mountain" at the service. WSM's Eddie Stubbs read a long eulogy. He is buried

Charlie Louvin outside
City Auditorium, Waycross GA, September 19, 2009

next to his brother, Ira, in Harpeth Hills Memory Gardens in Nashville, Tennessee.

I had a lot of fun with Charlie, and he taught me a great deal about music and life. It was an honor to work on his behalf and to be acknowledged in his book. He also wrote me a beautiful note after the first album came out, which is too personal to share. I have precious photographs of Charlie playing with my daughters in my apartment in New York City. Charlie achieved immortality through his music, even though he always said he and his brother were "just trying to make a living." I'll remember him most for his humility and his deep humanity.

Lucinda wrote this in the *Los Angeles Times* when Charlie passed:

> I got word of Charlie Louvin's passing today, which is also my birthday. Losing Charlie means that we have lost one of the last of the founding fathers of honest-to-god country music. Charlie was a legend as one half of the Louvin Brothers and left a deep impression on me. I had the honor of working with him in the studio and touring with him.
>
> Every show would end with the two of us trading out verses on his song "When I Stop Dreaming" followed by my song "Get Right with God." Charlie loved that song and he loved to dance, and as the band rocked out, he would grab my arms and spin me around.
>
> One time we were performing in Kansas City outdoors and it was very windy that evening. Charlie's set list kept blowing away. At one point, he'd finally had enough and he grabbed his pocketknife and planted that thing right through the set list into the stage floor to keep it from blowing away. Later, that same night, after the show, we sat on the bus and, with

sadness in his eyes, he told us that, on the way to Kansas City, we had driven right by the milepost where his brother, Ira, had been killed in a car wreck.

Charlie was eternally youthful, full of spitfire, vim, and vigor and, like Hank Williams, was a true punk, in the best sense of the word. We will miss Charlie but like he said, shortly before he left us, "I'm ready to go home."

● ● ● ● ●

"If you have any roses that you would like to lay in front of somebody or put in their hand, do it while they can still smell 'em."
—Charlie Louvin, 2008

Chapter 15:

1989–1997

Elvis Costello is responsible for my "career." Thanks, EC!

After graduating from Syosset High School, I spent one year at the State University of New York at Purchase. I felt alienated there, seeing as I wasn't a ballet dancer or a sculptor. "Performance artists" smashed plates of glass with sledgehammers and walked around downtown Rye dressed like Jesus carrying a gigantic cross. Everyone else in liberal arts was marginalized.

I tried to compensate for my lack of performing arts skills by writing a very long term paper on Eric Dolphy. There were many kids on drugs, even heroin; the campus felt cold to me; and their closed-circuit radio station sucked. Once, my friends broke into Campus North in the middle of the night to steal large amounts of breakfast cereal, and that was the most exciting night I spent at SUNY Purchase. I did enjoy regularly seeing a band called Asleep Standing featuring Chris Ballew, a wry, wiry kid who went on to form the Presidents of the United States of America. In a strange twist of fate, the group later signed to Columbia while I worked there.

Meanwhile, my friend Sean from Syosset was up at SUNY Albany, and my old mentor from PolyGram, Jack Isquith, was also an alumnus. He was among a crew of industry types who had worked at the Albany campus radio station, WCDB, and went on to jobs in the music business: Russ Rieger managed the Replacements, Craig Marks worked at Homestead Records, Diarmuid Quinn was at Epic. So I transferred to Albany for sophomore year and lived on Indian Quad.

My roommate, a kid named Oscar ("Oska T"), was Thelonious Monk's grandnephew. There's a Monk composition entitled "Oska T," first recorded in 1963, which Oscar was named after. He was pretty blown away that I actually had several Monk records in my two large crates of LPs. T. was a big Mets fan and idolized Darryl Strawberry and Doc Gooden. We used to play a very dangerous version of stickball out in the hallway, taking full swings at racquet balls and tennis balls in a space about ten feet wide. We had all kinds of complex rules for what counted as a single, a double, etc. Someone really could have lost an eye; it was that stupid.

I worked the overnight shift at WCBD that year, trudging back to my dorm as the sun was coming up, often in deep snow. Back in those pre-cell phone days, people would pull over and call a DJ from a payphone when they heard something interesting in their car: "Hey man, what was that song?" I played lots of Squirrel Bait, Big Black, Big Dipper, Slint, Descendents, Verlaines, Membranes, Volcano Suns.

I was appointed Music Director of WCDB in my senior year. I'd already been MD at my high school station on Long Island, and I had maintained some of those old label contacts. I interviewed bands playing on campus or at local clubs like QE2. Screaming Trees came up. Rick Danko played a live set. I interviewed Alex Chilton in his car. I did a phone interview with GG Allin from jail. He said, "My high school principal used to tell me I was a penny waitin' for change." Wish I still had that tape.

I heard that Elvis Costello was coming to the Palace Theatre on April 7th, 1989, in support of his recently released *Spike*. I contacted my Warner Brothers rep, Steve Tipp, and asked if Elvis would come up to the station. Steve told me he couldn't make it. I found this entirely unacceptable, so I found out where Elvis was staying and dropped off a bunch of cassettes for him (yes, cassettes—Pierce Turner, Neville Brothers) along with a note inviting him to come up and do a mellow DJ set with me before his gig. He called me at the station, and I arranged for a stretch to pick him up. His wife at the time, Cait O'Riordan of the Pogues, was in tow, but didn't say a word all afternoon. Elvis pulled stuff from the library (Randy Newman, Yo La Tengo), and we spent a very fun hour on the air, although I was pretty nervous. I bought a block of tickets, invited my label rep friends from New York City up for the show, and made a big party out of it.

Steve Tipp, who was based on the West Coast, heard about all this. A few months later, Tipp moved to New York City to head up the new Alternative promotion department at Columbia Records. He needed to hire an East Coast promo guy, and I guess because of the chutzpah I had demonstrated by going around him with Elvis, he offered me the job. Thing is, I had already accepted a job at A&M Records in Los Angeles. So Steve had the newly minted president of Columbia call me at my parents' house in Syosset. I wasn't home the first time he called, but he spoke to my dad and told him what a horrible mistake his son was making by going to A&M. Once he got me on the phone, he said, "You haven't even seen my face. At least come in here." I didn't know much about him, except that he'd worked at Arista with the Grateful Dead and Whitney Houston. At 36, he was the youngest president in the label's long history. I went up to see him at Black Rock on 52nd Street. He worked me over, and by the end of the meeting, I was a Columbia employee. The whole scenario was something he'd tease me about, even years later. I had to break the news to A&M, which was very awkward.

After the obligatory post-graduation European trip, I started work at Columbia on July 10, 1989. It was heady to walk around the halls and see photographs of Miles Davis, Simon & Garfunkel, Billy Joel, and Elvis Costello—artists that were so important to me growing up. I felt comfortable at Black Rock, having attended

"To Josh. Peace '93. Let's do work. Chuck D"

many press conferences there—Dead or Alive, Band Aid. For my first work-related event, I attended a dinner with about twenty executives and Kate Bush, whose album *The Sensual World* was released in October of that year.

Kate came to the States via ship from the UK, because she refused to fly. During her stay, I sat with her at the office while she called in to alternative radio stations around the country, smoked cigarettes, and signed stuff. The first few records I worked to radio at Columbia included the soundtrack for Spike Lee's *Do the Right Thing*; Bob Dylan's *Oh Mercy*, out in September of that year; and the Psychedelic Furs' *Book of Days*, released in October. I went on the road with Richard Butler for about ten days on a promotional tour. I was green, but Richard was very forgiving. Sometimes if the rock-radio folks needed a body, they would have me cover certain things, so I escorted Eddie Money to WDHA in New Jersey in a limo once, and I sat with Kenny Loggins while he did a round of phone interviews, extolling his New Agey credo.

Also released in October of '89 was the debut album by white rap duo 3rd Bass, featuring MC Serch and Pete Nice. I was exposed to a lot of hip hop at WCDB, and that prepped me to work all the stuff coming out on Def Jam and Ruffhouse, two labels that had recently signed deals with Columbia. College radio was pretty receptive to rap during this period, which is now referred to as "the golden age of hip hop," roughly the mid '80s to mid '90s. I got involved with promotional campaigns for 3rd Bass, the Afros, the hilariously filthy Bytches With Problems (BWP), Public Enemy, Cypress Hill, EPMD, and Tim Dog.

Back in those days, with enough money, commitment, and luck, you could almost will a record into becoming a hit. I recall Cypress Hill shipping around ten-thousand units upon release. No one knew what was about to happen. But if you could get MTV to start spinning a video on a specialty show and get the underground radio stations and club DJs on board, things could pop in a hurry, and you could really chase it. There was a lot of emphasis on targeting "the street," which is jargon you never hear from record companies anymore.

Tim Dog was a funny, foul-mouthed rapper who stirred controversy with his East vs. West anthem "Fuck Compton." Tim used to come up to my office with his posse to pick up 12"s, and I went to the Bronx a few times to watch him perform outdoors at various events. I was the only white person there, not that I cared. I would go to EPMD shows where there were almost no white people. I took a college music director from WUSC to see Public Enemy at an arena in Columbia, South Carolina, on their *Fear of a Black Planet* tour in 1990. The audience was about 10 percent white. Even post-Run DMC/Aerosmith, in the late '80s through the early '90s, hip hop hadn't fully "crossed over," and live audiences were still mostly black.

By the mid '90s, there was a lot of talk about hip hop being consumed mainly by white kids in the 'burbs, and the industry shifted focus from "the street" to making sure a release was prominently placed in the weekend circulars for mass merchants and chain stores. A 1991 *Newsweek* cover story on gangsta rap suggested that 80 percent of the buying audience for rap was white, which stirred wide debate over hip hop's supposed demographic shift. Journalist Davey D has presented interesting theories about how radio and advertisers factored into the trumpeting of these somewhat misleading statistics. In short, follow the money. The audience for hip hop was growing in every direction, and artists like LL Cool J, Public Enemy, and Cypress Hill were at the forefront.

In addition to now-classic hip hop, Columbia released a wide breadth of artists within those first few years: Kate Bush, Leonard Cohen, Bruce Springsteen, Alice In Chains, Mercury Rev, the Rolling Stones, the Psychedelic Furs, Big Audio Dynamite, Bob Dylan's Bootleg Series, and the Robert Johnson box set. Do you think I was a little excited to be there?

I went down to the old CBS Studios and watched the engineers remaster the Johnson box. When it came out in August 1990, I decided to work it to National Public Radio stations. There was no centralized promotion mechanism for NPR back then; it was a patchwork, whereas now it's the obvious go-to for a historical set. With a little help from Keith Richards and Eric Clapton, the entire industry was roundly shocked when the set went Top Ten and sold over 500,000 units. I got a gold record for the Johnson set, which rests among my plaques for Fiona Apple, 3rd Bass, Pearl Jam, and others in the closet—where tokens of past accomplishments belong.

My Incubus plaque is forever enshrined on the walls of Looney Tunes Records in Babylon, Long Island. Record executives still like to line the walls of their suites with plaques. I loved hanging out with Don DeVito, a veteran A&R guy who had worked at Columbia since the '60s. He told me his first A&R assignment was Moby Grape's debut album. He went on to work closely with the Byrds and Dylan and many of the label's top stars. Don had an original *Blood on the Tracks* gold record on his wall. He told me, "That's how it used to be—you got a gold record if you *worked on the record.*"

In 1990, producer Daniel Lanois brought Chris Whitley to Columbia. There was a lot of excitement around the signing, and I flew down with some execs to Lanois' neo-gothic home studio in New Orleans for a playback of Chris's debut album, *Living with the Law.* Chris had a well-rounded package—good looks, Texas grit, command of his National Steel, a soulful voice with a Prince-like falsetto and a Hendrix strut, solid writing. He was also sweet and charming, with big, wet, puppy-dog eyes, muscular arms, sunken cheeks, and a quiet, humble, retiring way about him. We hung out a few times at local West Village eatery Shopsin's, and I'd see him play in town.

Chris was sent out on a promo tour to set up the record, playing major market clubs and introduced nightly onstage by Columbia's colorful Artist Development VP, Kid Leo. Two singles from the album became mid-charters at mainstream rock, but he couldn't connect at other formats, and despite an aggressive publicity and marketing effort, the record underperformed. Chris was just way too fragile for the star-maker machinery, and I think ultimately he felt like he had failed somehow. It was no fault of the label—everyone worked hard and really cared about him.

There was talk that he had gone into rehab, which may be why it took four years for his next album to surface. The "failure" of *Living with the Law* led to his shedding the marketable version of himself and creating something totally indistinguishable—1995's *Din of Ecstasy*, released on the new SONY affiliate label WORK. The album took six months to make. Trading the pressure of "Big Red" for the boutique vibe instilled by WORK heads Jordan Harris and Jeff Ayeroff, Whitley essentially divined himself a cult artist, offering WORK little to work with. Gone were the dusty panoramic vistas and lyrical Americana of "Big Sky Country." Angular chords, feedback and distortion, a gunky, corrosive power-trio sound—Whitley pours motor oil all over his previous self. Complex melodies, made-up chords, and riffs—confounding ones that make you wonder how he could have even conjured them—unfold with repeated listening. 1997's *Terra Incognita* follows a similar blueprint but seeks more accessibility in songs like "Automatic," "Power Down," and "Weightless."

Everything he would do after the debut album was about "feel," a sound in his head, and less about what a lyric "meant," building impressionistic, rusted-out blues figures. His mom was a sculptor, which might explain something about his approach. He went on to record for various indie labels and for Dave Matthews' ATO Records. His stripped-down 1998 indie solo album *Dirt Floor*, made in one day, includes the great "Indian Summer," wherein he reminds us, "It's so hard to get warm where/It's so easy to get burned."

Today, Whitley seems forgotten. He was out of step with everything going on in the '90s in a great way, giving the finger to whatever was "cool." The records he made for WORK in particular deserve reappraisal. There's a documentary film about him in the works, *Dust Radio*. I have seen the trailer, where he describes having been through four rehabs. It's painful for me to watch and seems to dwell on Chris's dark side. Whitley died of complications from lung cancer in Houston, Texas, on November 20, 2005, age 45. Upon his passing, John Mayer spoke some eloquent words: "[Whitley's] somewhat prostrated place in pop culture earned him a sidebar of an obituary, but to those who knew his work, it registers as one of the most underappreciated losses in all of music."

In July 1990, Alice in Chains released their first EP on Columbia, *We Die Young*, followed by their debut album, *Facelift*, a month later. The label was peddling hair bands like Britny Fox and Warrant, and grunge had yet to crystallize as a genre, so Alice dangled for a good while. I would visit my friend's office a few floors down at Epic Records. The label had just signed a new band from Seattle, Mookie Blaylock, and my buddy had boxes of their T-shirts in his office. Wish I'd kept a few of those, since the band would soon change their name to Pearl Jam. *Ten* never reached me—it felt too formulaic—and something about Jeff Ament's cargo shorts, boots, and backwards baseball cap really bugged me. Then I heard their cover of "Crazy Mary" on Victoria Williams' *Sweet Relief* album, which came out three months before their second album, *Vs.* It's still one of Eddie's best vocal performances, and one that made me an instant fan.

The fact that the band would cover a Victoria Williams song was damn impressive all by itself. I moved over to SONY just in time to watch *Vs.* set the record for the biggest first-week sales of any album in history. I'll always admire Pearl Jam's integrity in how they dealt with their career, shunning videos and refusing to do certain things. They just wouldn't play the game, and it solidified their career for the long haul.

Also admirable was Eddie's passionate and fervent support of other, far less popular bands. At the height of all the heat around *Vs.*, they released a split 7" with the Frogs singing "Rearviewmirror" on the B-side. This actually happened. I love some of their songs, except when they try to sound punk, which is about 70 percent of the time—like on "Spin the Black Circle." Eddie is about my age, so

I've always been able to relate; he seems like a really sincere guy (we've never met, although we have been in the same room), and he plays a mean ukulele.

I also like Pearl Jam because, despite not having any singing ability, I can groan the slower-tempo songs along with Eddie and be more or less in the same vocal range as him, making me feel like I can actually sing. I'm especially fond of "Nothing as It Seems," "Just Breathe," "Nothingman," "Corduroy," "Better Man," "Immortality," "Animal," "Daughter," "Rearviewmirror," "Elderly Woman Behind the Counter," "Indifference," "Yellow Ledbetter," "Last Kiss," "Given to Fly," "Wishlist," "Present Tense," "Off He Goes," "Who You Are," "Smile" ... and the list doesn't go on.

Nirvana's *Nevermind* was not released until September 1991 and did not explode until January 1992. Alice in Chains was stuck between alternative, metal, and rock formats and was thus a hard sell at radio, competing for attention internally with bands like the Front and Love/Hate. The latter's "Black Out in the Red Room" is still hilarious, and you gotta love lead singer Jizzy Pearl's legendary fake crucifixion stunt on the Hollywood sign's "Y." Alice's amorphous status was temporary, but it was underscored by the variety of bands they opened for early on: Iggy Pop, Van Halen, Extreme, Poison. Where they "fit" suddenly stopped mattering as soon as MTV started spinning "Man in the Box." I first saw them in Boston on November 17, 1990, opening for Iggy. You knew they were unstoppable.

Dirt, Alice in Chains' stone classic released in 1992, doesn't sound dated at all, especially compared to mainstream rock from that era. Close vocal harmony was their secret weapon and something that still sets them apart. Layne Staley was a deeply soulful blues moaner, and I hear his truth in everything he sang. Layne and Jerry's work apart from each other is interesting too. Listen to "River of Deceit" from "super-group" Mad Season's *Above*, perhaps Layne's most confessional vocal. Jerry Cantrell's 1998 solo release, the double-LP *Boggy Depot*, is totally forgotten, but it was a ballsy detour while Layne was sidelined due to substance abuse: long, ripping guitar solos and a lyrical, sensitive side ("My Song," "Settling Down"). I followed the band around on a couple of Lollapalooza shows in 1993, their last major tour with Layne before heroin addiction did him in on Kurt Cobain's birthday—April 5th, 2002. I was born within a few months of both Cobain and Staley, and always felt a kinship with them, like they were "my generation." When they passed, I felt that metaphysical shudder you experience when someone your own age dies young.

T Bone Burnett released *The Criminal Under My Own Hat* in 1992, and I worked on setting up a promotional tour for that album. T Bone's idea, or somebody's, was to run a contest on a local radio station to win a house concert, then invite the local TV news station over to film and broadcast a story on it—a perfectly workable 1992 marketing concept. I traveled around the US with T Bone and his tour manager, a guy who had worked with Dylan and Bruce, for about two weeks. I learned a lot from him, just talking music and studio concepts, listening to his stories, and laughing.

T Bone played a show in Atlanta, and the next evening, we stopped in Athens, Georgia, for a house concert at the home of R.E.M.'s lawyer, Bertis Downs. River Phoenix and Mike Stipe were there, and we all went out to a bar afterward. (River wrote down his address for me—a Florida address—and I sent him some CDs when I got home.) When T Bone played the eTown NPR show, we stayed at the fabulous Brown Palace in Denver, and his then-wife Sam Phillips came out to visit. We went out shopping, and Sam talked me into buying a women's tweed jacket. It looked ridiculous on me. Thanks, Sam.

I spent some more time with T Bone in the early '90s in Bearsville, where he was producing Bruce Cockburn's excellent albums *Nothing but a Burning Light* and *Dart to the Heart*, and later when he signed Ralph Stanley to Columbia. I wanted to do something extra special for Ralph's album, so I had a few hundred life-size cardboard standup displays of Ralph's likeness made up for record stores. When I visited T Bone in LA, he had the standup I sent him propped up in his living room. Around that time, he invited me to the studio where he was working with Autolux. He played me their rough mixes at excruciating levels. I must have sustained some hearing loss that day. He likes it LOUD.

Through *O Brother Where Art Thou*, he exposed millions to Ralph Stanley and traditional American music, and who could forget his early work on the 1968 Legendary Stardust Cowboy single "Paralyzed"—one of the few regional hits ever to feature a bugle. I took my daughters to meet T Bone at Hardly Strictly in San Francisco last year. I hadn't seen him perform in over twenty years, and it was amazing to see his total command over his own material. He doesn't play that many shows, yet there was no rust on him whatsoever. He was pleased to hear that my younger one's name is Hazel, which was his mother's name. And Hazel asked him for Taylor Swift's autograph, of course.

Around 1992, I moved out of promotion and into an artist-development role, working for veteran rock-radio promotion VP Paul Rappaport. "Rap" started his career as a college rep for CBS Records in the late '60s and worked his way up, promoting hits for all the heavy hitters over the years: Aerosmith, Billy Joel, Journey, Pink Floyd, the Rolling Stones. He had a signed Keith Richards photo on his wall: "To Paul, 5 strings, 3 notes, 2 fingers, 1 asshole. Love, Keith." He first met Keith on the New Barbarians tour in support of Ron Wood's solo album, and they reconnected when the Stones signed with Columbia in 1986. The first time they met, they snorted two lines of blow off a drum stand. Good start! Keith taught Rap how to play in a G tuning with 5 strings, and showed him some of his tricks. Rap was also inner circle with Pink Floyd, who invited him onstage to play a guitar solo once, and he was one of the guys responsible for launching large inflatable pigs over cities during the *Animals* promotional campaign.

Rap is a fencer, surfer, magician, guitarist, and sports-car enthusiast. He's OCD in a charming way, very cerebral, always overanalyzing everything. He will get stuck on one small thing for an entire day, or he'll have a two-hour conversation with someone on the phone that should have taken three minutes. He came up with an idea to start a nationally syndicated live radio show featuring Columbia artists and guests that beamed out via satellite, pre-Internet. We produced shows by Bruce Cockburn, Judas Priest, Leonard Cohen, Jeff Buckley, and fIREHOSE, among others. The first show was "Christmas with Cockburn." Bruce invited Lou Reed and Rosanne Cash on as guests. All three sang "Cry of a Tiny Babe," Bruce's 7:41 retelling of the nativity story, and Lou sang a Hanukkah song as well. He was hungry when he showed up, so he asked for some latkes. I was eating latkes with Lou Reed—this was a special moment!

We put together a radio show live from Electric Ladyland Studios in New York with fIREHOSE, Gumball, and J. Mascis. J. requested cereal with "lots of milk" and a timpani drum, which we gladly rented for him, although he did not touch the timpani drum once throughout the session. I spent two years with Rap, and it was fun, but as in any big company where everyone has a specific role, mine seemed ill defined. So I went to work for SONY Music Distribution for the next ten years, heading up their Alternative Sales and Marketing area. I had a staff of 15 or so between HQ and the field, and it was a big step into management for me at 27. But it was the '90s, and we were selling shit tons of CDs. I loved working all the aforementioned, and there were so many other highs. It's easy to like your job when you're involved with Patti Smith, Bruce Springsteen, and David Bowie. There were plenty of bands I couldn't stand as well that took years off my life.

Most of the joy, however, came from interacting with the independent record store community. I loved getting on a plane and going into a market and hitting record stores. I got paid to do it! I was seeking new challenges too. Shortly before splitting the company in 2005, I brought Lamb of God to the attention of their A&R guy at Epic; he signed them, and they sold millions of albums.

I'll tell you about it someday.

As I was transitioning from the Columbia label to distribution, my first task was to spread the gospel on Jeff Buckley's new EP *Live At Sin-é*, released on November 23, 1993. I was present the day he recorded it, with cables running out into the street, down St. Marks Place and into a bar with a mixing board a few doors down. I first became aware of Jeff during the signing derby, when labels were checking him out. He was still playing with Gary Lucas as a duo, Gods and Monsters, and I first met him at the Knitting Factory on the night of what was to be their final show. We chatted. I gushed about his dad, which he tolerated, and told him I hoped he would sign with Columbia.

Sin-é was a very cramped, uncomfortable place to see a show, and once the labels started sending black cars to the venue, it became rather strange in there. You had all these record executives impatiently tapping the table, listening to Jeff perform elongated covers of Nusrat Fateh Ali Khan and Edith Piaf tunes. There was something formative about playing in such a tight environment though, as he explained to Bill Flanagan in 1994:

> I went into those cafes because I also really felt I had to go to an impossibly intimate setting where there's no escape, where there's no hiding yourself. If you suck you need work and if you don't then you have to work on making magic and if you make magic then everybody has this great transformative experience.

Jeff had a very goofy side on stage, but once he got inside a song, he was all in, and I think that's what folks remember most about his performances.

I was involved in setting up *Grace*, and there were lots of meetings around that. We were looking at various comps of the cover art, and a consensus developed around the image that eventually became the cover. I expressed my displeasure with this choice, stating that

I thought Jeff looked too glammy, the old microphone was too stagey, and while his good looks could be emphasized, he was too dolled up. The President said, "When you make an album this good, you can pick any cover you want." Fair enough!

There was also debate around whether the album should include "Forget Her," and Jeff decided to leave it off the album. It ultimately wound up on the expanded version of *Grace,* released in 2004. It's my favorite song of his. Was it a hit? We'll never know. A few months later, we sat around a table on the executive floor with Jeff, discussing his upcoming tour. He turned to me mid-meeting and said, "You have the most beautiful eyes for a man I've ever seen." I think he was just fucking with me and trying to bring some levity to the proceedings.

Jeff, Rap, and I hung out on the beach in Boca Raton during the SONY Music Convention on June 18, 1993. He played a few songs for the company, which you can miraculously hear online. We talked about his dad, Tim Buckley, and he eerily sang a few lines from one of Tim's songs. While Jeff always showed his appreciation to the label folks, I know he was deeply distrustful of the music business, not that that's at all unusual. He did have a great champion—his Columbia A&R man, Steve Berkowitz, who's as music-centric as they come. Jeff was burdened by his father's fame and haunted by a dad he had only met once at eight years of age, two months before Tim's death. It was hard for him to reconcile all that with his own creativity and fame.

Released on August 23, 1994, *Grace* would be Jeff's only studio album. It was frustrating to be on the marketing end of the project, as sales were initially disappointing. The album peaked at #149 on the Billboard chart, and radio had no obvious hit to run with. The reaction seemed better overseas. Although there was plenty of critical acclaim, and the album made many "Best of 1994" lists, *Grace* did not achieve its vaunted status until years later, with some help from Britain's *X Factor* and steady posthumous releases of archival material.

In January 1997 I got a phone call at home from Steve Berkowitz, asking if I wanted to come down to a low-key show uptown at the Sunshine Café. It was a small, intimate show with a secret, insider vibe. Jeff was headed down to Memphis to do some recording with Tom Verlaine for his follow-up LP. This would be one of his final shows in New York, and the last time I saw him alive.

It's strange to think about Jeff pushing 50, but he'd be doing that now. I wonder where he would have traveled musically. He had a four-octave range, and a four octave-personality: tortured, philosophical, gentle, silly. He was a dreamer and seeker at a time when those things were unfashionable or even a career liability.

From an Italian radio interview in 1995:

> It's just that, when you get to the real meat of life, it's that life has its own rhythm and you cannot impose your own structure upon it—you have to listen to what it tells you, and you have to listen to what your path tells you. It's not earth that you move with a tractor—life is not like that. Life is more like earth that you learn about and plant seeds in ... It's something you have to have a relationship with in order to experience—you can't mold it—you can't control it ...

Chapter 16:

Mickey Jupp

What becomes a legend most, after playing in a band called Legend? Working in a record store, naturally.

By 1975, former Legend front man Mickey Jupp was slinging discs at Music Centre in Queens Road, his Southend-based band having broken up in 1972 after releasing three albums. Although Legend was a commercial failure, Jupp was already a bona fide local hero, having influenced scads of pub rockers throughout the UK as well as local talents from Southend. The area, also referred to as the Thames Delta, spawned folks like Robin Trower, the Records, Procol Harum, and Dr. Feelgood, all having tenuous or tight connections to Jupp as a key player on the music scene.

He first established himself as leader of the popular local R&B combo the Orioles, who went through four lineup changes in the mid '60s. Legend bassist John Bobin recalls Jupp's stage antics in his book, *Bark Staving Ronkers: A Music Memoir*:

> The bashing away at the piano Jerry Lee Lewis style was the forte of Orioles singer Mick (later Mickey) Jupp ... He had fiery red hair and flailed away at the keyboard like a demented younger brother of Jerry Lee and even included the odd few notes played elbows-style or with the toe of a boot.

Mickey Jupp *Long Distance
Romancer*, Chrysalis, 1979

Although Jupp gets lumped into the pub-rock movement, he was never actively part of it. He's not the only guy who's been mistakenly filed under pub rock. I asked Graham Parker if Jupp influenced him. "I just wasn't clued up on the 'pub-rock' scene until my career began and I saw those words pop up in things written about me. Which was very odd!" While Graham may not have been under Jupp's influence, Brinsley Schwarz, Nick Lowe, Dave Edmunds, and Rockpile certainly were, and you can clearly hear Jupp phrasing and stylings in their spit-polished rockabilly. Legend disbanded well before pub rock took hold in the UK, but they made their mark. Since dubbed "the Godfather of Southend Rock," Jupp wrote tunes that have been covered by Lowe, Edmunds, Joe Cocker, and the Judds. His slavish, unabashed (some might say shameless) worship of '50s rock and roll—especially Chuck Berry—pulses through everything he's done.

In a 1975 *NME* interview, Jupp sounds washed up at the ripe old age of 31. "Most of my good songs were written when I was down, I think most people's are. A lot of it was reminiscing. I was 27 and beginning to realize it was the last chance. I'd never make it now." The article goes on. "Despite dissatisfaction with the way they were managed at Vertigo (Legend's second label), Jupp resolutely refuses to be bitter. He merely says: 'In the end we got pissed off and these gentlemen here (indicating the passing figure of Chris Stevens) offered me a job at the Music Centre. Been here ever since.'"

Jupp's stint at the Music Centre was interrupted, however, when he was "re-discovered" and signed to Stiff Records in 1978. They issued a compilation LP, *Mickey Jupp's Legend*, consisting of four tracks from each Legend LP, and he was part of the 1978 *Be Stiff* UK tour featuring Wreckless Eric, Lene Lovich, Rachel Sweet, and Jona Lewie. The tour made it all the way to New York's Bottom Line, but not with Mickey—he hated flying (see his song "You'll Never Get Me Up in One of Those"), so he bailed.

Legend released their eponymous debut in 1969 on Bell Records. An ad in the May 24, 1969, issue of *Billboard* read, "A new long-distance hit group from England that takes its toll." Get it? Bell/toll? Ugh. The album stiffed, and Mickey took a job in Bath, until Robin Trower tipped him that Procol Harum's bass player, David Knights, was going into music management. Knights landed a deal with Vertigo Records for a newly configured Legend featuring Bill Fifield—who later became drummer for T. Rex—renamed "Bill Legend" by Marc Bolan. The resulting album, produced by Tony Visconti and also titled *Legend*, is referred to as the "Red Boot" album, because of the red-boot-on-fire cover art. The title and artwork were ill advised, but the record is now considered a classic. A mint copy just went off online for $610. Up until a few years ago, you could still find a copy for cheap in cutout bins across England. A third album, *Moonshine*, was released in 1971. Legend disbanded in 1972.

In interviews, Jupp bristles at being pigeonholed as a retro-rocker, and if you pay attention, he's right—there are a lot of diverse textures in his repertoire. For example, the best song on Legend's *Red Boot* and his greatest vocal performance, "Life" is a moody, smoldering R&B ripper in the mold of "I Put a Spell on You," but he's directly singing to "life" in a way I've never heard anyone attempt, as if life were a girl. The song was the closest thing Legend ever had to a hit, reaching #12 in Italy.

Oddly, the track was sampled by Spanish hip-hop act Nitro in their song "Margot," distributed by SONY Music Spain in 2013. They use so much of Jupp's vocal, you could almost consider it a duet instead of a sample. It's pretty cool, and you'll hear the song in an entirely new context that totally works. YouTube it!

Mickey also knows his way around a ballad. "Pilot" is an arresting, piano-powered heartbreaker from his 1978 solo album *Juppanese*, featuring all-star backup from Gary Brooker, Chris Spedding, and Dave Mattacks.

The chorus:

I'm a summer

Ruined by rain

I'm a pilot, baby

Shot down in flames

I'm a sailor

Sunk without trace

The last time I saw your face

It was during the sessions for *Juppanese* that Jupp's "Switchboard Susan" became a Nick Lowe favorite. Lowe explained in 2011:

> Mickey recorded *Juppanese* with one half produced by Gary Brooker, and I think he did that half first. It's rather unusual to have half a record done by one producer and the other side done by another. Plenty of records have multiple producers, but they are all jumbled up. I was wheeled in to do the other side of the record, and Rockpile was hired to be the backing group. We cut "Switchboard Susan," and we all thought it was great, and we were jumping up and down. The next morning we went to the studio, and Mickey pronounced it shit from top to bottom. I waited until he calmed down a bit and told him if he didn't want it I would buy the tape and put it out myself. He said "Alright, alright. I never want to hear it again, it's rubbish." But he was wrong about that one. It's cracking.

"Make It Fly" from 1979's *Long Distance Romancer*, on Chrysalis, is a surprisingly tender fingerpicked ballad that veers as close to British folk as Jupp ever got. 10cc's Kevin Godley and Lol Crème produced the album, offering Mickey a diverse and adventurous sonic canvas for sweet ballads like "Make It Fly" and "Barbara," fun Bo Diddley–beat numbers like "Chevrolet," and my very favorite Mickey Jupp song, a totally un-Jupp Jamaican dub-sounding jam, "I'm in Control." For those who prefer Jupp the rock-and-roll purist, this album is probably not for you. But it's his most well-rounded solo effort. The record also includes a new version of Jupp's least favorite song from the *Juppanese* sessions, "Switchboard Susan."

Although Jupp maintains he's a "dead loss on guitar," I tend to differ. Witness, for example, "Taxi Driver"—a riff like "Lay Down Sally," but then he slides the note all the way up the neck inside the riff, and each note in the slide is spot-on. Listen and you'll hear it. I wonder if there are any other recorded examples of this precise technique. There's clever, biting guitar flash all over his catalog.

Lyrically, although his ballads are few, the aforementioned ones are surprisingly confessional and mature, especially when contrasted with the sly-dog nature of some of his rock numbers. These are split between macho bravado and an awkward vulnerability. With some of the lines, you can imagine a woman staring back at him going "Eeeew." When you see Mickey deliver some of these lyrics in live video from 1994, you envision women in the crowd (if there are any) going, "Uhh, please don't do that." In other words, this is guy music. Jupp sums up his endearing loser vibe in 1991's "Standing at the Crossroads Again":

Well here I am on my own again
Where did I go wrong this time
Treat em good like a gentleman should
I never ever step out of line
I'm no kid, I know my way around
I'm 6 feet nearly, I weigh 200 pounds
But I can't hold no romance down
Maybe I should give up tryin'
I'm standing at the crossroads again

Jupp has been described by former band mates as difficult to work with, with a dash of stage fright and a general disdain for the limelight. "I'm in the wrong business," he said in 1994, "cuz there's so much of it I don't like. I really don't enjoy making records that much, I don't really enjoy having to record the 'finished song.' The writing is the great thing." Writing is one of many things that Mickey Jupp did well. The scant performance video footage available online from the early '80s reveals a confident and kick-ass performer.

A three-CD + DVD box set of Jupp's work, *Kiss Me Quick, Squeeze Me Slow: the Collection*, was released on Repertoire Records in the UK in 2014. A non-chronological survey of his entire career, including some Legend tracks, I recommend it simply because such a thing exists. Not the sequencing I'd choose, nor the track selection, but a Mickey Jupp set exists; therefore, buy it. The DVD contains a 1994 documentary illuminating, as there is no Jupp interview footage online. Unfortunately, there is no vintage performance footage on the DVD, only live footage from a pub gig in 1994. Some of his television performances from the early '80s can be found on YouTube, and you get a sense of what it would've been like to see the R&B wonder in the flesh, in his prime.

I reached out to Mickey, who turned 70 in 2014. I wanted to ask him about "Pilot," about "I'm in Control," about touring with Elvis Costello in 1978, about how he felt about Joe Cocker covering his songs, did he ever get to see Eddie Cochran or Chuck Berry live, had he heard Nitro's sample of "Life"? He was gracious enough to reply:

Hi Josh
I have the impression that L.K. has not really informed you of my present feelings/philosophy regarding music in general, and mine in particular—which is as follows: My musical "career" has come to an end, and I do not feel any sense of loss or remorse. Apart from a gig in my local pub from time to time, I don't involve myself with music

anymore. Songwriting no longer interests me. The box set was none of my doing—that was Repertoire. I drifted into the world of rock'n'roll in the 1960s, and now I've drifted out again.

Your questions seem to mainly dwell on the 1970s. An awful lot of water has passed under the bridge since then, and I am afraid that the answers to those questions have long been washed away with it.

And so—I apologise for seeming to be uncooperative, but Mickey Jupp—the songwriter/recording artist—no longer exists. Mickey Jupp—the grumpy old man—is still alive and reasonably well and living in the English Lake District!

As an afterthought, I seem to recall that I have been misquoted in every interview I have ever taken part in—but I guess that happens to everyone!!

Cheers
Mickey
P.S. Feel free to print this, if you wish!!

There'll be no misquoting this time around, Mr. Jupp. You are a LEGEND.

Chapter 17:

Bill Fay

British singer/songwriter Bill Fay recorded two albums of musical interest in the early '70s. His eponymous debut (1970) followed by *Time of the Last Persecution* (1971), both on Decca, are remarkable in their own right, and even more so considering how different they are from each other, released just one year apart. They represent one of the most compelling left-right combinations in rock music history, akin to how Leonard Cohen's raggedly glorious *Songs of Love and Hate* immediately followed the well-mannered *Songs from a Room*.

Fay's debut features grandiose orchestral arrangements that blast his miniature character studies into the stratosphere. Like Scott Walker's early solo LPs, it's cerebral, rococo English orch-pop. The second LP is experimental, spontaneous, and influenced by acid rock and Bob Dylan. Pictured on the cover of the self-titled debut album wearing an overcoat, walking over shimmering water in Hyde Park, a clean-cut Fay gazes wistfully into the camera. By contrast, on the second album we find him with downcast eyes, unkempt beard, and wild hair. "It wasn't a setup or a pose," Fay told *Flashback* magazine in 2014. "It was serious music, and I was concentrating. But people always read meanings into things, and they assume that because I had a beard I was undergoing a drug meltdown or personal problems of some sort. I wasn't."

Bill Fay in the studio
(Photo courtesy of Joshua Henry)

That same sort of speculation swirled around Fay's conspicuous decades-long absence after Decca dropped him in 1971. Fay dismisses the typical "script" that often accompanies commercial failure and disappearance—the descent into drugs and mental illness—rejecting any portrayal of himself as a "tortured artist." Instead, he never stopped writing or recording. The period of 1977 to 1982 was especially fruitful, but no record company was interested in releasing his work. It wasn't until the late '90s that whispers of Fay's legend started circulating, the result of various archival CD releases and *MOJO* magazine mentions. A collection of early demos from the first two albums along with other material, *From the Bottom of an Old Grandfather Clock* was released in 2004. A "lost" third album under the moniker of Bill Fay Group, *Tomorrow, Tomorrow, Tomorrow*, featuring the magnificent "Isles of Sleep," surfaced in 2005, as did reissues of the Decca albums. Incredibly, Fay released a whole disc of unreleased demos from the *Time of the Last Persecution* sessions in 2010 as *Still Some Light*, which included a few never-before-heard songs that were left off the album, such as "There's a Price upon My Head" and "I Will Find My Own Way Back," both as great as anything on *Time*.

Jim O'Rourke played Fay for Jeff Tweedy in 2001 while mixing Wilco's *Yankee Foxtrot Hotel*, and Tweedy would go on to play a key role in generating renewed interest in Fay's work. Wilco performed Fay's "Be Not So Fearful" together on May 24, 2007, at Shepherd's Bush Empire, with Tweedy gushing from the stage, "Since we discovered this man's records six years ago I can't think of anyone whose records have meant more in my life." Fay returned the favor by recording the band's "Jesus, Etc." for his widely praised 2012 Dead Oceans "comeback" album, *Life Is People*. Fay looks like a young Jeff Tweedy on the cover of his debut, and Fay sounds like an old Jeff Tweedy at times on his last two albums. Check it out; it's kind of eerie.

Growing up in North London, Fay's mother had a knack for playing tunes by ear on the piano, and her siblings played various instruments. Fay would write songs on the piano, eventually recording some at home in 1966. Terry Noon, manager of Honeybus and former drummer for Them and Gene Vincent, heard Fay's demos and arranged a recording contract with Decca, which released his first single in 1967, "Some Good Advice" b/w "Screams in the Ears," produced by Peter Eden and featuring a Southend-based band called the Fingers. The single went quietly, and Fay spent the next few years playing with Honeybus, demoing new songs and working odd jobs.

Through this period, Fay refined his songwriting, inspired by Procol Harum and books by French philosopher and Jesuit priest Pierre Teilhard de Chardin. Several songs on the debut LP, such as "Garden Song," dwell on the natural world, often with vague religious overtones. "It amazes me that that song could appear within ten minutes. It was a big step forward," Fay shared with me. "It expressed lyrically more where I was as a seeker. There's a lot of depth that would take ages to explain." *Record Mirror* was rather unforgiving of the song's naturalist metaphors in a review from 1970: "'Garden Song' commences, 'I've planted myself in the garden, between the potatoes and parsley.' Pass the weed killer, please!"

While that lyric may not be for everyone, it's an example of Fay's knack for building out a pithy phrase or idea, letting it sit there quietly for a minute or two, and then suddenly whipping it into something grand, both lyrically and by way of jazz composer Michael Gibb's swirling horn and string arrangements. "Methane River" also achieves these heights, moving from a plaintive woodwind intro to a cascade of brass and strings with the alternating anthemic chorus—first, "I cannot make it" (as in, make it across the poison river), and then a triumphant, rousing "You can make it" in the final chorus.

A man he told me it's not the methane
It's your knowledge that blocks your way

"The song came from talks I used to have with a friend, about how we name things and explain them away," Fay told me. "It's knowledge that blocks your way. Look at a tree—what is it?—it's a living thing. You're trying to reach a deeper reality, trying to wake up to the natural world around you, trying to get out of your own head. Not in a drug way. Seeing the impact of the natural world."

Fay's debut album was recorded in one day with an assembled crew of about 30 musicians and mixed the next day. Guitarist Ray Russell was brought on board by Mike Gibbs and became friendly with Fay during those sessions. Russell took over production chores on *Time of the Last Persecution* when Peter Eden bowed out, apparently uncomfortable with Fay's overtly religious lyrical content. *Time* is influenced by Biblical themes, including references to Daniel and *The Book of Revelation*. "Lyrically, I now feel it's immature in part, and was conveyed more perfectly on (Dylan's) *Slow Train Coming*," he says, in typical self-effacing fashion. Ray Russell remembers:

> We had long conversations, along with drummer Alan Rushton, who was also a big influence on Bill. Our talks would see the dawn rise many times. Bill talks about the Second Coming many times in his songs, but songs like "Tell It Like It Is," when he says "Peace be in your bike and in your door keys and old friends that have passed away," show his commitment to people and that humanity and social commitment is where the basis of change will come from. He practices what he preaches.

Like the debut, *Time* was also recorded in one day, live in the studio, without the 30-piece string section and gaudy arrangements, most likely with a fraction of the budget. There are still some horns, and Ray Russell's guitar work is much more prominent. "The wailing guitar lines are based on the emotional content of Bill's music," Ray explained to me. "He wanted me (us) to have these very varied dynamics. Very few songs have that freedom. The restless nature of the music was really a demand for change."

The opening track, "Omega Day," likely refers to de Chardin's concept of the Omega Point, the point at which our consciousness and spirituality are heightened and converge. This theme runs through the album, played out in dust-filled rooms, bars, at Kent State, in concentration camps, "Inside the Keeper's Pantry"— songs with souls all looking for higher meaning while confronted with forces of evil. He reprises the idea of "getting up out of your chair" on a few songs, beckoning the listener to find spiritual enlightenment. Musically, the shift in instrumentation and studio approach reflected the fast-moving changes of the times. Fay told me, "When our second album came out, I felt it was progress in the wider world of music. It deserved more attention. It was very innovative and progressive. Within a few years, music was really progressing."

He goes on to cite *Abbey Road* and Procol Harum's *Home* as important markers, although he bristles at the notion of any direct influence.

> I definitely appreciated what others were doing, but I was finding more from the piano. I was looking for answers, so lyrically the songs would reflect that. I don't think anything influenced me. I was bringing in the spiritual aspect. Around that time, it was like it all stopped—the labels didn't know what was going to be successful. The music got more and more replaced by conscious songs replacing unconscious. I've always considered myself a "song-finder."

Keith Richards and Bob Dylan have talked about this idea of songs existing outside the self, waiting to be siphoned, just as "Garden Song" came to Bill in ten minutes.

Ultimately, *Time of the Last Persecution* is a plea for spiritual awakening, a roadmap for locating that Omega Point. Bill comes full circle with this idea on his 2015 album *Who Is the Sender?*, which can be thematically summed up as follows: The path mankind is staking out (wars, wrecking the environment) is unsustainable, and everything WILL change if people seek their Omega Point. Fay's world-weary condemnations of man's endless folly (think Randy Newman sans humor or irony) take on a Voice of God quality on the recent albums, his earthy croak giving authority to even his most mundane lyrical turns. On *Who Is the Sender?* he repeats phrases—"It's all so deep," "He gonna change this world," "Bring us peace on earth," "This can't be all there is"—that in the hands of others might sound trite. But there's nothing trite about an album that uses the word *saxifrage* in a song, or devotes a whole song to William Tyndale, executed in 1536 for first translating the Bible to English from Greek and Hebrew texts.

Unlike many tragic music heroes of the '60s and '70s, Bill Fay is still alive to enjoy an overdue round of acclaim here in the 2010s, made possible by producer Joshua Henry and Dead Oceans. Bill's incredulous response to all the dripping accolades is sincere and very charming. When asked recently what he thinks of *Time of the Last Persecution*, now routinely referred to as a masterpiece (and one that commands four-figure sums for an original copy), he politely demures, "'Masterpiece' is a journalistic overstatement—I'd say 'of musical interest' myself."

Billy Bragg and me in NYC, 1985

Chapter 18:

Gigs

My first concert was Tom Petty & the Heartbreakers on the Hard Promises Tour at Nassau Coliseum on Long Island, August 6th, 1981. Joe Ely opened. Petty was a huge hero of mine. I had worn out *Damn the Torpedoes*, and his new one, released May 5th, 1981, was just as good. In a highly publicized tussle, Tom took on his record company, MCA, for trying to raise the list price on his new album to $9.98. He publicly shamed them, and the price remained at $8.98. Petty is pictured on the cover of *Hard Promises* in a record store, "$8.98" faintly scrawled on a record bin next to him. The whole saga was laid bare in a *Rolling Stone* cover story, and we fans ate it up.

Nassau was a fucked up place to see a show in those days. Broken glass strewn all over the parking lot, no crowd control, weed and drug dealers everywhere. Shows today are so much more controlled in every aspect, less chaotic, and arguably less fun. To this 14-year-old, it was all pretty intimidating and exhilarating. I felt like a big kid, hanging with my best friend at the time, Scott. Our dads carpooled us each way. How'd we manage to find his dad after the show without cell phones?

I've kept some of my ticket stubs, including that first one. Around 1981 to '83, we would wait in line for hours at the Hicksville

Mid-Island Mall Ticketmaster location for our Cars, Police, Kinks, or Neil Young tickets before they went on sale. My fellow Mid-Islanders may recall a nasty guard in a dark blue pantsuit who would limp up and down the line telling us kids we couldn't sit on the floor while we waited. What a wench!

I have a friend who saw Jimi Hendrix. My uncle saw Charlie Parker many times. Looking through my ticket box, which only represents a fraction of the shows I've actually attended, I remember so many shows. But there were a few times when I felt like I was actually a witness to history (of sorts). For example, I was in the Green Room with Nirvana when they played *Saturday Night Live* on January 11, 1992. Mark Kates dragged me along. He worked at Geffen Records, went on to run the Beastie Boys' record label, Grand Royal, and now manages MGMT. We had a meal in the NBC commissary with Krist Novoselic, but I didn't have any interaction with Kurt; he was really withdrawn. If you had asked me whether I knew I was witnessing something historic that night, I would have said, unequivocally, "YES!" We all knew. A rock band will likely never be as big as Nirvana was that night.

I had seen Nirvana two years prior, before they were signed to Geffen, at the Kennel Club in San Francisco on February 14, 1990, during the Gavin Convention, an annual industry confab. The major labels were starting to circle them, and industry reps were on hand. The entire show is up on YouTube. At 43:15, Krist smashes his bass and walks off stage. After a minute or so, Kurt says, "Would the legend like to play again?" Krist returns with a new bass and quips, "You get what you pay for." I really didn't think much of them that night. I was just attending another buzz-worthy band showcase. I thought they were loud, sloppy, and immature, especially the smashed bass part. In a bit of foreshadowing, Mark Kates would see the band for the first time that night as well and later become their A&R guy at Geffen.

I saw the eighth-ever Foo Fighters show at Gibson's in Tempe, Arizona, on April 12th, 1995, notable for a guest appearance by

Eddie Vedder playing (drums?) in his first wife's band, Hovercraft, who opened the show. Mike Watt was also on the bill.

I was in attendance at the Madison Square Garden Bob Dylan 30th Anniversary Concert on October 16, 1992. I've seen Dylan in all kinds of settings: on tour with the Grateful Dead; at Tramps, the Beacon, and the Supper Club; I met him backstage in Dallas in 2002, and handed him a copy of Kinney Rorrer's book, *Rambling Blues: the Life & Songs of Charlie Poole*, which he seemed to appreciate. This was a special night, however, because I was rolling with my boss, longtime Columbia Records promo VP Paul "Rap" Rappaport. We were going from one dressing room to the next: Lou Reed, Neil Young, Ron Wood. Quick handshake with Johnny Cash. I told Neil how much I loved "Ambulance Blues" from his album *On the Beach*, and we spoke of our mutual admiration for Bert Jansch.

Rap knew Ronnie from his years promoting Stones records, and he also introduced me to Keith Richards at a Beacon Theater date on his *Main Offender* tour in 1993. Keith saw Rap and just started cracking up; they didn't have to say a word to each other. Rap had worked the *Steel Wheels* album, and years earlier he'd been out with Keith and Ronnie in 1972 on the notorious drug-and-booze-fueled New Barbarians tour. Rap told me he needed to be re-introduced to Keith on a daily basis during the tour. "Keith, this is Paul." Keith referred to Paul as "CBS" (the then-parent company of Columbia). "Hey CBS, you stole my Rebel Yell ..." There was an after-show for Dylan's 30th at Tommy Makem's Irish Pavilion, and everyone was there: Petty, George Harrison.

I was there on July 21, 1994, when Oasis played their first US show at the tiny Wetlands club in New York City. It was packed beyond capacity and was the hottest (temperature-wise) show I ever attended. A couple of months later, I took Noel and Liam around to some local record shops like Mod Lang in Berkeley, California, on their first US West Coast tour. The guys were really polite. Noel was a sweetheart, and Liam was very reserved. Of course, it was their first US trip, no one knew who they were yet, and they were just taking it all in. The band played Bottom of the Hill in San Francisco, capacity 350.

The second-hottest gig I ever endured was Manic Street Preachers in Cardiff, Wales, on October 20th, 1994. It was deadly hot inside the venue, odd because it was only about 60 degrees outside, mild for October in Cardiff, but still. It would be the last show that guitarist Richey Edwards would play in his hometown before his mysterious disappearance four months later, on February 1, 1995. His body has never been found, and no one knows what happened to him. I remember hanging out with the band after the show, but Richey was not around.

I saw R.E.M. and the Dream Syndicate play the Good Skates Roller Rink in Setauket, Long Island, on July 17, 1984, on the Reckoning tour. After the show, I interviewed Bill Berry for my high school radio station, WKWZ. I also interviewed Steve Wynn, who went on and on about Dock Ellis throwing a no-hitter while on acid. I attended the CMJ New Music Awards show on November 9th, 1985, at the Beacon Theatre in New York, where Peter Buck chucked his Rickenbacker full throttle across the stage and walked off mid-song.

My friends dragged me to see the Replacements at Heartbreaker's in Oyster Bay, Long Island, on June 19, 1986. I didn't think much of it, just thought they were drunk, sloppy, and loud. Through the miracle of technology, we can now hear that show online. One thing I did remember vividly upon hearing it again was Paul (I guess) playing the first few bars of U2's "I Will Follow." The crowd thought that was pretty funny. I saw them three years later, on March 17, 1989, at the Palace Theatre in Albany, New York. Paul made some snarky comment about Albany, like "Great to be back in Albany. Feels like we never left." Alas, they would never play the city again. My friend Russ Rieger was their manager at the time, so I went backstage and met the guys, who were smoking and wearing excessive eye makeup.

I saw the Smiths play their fourth show in the United States at the Beacon Theatre in New York on June 17, 1985. Billy Bragg opened, playing his fifth gig ever in the States. I bootlegged the entire show on cassette, which I should digitize someday. I was something of a Billy Bragg groupie around then, and conducted several interviews with him on his first trips over. Former Pink Floyd manager Peter Jenner would set us up at the Gramercy Hotel, and Billy would talk my ear off about unions, Labour, and the Tories for hours. I really didn't understand what he was talking about, and he would give me long, dense articles about British politics that only confused me further. But I followed Billy around to all his gigs. I would also probably qualify as a groupie for the Mekons during the late '80s as well. Their shows at Tramps during that period were so uplifting and joyous. The band came up to stay with me at my place in Albany when I was in college there in 1989. They listened drunkenly, reverently to my copy of Springsteen's *Nebraska* deep into the night, and I gave Sally Timms and John Langford my bed. Sally signed my *Curse of the Mekons* LP: "Josh, Thanks for putting it up us [sic].—Sally"

I'm not much of a Bjork fan, but I did witness the first US Sugarcubes show ever on August 15th, 1988, at the I Beam in San Francisco, and I met her that day. She was so cute and nice, but I couldn't really understand what she was saying.

I saw Kris Kristofferson play the Continental Club (capacity 300) in Austin, Texas, in 2004. It really brought home for me the idea that these giants can never, ever be replaced. Kris, Willie, Merle. When they're gone, it's over. The way they carry a song, the authority with which they deliver it, their stature, their roots. Young singer/songwriters in their wake will always come along with something to offer, and I'll be listening. But those guys are like Mount Rushmore: for all eternity.

Other top SXSW gigs: Jeff Beck at La Zona Rosa in 1999; the Legendary Stardust Cowboy there in 2000; Roger McGuinn at Stubbs in 2000; Ray Price at Stubbs in 1998; Harvey Sid Fisher (my favorite astrological songsmith), 2000. I hosted a label show at SXSW in 2013 with Alice Gerrard, Luther Dickinson, Hiss Golden Messenger, and Harry Taussig. It was Taussig's first public appearance since his first album was released back in 1965. Speaking of Texas, I saw Townes Van Zandt at the Bottom Line, NYC, on November 7, 1990.

I saw the Pogues in their prime on June 27, 1986, at the Ritz, back when it actually felt dangerous to go to a Pogues show. Complete mayhem. Years later, I saw Shane MacGowan at the Viper Room. He was a mess. His face was all jaundiced, but his singing was still great. I saw Harry Dean Stanton sing at the Viper Room too, and met Jeffrey Lee Pierce (the Gun Club) there once.

Then there are the countless indie rock gigs. I saw David Kilgour of the Clean play songs from *Here Come the Cars* at a short-lived space called the Garage on Avenue B in NYC. I saw Live Skull at the Ritz on August 15, 1986. I would never miss Royal Trux. I saw Elliott Smith numerous times, most memorably at Brownies in NYC on March 3, 1996 (I have a tape of it). I saw Palace (Will Oldham) at Thread Waxing Space on June 24th, 1994. I can't believe it's on YouTube. He looks like a child. I saw the Frogs at CBGB in 1989, wearing wings, and I saw Uncle Tupelo at CBGB on July 17, 1990. I also saw John Fahey at CBGB—the only time I ever saw him—at a gig that Thurston Moore set up. The room was packed, and I was all the way in the back by the pool table. Fahey was just wanking away on the electric guitar, being "experimental." A couple of years later, I attended his last show ever in New York City—which he did not show up for. We waited patiently on line for an hour or so outside the Knitting Factory before it was announced that Fahey was "on a train somewhere in North Carolina." How fitting. I saw Sonic Youth around the release of *Daydream Nation* at the Ritz in NYC on October 29, 1988, which was just one big mosh pit, and then went twenty-two years without seeing them again until July 31, 2011, at the Prospect Park Bandshell, where they absolutely destroyed. Steve Shelley was especially animalistic on this night. So underrated.

On November 15th, 1997, I was on the road with a local SONY rep, driving along Route 46 from Columbus to Bloomington, Indiana. There were squalls along the way, and visibility started getting really bad. All of a sudden, I look out the window and see a sign: "Tonight: George Jones." We're saved! We pulled in to the parking lot and found out we were in Nashville, Indiana. Tickets were sold out, but we got in, somehow. We were completely out of place, especially my colleague, who was wearing purple knee-high Doc Martens. The venue was one of those joints where all the locals buy a season pass and go to every show. Lots of blue hair. It was the one and only time I'd ever seen George Jones, and yes, he did show up. But he was real ornery—chewing out his band, the sound guy. He was just really pissed that night.

I saw Roy Orbison twice: once in Albany, New York, on February 25, 1988, and again, with Chris Isaak opening, in August 1988 at the Paul Masson Winery in California, four months before Roy died. I was attending SUNY Albany, and as Music Director at the campus station, I was excited that Roy was coming to town for the Albany show. I promoted the hell out of it. When the date came around, I asked the promoter if I could meet Roy. For some reason, I couldn't get backstage, and I remember looking up from the street outside and seeing his silhouette in the window with someone else getting their picture taken, flashbulbs going off. I stalked him outside the backstage door, but he snuck out the front door of the venue and got in a car. Damn! Management heard about the snub and sent me an autographed picture, which I had framed, but my framing guy decided to bake the 8x10 onto a piece of cardboard, which ruined it. I should have sued that motherfucker. Anyway, Roy Orbison is the greatest vocal performer I have ever seen. I consider myself hugely fortunate to have seen him twice in the months before he passed.

I've seen lots of memorable jazz: Cecil Taylor, Sonny Rollins, Pharoah Sanders, Archie Shepp, Hank Jones, Mal Waldron, Mose Allison, Sam Rivers, McCoy Tyner, Art Farmer, Ran Blake, Charles

Gayle, Burton Greene, Dizzy Reece, Henry Grimes, Sunny Murray, Andrew Hill, Les Paul. The earliest was Art Blakey & the Jazz Messengers on Long Island in August 1983. He wasn't walking too well, but when he got behind the kit, he was explosive! I remember him sitting backstage signing a big stack of LPs for somebody. He signed a show flyer for me; still have it.

Ornette Coleman's performance at Carnegie Hall on June 20, 2004, was the greatest of all. I have rarely been transported like that at a concert. Part of the thrill was that I couldn't exactly decipher what I was hearing. It was a trance-induced musical coma of pleasure, but it was also very dense and abstract. I remember seeing a lot of colors in my eyes during the show. The same group configuration—two bassists, his son Denardo on drums, and Ornette—can be heard on the album *Sound Grammar*, recorded in Germany a year later. I was so glad to get ahold of that CD, just so I could unlock the throbbing intensity of that show and try to piece together what I had witnessed and heard. Even on record, it's still mysterious and challenging. That album won the Pulitzer Prize for Music in 2007.

The only time I've had a similarly ecstatic, near out-of-body experience at a show was seeing Terry Riley play solo piano on September 9, 2011, at the UC Berkeley Art Museum. I'd seen him once before, in March 1997 at Merkin Hall in New York City. La Monte Young was in the audience. Parts of the Berkeley show can be found on YouTube. His solo piano appearances are rare. Although tagged as a minimalist, his piano performances are anything but, bursting with all sorts of influences—jazz, classical, Indian, modal patterns, complex improvisation. Not to sound ageist, but it's truly remarkable that he had such command of the keyboard at age 76. He turned 80 this year and keeps up an active performance schedule. 1969's *A Rainbow in Curved Air* is salve for the soul. Get yourself a copy, right this minute!

I'm gonna list some of the shows I have stubs for—'cuz why not?—in the order in which I pulled them out of the box, with notes here and there. They represent a small fraction of the shows I've seen. I had another box with more stubs, mostly indie rocks shows from the '90s, which probably got ruined in the flood (Sandy).

● ● ● ● ●

Yes : Madison Square Garden, NYC, May 13, 2004
  I believe this, their 35th Anniversary Tour, was the last tour with Jon Anderson. Took my brother backstage, where he asked Jon Anderson if he wanted a drink. Got Chris Squire to sign cool Roger Dean postcard.

Radiohead : Hammerstein Ballroom, NYC, August 26, 1997

Plush : Mercury Lounge, NYC, November 21, 1998

Bob Dylan : Tilles Center, Long Island, January 30, 1998

Tom Petty & the Heartbreakers : Irving Plaza, NYC, April 15, 1999

Tame Impala : The Fillmore, San Francisco, November 15, 2012
  This show was boring.

Van Morrison w. Georgie Fame : Beacon Theatre, NYC, November 30, 1989

Pearl Jam w. Band of Horses : Madison Square Garden, NYC, May 21, 2010

Pearl Jam w. the Buzzcocks : Madison Square Garden, NYC, July 8, 2003

Big Country : The Ritz, NYC, September 9, 1983

The Police : Nassau Coliseum, Long Island, February 23, 1983

John Martyn : Joe's Pub, NYC, October 9, 2008
  He died about four months later. I'd seen him in the '90s at Tramps as well. Played in a wheelchair, was missing a leg. He told the crowd, "I'm a living leg end."

Richard Thompson : Beacon Theatre, NYC, April 20, 1985

Paul Weller : The Wiltern, Los Angeles, February 7, 2003

Oasis : Radio City Music Hall, NYC, June 8, 2001

Leo Kottke : Fredcrick Meijer Garden, Grand Rapids, Michigan, July 16, 2004
This is the only time I saw Kottke. A toddler ran across the front of the stage and Leo yelled, "Security!"

Rush : Jones Beach, Long Island, July 15, 2002

Rolling Stones : Madison Square Garden, NYC, Sept. 26, 2002

Nick Cave w. Low : Town Hall, NYC, March 31, 2001

Oasis : Madison Square Garden, NYC, December 17, 2008

Lucinda Williams : Radio City Music Hall, NYC, March 23, 2007

Lucinda Williams : The Fillmore, NYC, September 29, 2007

Jerry Lee Lewis : B.B King's, NYC, September 13, 2010
My girlfriend saw a rat at this show.

Willie Nelson : "Live By Request" taping at SONY Studios, NYC, August 14, 2000

Neil Young : Nassau Coliseum, Long Island, April 22, 1983
First time seeing Neil. *Trans* tour, half acoustic, half electronic. I had nosebleed seats, but the show stays with me. I remember seeing his knee bouncing back and forth playing solo acoustic, and then he completely flipped everyone out with the *Trans* material. It was so weird for the time.

Mars Volta : Irving Plaza, NYC, July 18, 2003

Elvis Costello : Broadway Theatre, NYC, October 25, 1986

Bruce Springsteen and the E Street Band : Meadowlands, New Jersey, August 17, 1984

Camper Van Beethoven : The Ritz, NYC, June 17, 1988

Talking Heads : Forest Hills Tennis Stadium, NYC, Aug. 21, 1983

Graham Parker : The Ritz, NYC, June 27, 1988

Donovan w. Loudon Wainwright : Carnegie Hall, NYC, December 8, 1984

Bruce Springsteen and the E Street Band : Madison Square Garden, NYC, June 17, 2000

Dylan & The Dead : Anaheim Stadium, Anaheim, California, July 26, 1987
First time I saw the Dead.

Jeff Beck : B.B. King's, NYC, September 10, 2003

Lucinda Williams w. Charlie Louvin : Brookhaven Amphitheatre, Farmingville, New York, July 28, 2007

AC/DC : Roseland, NYC, March 11, 2003

Christy Moore : Carnegie Hall, NYC, June 11, 1988

The Kinks : Nassau Coliseum, Long Island, May 7, 1983

Trio : The Ritz, NYC, November 11, 1983

Leon Redbone : Joe's Pub, NYC, January 6, 2004

Robyn Hitchcock & the Egyptians : Beacon Theatre, NYC, March 31, 1988

Rolling Stones : Shea Stadium, NYC, October 10, 1989
Nikki Sudden was sitting nearby.

Bob Dylan : Tramps, NYC, July 26, 1999
Elvis Costello popped onstage.

JJ Cale : Bottom Line, NYC, August 1, 2002

Ralph Stanley : Bottom Line, NYC, June 12, 2002

Eric Clapton : Fleetcenter, Boston, June 12, 2001
This show was boring.

Bruce Springsteen (solo acoustic) : State Theatre, New Brunswick, NJ, November 21, 1995

Orchestral Manoeuvres in the Dark : Beacon Theatre, NYC, June 10, 1985
I wish I could remember anything about this show.

Billy Joel : Nassau Coliseum, Long Island, December 29, 1982

Joan Armatrading : Radio City Music Hall, NYC, April 23, 1985

Roger Waters : Radio City Music Hall, NYC, March 26, 1985

Bob Dylan and Paul Simon : Jones Beach, NYC, July 30, 1999

Radiohead : Madison Square Garden, NYC, August 7, 2001

Tori Amos : Riverside Church, NYC, November 13, 2002

Bob Dylan : Madison Square Garden, NYC, November 11, 2002

Bob Dylan : Beacon Theatre, NYC, October 10, 1989
The first known live performance of "Broken Days." Isn't the Internet helpful?

Elvis Costello w. Nick Lowe : Radio City Music Hall, NYC, August 16, 1984

The Who : Madison Square Garden, NYC, October 6, 2000

Billy Joe Shaver : Village Underground, NYC, May 15, 2001

Otis Rush : Village Underground, NYC, February 17, 2001

Tony Joe White : Village Underground, NYC, December 2, 2000

Tom Waits : Paramount, Austin, March 20, 1999
Heckler goes off about the ticket price.

Michael Chapman : Knitting Factory, NYC, November 10, 2005

Bert Jansch : Southpaw, Brooklyn NYC, November 13, 2006
Met him earlier that day at WFMU. Also saw Bert at the Knitting Factory in the early '90s when no one cared, maybe 30 people there.

Rick Danko : Bottom Line, NYC, June 27, 1998

Loretta Lynn : Bottom Line, NYC, October 2, 2000

Bob Dylan and Tom Petty : Greek Theatre, Los Angeles, California, June 14, 1986
First time I saw Dylan.

Elton John : Madison Square Garden, NYC, August 2, 1982
Mom took us. Thanks, Mom!

Bob Dylan and His Band : Shoreline Amphitheatre, Mountain View, California, August 4, 2013
Probably my last Dylan show.

Bruce Springsteen and the E Street Band, Oakland Arena : Oakland, California, October 25, 1999

Aerosmith : BJCC Arena, Birmingham, Alabama, April 19, 1999
Oddly, this is the only time I ever saw them.

Rush : Jones Beach Theatre, Long Island, July 24, 2010

Randy Newman : Town Hall, NYC, November 10, 1998
I took Emma to see Randy Newman at Carnegie Hall in 2008 when she was seven. Taking little kids to shows always looks better on paper. About a half hour in she said, "Daddy, I'm tired."

U2 : Nassau Coliseum, Long Island, July 3, 1985

Neil Young (solo) : Theatre at Madison Square Garden, NYC, April 22, 1999
Complained about farming.

Jorma Kaukonen : Bottom Line, NYC, June 13, 2002

Aztec Camera : Bottom Line, NYC, April 10, 1985

Portishead : Roseland, NYC, July 24, 1997
In-the-round performance filmed for a DVD.

Cheap Trick w. NRBQ : SUNY Albany, May 6, 1989
(MAYFEST!!!)

Van Morrison : Beacon Theatre, NYC, May 19, 1985

Scanner : The Anchorage, NYC, June 27, 1997

R.E.M. : SUNY West Gym, Binghamton, New York, April 26, 1985

Leonard Cohen : Carnegie Hall, NYC, July 6, 1988

Lou Reed : Beacon Theatre, NYC, October 17, 1984

Tom Waits : Beacon Theatre, NYC, November 20, 1985

The Who (Quadrophenia) : Madison Square Garden, July 20, 1996

Pearl Jam : Fiddler's Green, Denver, Colorado, June 23, 1998

Black Sabbath : Jones Beach, Long Island, August 24, 1999
Backstage after the show, Ozzy could not walk.

The Cars : Nassau Coliseum, Long Island, March 24, 1982
The band did not move. I was fine with that. But band did not move.

Bob Dylan w. the Alarm : Jones Beach, Long Island, July 1, 1988

Bob Dylan w. Patti Smith : Beacon Theatre, NYC, December 14, 1995
They sang "Dark Eyes" together, and I have never forgotten it.

Bob Dylan : The Supper Club, NYC, November 17, 1993

Merle Haggard : Tramps, NYC, April 19, 1996

Fiona Apple : Palace Theatre, Albany, NY, October 18, 1997

Bruce Springsteen and the E Street Band : Shea Stadium, NYC, October 1, 2003
This show was awful. I left early.

The Pogues : Roseland Ballroom, NYC, June 23, 1988

Ray Charles : Avery Fisher Hall, NYC, June 28, 1985
Attended this show with Judd Apatow. The Commodores opened with way too many instruments on stage. Ray's set was about 30 minutes.

The Smiths : The Pier, NYC, August 6, 1986

Phil Lesh & Friends : Irving Plaza, NYC, May 21, 2002

Porter Wagoner : Joe's Pub, NYC, March 30, 2007
Wagoner died seven months later.

David Bowie : "Live By Request" at SONY Studios, NYC, June 15, 2002
I was involved with marketing *Heathen* in 2002, and Bowie was performing *Low* on that tour. His people invited me to a small rehearsal space downtown, where he performed *Low* in its entirety.

Bruce Springsteen : Nassau Coliseum, Long Island, April 2, 1988

The Strokes : Apollo Theatre, NYC, December 30, 2001

The Blasters : Slim's, San Francisco, California, March 9, 2002

Bert Jansch : Bowery Ballroom, NYC, June 10, 1997

Echo & the Bunnymen : Savoy, NYC, March 31, 1984

Steve Winwood : The Warfield, San Francisco, California, November 12, 2012

Van Morrison : Irving Plaza, NYC, March 30, 2004

Hazel Dickens / Bonnie Prince Billy : Joe's Pub, NYC, August 6, 2006

Hot Tuna : The Fillmore, San Francisco, California. January 3, 2015

Chapter 19:

Start a Label If ...

 ... you like being ignored.

Tompkins Square is a pretty niche operation, but even the higher-profile releases I put out are mostly ignored. When I send out a press release to media outlets, about 20 percent open the email. This is considered an average open rate for entertainment media companies. Of those folks, maybe 2 percent will email back with interest.

Luckily, we have received tons of great press over the years, for which I am extremely grateful. But the vast majority of media and consumers don't care and are ignoring me, and will probably ignore you as well. If you are lucky enough to get people to care, in general they will only do so for a few days, and then your project will become a catalog item. Most journalists will treat an album that's already out like rotten vegetables. "Stay within yourself," as they say in baseball. Concentrate on releasing quality and pleasing yourself first, regardless of the response or lack thereof. The only thing more likely to get ignored than your label is your book.

... you enjoy owing someone money at all times.

A manufacturer, a producer, an artist, a studio, an engineer, an art director. Pay up.

3   **… you like dealing with the same people over and over and over.**

The music business is a closed system. You are pitching the same people year in and year out. Coming upon a new media person or retailer who's enthusiastic about your work is incredibly refreshing. Most writers and editors seem like nice, passionate people, and I enjoy interacting with them, although I've never met most of them in person. But you are pitching the same people over and over.

I don't like hiring publicists because I like driving the narrative, having my own relationships, and saving money. I'm not convinced that I'll get incrementally more press by hiring someone. Plus, there are very few press hits that actually move the needle. If your music is any good, certain outlets will embrace it without a middleman.

Social media is effective at spreading terrorist propaganda. For music, not so much. There's too much chatter; nothing sticks. Is it helpful? Yes. But if you're relying on it, that's really sad. Note: This does not apply to stars.

4   **… you enjoy engaging in unhealthy "competition."**

Have you ever heard the Morrissey song "We Hate It When Our Friends Become Successful"? Such an elegantly expressed dark truth. I have never felt in competition with any other independent label. I have respect and reverence for quite a few of them, and I know a few of their proprietors. Some of them seem incredibly insecure though, and when you meet them, the interaction often devolves into a very awkward dick contest. Somewhere in the conversation, they'll start in with my favorite: "So, is Tompkins Square all you do?" You look into their eyes and listen to them, and you can tell they're not rooting for you. Not at all.

5   **... you enjoy having things go wrong.**
Any small business is fraught with daily challenges. In this racket, your print work will come out a funny hue, your test pressing will sound bad, your vinyl will be warped or the corners dinged, your shipments will be late, the wrong master will be uploaded, there'll be a typo you missed, or a vendor will return unsold goods. Ah jeez.

6   **... you enjoy selling a worthless product.**
My label has enjoyed extremely good fortune over the past ten years. But the CD is almost done; the LP is an unwieldy, low-margin production nightmare; the download is disappearing; and everyone on the planet can listen to all the music they want for free.

You can still make money selling pre-recorded music if you know what you're doing. I embrace all forms of technology that allow people to hear more music, even if it's free. Music content will be owned by technology companies eventually. There's already this morphing of digital services and the major content holders, which are buying stakes in said services.

Forget the delivery method; you can't control that broadly. Keep up with developments in technology, but don't let them guide your creative principles. If you can't make money using the present-day delivery systems, innovate or go do something else. Old-world constructs made musicians and labels feel entitled to reliable income, but that doesn't mean it will be that way going forward.

7   **... you enjoy taking naps.**
I love a good nap. Napping is the best "fuck off" you can offer the universe. You're losing consciousness, you know you're going down, then that warm twilight. It's like free, un-dangerous heroin. You will be a more efficient businessperson if you can fit one into your day.

Ah jeez ...

There are a few different kinds of naps. There's the 20-minute power nap from which you awake re-charged and refreshed. There's the slightly longer 30- or 40-minute nap, from which you awake disoriented, disheveled, and wobbly, and all you want to do is get back under the covers for another six hours or so. So set your alarm for 20. When I worked for a big corporation, one of the few ways I maintained my humanity was by telling my assistant to hold my calls, and then I'd take a snooze. When you run your own label, you can take a nap anytime.

8 **... you don't like music that much.**
This isn't a pre-requisite per se, but it will make your job a lot easier. There'll be no heartache if some artist or compilation you love is ignored or doesn't sell. By not caring as much, you'll have less skin in the game, and you'll be more nimble and ready for the next challenge.

 ... you have no talent.
I can't really play an instrument. I play chords on the guitar, that's it. I can't sing. My mom bought me a ukulele recently, but I can't figure out how to play it. I have no talent, so I'm perfectly suited to run a label. (Note: I did play guitar in a band, the Felt Bads, in high school/early college years with my friends Al Griffin and Sean Griffin. Tompkins Square released the recordings digitally—you can go listen and tell me what you think. We were heavily influenced by the Fall and Happy Flowers.) As my friend the legendary producer Bob Johnston (Dylan, Cohen, Cash) likes to say, all the record company brass he ever answered to couldn't sing, couldn't write, couldn't play—yet they had an opinion about just about every aspect of what the artist was doing.

I've always regretted the fact that I can't really talk on the level with a musician about the technical aspects of reading, writing, or performing music. You can be an "executive appreciator" and work the business side, but to be a true "music executive" you better know something about actually playing, writing, and performing. Otherwise, never tell the artist what to do with their music, because you don't know what the fuck you are talking about. Therefore, if you have no talent, you will be following a long succession of very successful professionals in our industry, and you'll be well qualified.

 ... you like bands.

I have never signed a band in ten years running the label. The closest I came was Prefab Sprout (a guy, not a band) and Hiss Golden Messenger (more a guy than a band). I don't like the sound of most new ones. Most indie rock is just retread, with nondescript singing and playing. I'm also firmly out of the demo. But it seems like bands are where the money is, so sign one!

11 **... you like these acts.**

I'm always amazed by the faces people make when I tell them I don't like certain artists. You would think I did something truly horrible to them, when in fact we're discussing music, and music is about taste. Don't debate zucchini with me. If you don't like it, I'm not gonna torture you, wonder about you, look at you askance, or try to marshal you over to my side and convince you of how great zucchini tastes. Music is the same. My list is comprised of (artists I dislike) + (how indignant/nasty their fans are when I tell them I don't like them), and that fetid equation makes them eligible for this list. The jerky fans of these artists intensify my dislike for the music, which is already substantial. If you like these artists, it's probably a tip-off that there is a deep cultural chasm between us. We can be friends, but only to a point, because we will always be deeply suspicious of each other. But if you start a label and you like these acts, you will be very successful.

The Beach Boys *

Arcade Fire

Neil Diamond

Nine Inch Nails

Ryan Adams

Swans

Dave Matthews

Afghan Whigs / Greg Dulli

Frank Sinatra

* Dennis Wilson's *Pacific Ocean Blue* is sublime, though. Sublime defined as "impressing the mind with a sense of grandeur or power; inspiring awe, veneration, etc." All those things.

Chapter 20:

Of Musical Interest

To cop a phrase from Bill Fay, these records from my collection are "of musical interest." My hope is that folks will pull this book off the shelf and treat it as a reference volume, leading to an exploration of some of my lists. All are original pressings unless noted otherwise.

Terry Allen : *Lubbock (on everything)* – Fate Records
Terry Allen, Joe Ely, Butch Hancock, Jimmie Gilmore, the Legendary Stardust Cowboy—they all went to Monterey High School in Lubbock, Texas. Leaning toward the "outlaw" side of country, Allen wrote most of the songs on this 2-record set in the '60s and released them on his own label in 1979. Cited as one of the pioneers of alt-country, Allen delights with his cutting observational humor and regional storytelling.

Mose Allison : *Local Color* – Prestige
As of this writing, Mose Allison is one of the oldest living "rock stars" at 87 years of age. I say "rock" even though he's technically a "jazz" practitioner, or as Pete Townshend refers to him on *Live at Leeds*, a "jazz sage." I just think of Mose as a great Southern singer/ songwriter from Mississippi who happened to choose jazz as his medium. I've seen him play a bunch of times and met him as well. I approached him a few years ago to record an album, right around the time Joe Henry moved in to do one last one with him. He's now retired from live performance after 65 years on the road. Mose's records are still easy to find—and cheap, for some reason, except for original pressings of this one, and his 1957 Prestige LP *Back Country Suite*.

Duane Allman : *An Anthology Vol. I & II* – Capricorn

Duane has been anthologized with a mammoth multi-CD box set, but for me, these double LPs are essential for their fine sequencing, detailed personnel, cool art, and un-remastered sonics.

Stephen Ambrose : *Gypsy Moth* – Barnaby

My friend Sean sent me a nice YouTube on this, so I took the Stephen Ambrose plunge and bought the LP online for $3. Pleasant singer-songwriter fare from 1972 staking out a sound somewhere between Bread and Tim Buckley, *Gypsy Moth* has a couple of classic moments, especially "Mary," with its sweet finger-picking, strings, and pedal steel. This was his only album before moving on to become an innovative audio engineer big shot.

Al Anderson : *s/t* – Vanguard

This LP pops up rarely in a shop, but when I see it, I want to buy it again, even though I already own it. The NRBQ guitarist/vocalist's first solo LP from 1972 has a great vibe with some jumpers and laid-back, soulful ballads. This LP is on a list of titles that were supposed to come out in Quad and never did, just as Quad was dying out. It's never been reissued on vinyl.

Ran Blake : *Open City* – Horo

Ran Blake is one of the first artists I sought out when I started the label in 2005, and we made three records together. Legendary for his 1962 RCA debut with Jeanne Lee, *The Newest Sound Around*, as well as his prolific solo output, the 80-year-old educator, author, composer, and pianist taught at New England Conservatory of Jazz for over 40 years. There are very few artists who can legitimately lay claim to inventing their own musical language. He did. The finest solo albums among the forty or so in his discography are the double LP *Open City* and *Crystal Trip*, both released in 1977 on the Italian Horo label. Exquisitely recorded and intensely performed, check out the distant thunder of Ran's left hand, the stabbing dissonance of his right, and how he works

"That's OK . . .I'll come back another time."
The Thrifty Hippy, Petaluma, California

the pedals. Noirish, nightmarish, at times inert and barely there, these LPs are tough to locate and have never been reissued on CD, but they represent the artist at his peak.

Lenny Breau : *Cabin Fever* – True North (CD)

I have a lot of Lenny Breau titles, but none I like better than *Cabin Fever*, a barebones solo set recorded in a log cabin somewhere deep in the Canadian wilderness, where he was cooling out from his drug-addled lifestyle. Some folks close to Breau claim this album was actually recorded in a Toronto studio. I wish I had never heard that, although nothing could ever taint the pure intimacy of this recording. Check out the Breau documentary on YouTube detailing his brilliant musicianship and tragic early demise. When mentor Chet Atkins talks about Lenny, choking back tears, it'll rip you apart.

Bob Brown : *The Wall I Built Myself / Willoughby's Lament* – Stormy Forest/MGM

As I write, Tompkins Square is readying reissues of these Richie Havens-produced albums from the early '70s, heretofore overlooked singer/songwriter LPs released in an era of great ones. Brown achieves a dynamic, floating, layered sound as backdrop for his lonely lovelorn ballads, guided by ace musicianship.

Bobby Charles : s/t – Bearsville/Rhino

A swampy 1972 classic by the author of "See You Later, Alligator" and "Walking to New Orleans," featuring members of the Band and produced by John Simon. Instead of hunting the original LP or a reissue, grab the 2011 3-CD set on Rhino. The re-mastering job is unobtrusive, plus you get 17 previously unreleased bonus tracks, cool pix from *The Last Waltz*, an interview CD, and some very informative session notes. "I remember copious amounts of drinking," says guitarist Amos Garrett.

B.J. Cole : *The New Hovering Dog* – United Artists

I almost fainted when I found an original copy of this 1972 LP for a good price in the New Arrivals bin at Freakbeat Records on Ventura Boulevard. When I brought it up to the counter, a gaggle of onlookers were like "Man, that's a great record!" "Great price for that!" "Can I see that for a second?" The guy at the register had that "maybe I shouldn't be selling this ..." look to him. Hey, can I just buy a fucking record? Anyway, with string arrangements by Robert Kirby (Nick Drake), the album kind of operates like an early Eno record, very progressive and dreamy. And of course, there's some stellar steel guitar work. There's a reason people hire B.J. Cole as a session player, and I don't believe it's just because he's B.J. Cole. He's got concepts and a knack for melody. *Transparent Music*, his next solo album, released 17 years later in 1989, is great too.

Cowboy : *Why Quit when You're Losing* – Capricorn

Duane Allman had a hand in getting these guys signed to Capricorn, and they toured as Gregg Allman's backing band in 1974. Their 1971 debut, *Reach for the Sky*, is an unconventional Southern rock stew, steering clear of any commercial ambitions— weird interludes, a laid-back CSNY vibe, and off-the-cuff hoedowns about being in a band. "Everything here is getting kinda crazy/ Everybody's close/But everybody's too damn lazy." The one I listed here is a double LP consisting of the first two albums. File next to New Riders of the Purple Sage under "Non-threatening country-rock boogie."

David Crosby : *If I Could Only Remember My Name* – Atlantic

It took decades, but this album is now enshrined in the pantheon as one of the most influential records of the '70s. It seems one can't read about a young musician playing psych-folk these days without some reference to this LP. File next to Gene Clark's *No Other*.

Jesse Davis : *s/t* – Atco

The great Native American guitarist from Oklahoma seems totally forgotten, even though he produced Gene Clark's *White Light* and played on sessions with George Harrison, John Lennon, Bob Dylan, Leonard Cohen, Harry Nilsson, and many more. He released this debut solo LP in 1970 featuring Eric Clapton, Leon Russell, and Gram Parsons, and released a second Atco LP, *Ululu*, before OD'ing in 1988, age 43.

Richard Dobson : *In Texas Last December* – Buttermilk

I nearly jumped out of my skin when I found Richard Dobson's 1977 debut LP for $4 at A-1 Records in the East Village. You can do that sort of thing there, cuz it's mainly a hip-hop/R&B shop frequented by DJs. His tune "Baby Ride Easy" was recorded by Johnny Cash and Father John Misty, to name a couple. (The song is mislabeled on the back cover as Song 2 on Side Two, but it's actually Song 1.) His buddy Townes Van Zandt wrote some notes for the back cover: "There is no such thing as a best songwriter. My favorites are David Olney, B.W. McTell, P. LaFarge, and R. Dobson ... Richard, please get them to spell my name right. " – Townes Van Zant. (Sic!)

Bobby Doyle : *Nine Songs* – Bell

Kenny Rogers sidekick Bobby Doyle was a versatile blind session pianist from Houston who only made three albums under his own name. This one from 1973 is the one to check out, with warm, intimate low-down ballads and funky breaks all over the place. Seek out Austin writer Michael Corcoran's insightful online article "Make It Beautiful: the Bobby Doyle Story" to go deeper.

Peter Green : *The End of the Game* – Warner Bros.

This 1970 set by the former Fleetwood Mac guitarist is an elongated two-sided psychedelic freak-out, and I have fantasized about someone releasing a multi-CD reissue with all the leftover jams from this session. Green is muted, ripping back behind the rhythm section in a perfect spot—not all up in your face. Some of his greatest work is here. Check out the delicate phrasing in "Timeless Time," the warm pulses of echoey flange in "Hidden Depth." *All Music Guide* gives this album one star, and Christgau gave it a "D." Fuck them both.

Hampton Grease Band : *Music to Eat* – Columbia

I was turned on to this adventurous 1971 double album by producer Brendan O'Brien (Pearl Jam, Springsteen), who I met briefly during his tenure at SONY Music. His first move upon starting his own imprint at SONY, 57/Shotput Records, was reissuing *Music to Eat* by his fellow Atlantan Bruce Hampton and Co. One of the strangest and, according to sources, worst-selling albums in Columbia's long history, Hampton reminds me of a cross between Beefheart and a southern David Thomas (Pere Ubu), all three possessing a penchant for weird time signatures, abrasive vocals, and nonsensical lyrical content. Key line: "He made me vomit / Riding in his comet." File next to *An Evening with Wild Man Fischer* in the "Insane-double-albums-on-major-labels" section.

Cal Hand : *The Wylie Butler* – Takoma

Besides the unsightly tuft of chest hair poking out of his shirt on the cover, Hand's Leo Kottke–produced LP from 1977 is notable for some extraordinary pedal-steel playing. This is really a Hand/Kottke duo album, with lots of hot exchanges between these masters. Never been reissued, and his only album, to my knowledge.

Gary Higgins : *Red Hash* – Rufusman

I'm not a real big psych-folk "private-press" collector, as I find so many of these LPs over-hyped and overpriced, but this 1973 beauty deserves its stellar reputation. A little CSN feel leavened with psychedelic tones, it's equally tuneful and damaged "downer-folk." Higgins had a "comeback" moment a few years back. File next to Dennis Wilson's *Pacific Ocean Blue.*

Bill Jennings : *Enough Said!* – Prestige

The 1959 debut LP from this left-handed Indianapolis guitar master was reissued on CD in 2000 by Prestige as *Legends of Acid Jazz.* A double CD of his King and Gotham recordings recently surfaced, *Architect of Soul Jazz: the Complete Early Recordings, 1951-1957.* Yet Jennings is sadly neglected today, as he was during his career. Supposedly a favorite of B.B. King, Jennings had a clean, warm technique with clever and innovative phrasing. At some point he lost a finger on his fretting hand. His last recordings were made in 1968, and he died from stomach cancer after years of heroin addiction around 1979. (I found this LP for $2).

Mark Knopfler : *From the Film Cal* – Mercury

This is a mellow, Celtic-tinged Dire Straits album without the vocals, if that sounds appealing to you. Band members Knopfler, Guy Fletcher, and John Illsley team up with Paul Brady and Liam O'Flynn to create a mesmerizing instrumental song cycle.

Kossoff : *Back Street Crawler* – Island

One of the greatest Jewish guitar players ever, alongside Peter Green, Harvey Mandel, and Mark Knopfler (half), Paul Kossoff released his solo debut in 1973. He was on fire around this time, having played his ass off on five of eight tracks on Free's best album, *Heartbreaker*, in 1972. This set features vocal tracks by John Martyn (!) and Paul Rodgers, but the real magic starts to happen at 9:34 into the 17:32 A-side jam, as a pedestrian garage rock jam morphs into a spaccy lysergic funk groove. Kossoff died on a flight from Los Angeles to New York on March 19, 1976, age 25.

Bruce Langhorne : The Hired Hand – Scissor Tails

This 1971 instrumental masterwork by the former Dylan sideman is right up there with *Paris, Texas* as a landmark movie soundtrack consisting of spare, haunting Americana. The film, the recording, and the artist may be less familiar than *Paris, Texas*, but a couple of listens and the banjo, slide, and piano themes will burrow into you. Try it on your next rural drive.

Angus MacLise : Dreamweapon III – Boo-Hooray

Velvet Underground's first drummer's legacy was given a recent boost by New York collective Boo-Hooray, which reissued some of MacLise's droney experimental work in 2011. This one features a jam in Tony Conrad's New York City apartment in 1968 with some beautifully harrowing viola. So mysterious and tripped out. He died in Nepal in 1979, age 41, of TB and "malnutrition" after years of drug abuse.

Bob Martin : Midwest Farm Disaster – RCA

The cover of this 1972 cult fave by Lowell, Massachusetts' Bob Martin pictures our hero seated on a giant hog, playing guitar, with a rope around the hog's neck tied to a human skeleton. Featuring crack Nashville session dudes like Kenny Buttrey and David Briggs, the album draws its power from heartbreaking depictions of rural life with a poetic streak, much like John Prine, and heavily inspired by Martin's Lowell neighbor, Jack Kerouac.

Vince Martin : *If the Jasmine Don't Get You ... the Bay Breeze Will* – Capitol

Here's one of those LPs that I've only ever seen in my own collection. Martin was Fred Neil's singing buddy, recording one OK album together in 1964 for Elektra, *Tear Down the Walls*. *Jasmine* was cut in 1968 with Dylan's *Nashville Skyline* crew— Kenny Buttrey, Charlie McCoy, etc.—and has a kind of innocent, yearning magic. Yes, it's in the Tim Buckley vein of free-range folk, but *Jasmine* occupies its own quiet space. The title track, clocking in at 13:07, is fearless.

John Mayall – Bare Wires – London

I'm a latecomer to Mayall, someone whose awesome-looking record covers I've always admired and whose music I've roundly overlooked. I have really come around to his voice, and the sheer musicality of this particular LP. He plays harmonica, piano, guitar, harpsichord, organ, and harmonium on *Bare Wires*, and moves through ripping solos and mellow psychedelics with equal passion. It's the dreamy, unconventional, un-bluesy numbers that really resonate, like "I Know Now."

Augie Meyer : *Augie's Western Head Music Co.* – Polydor

Sir Douglas Quintet keyboardist Augie Meyer—who would later add a letter *S* to the end of his last name, much like Keith Richard—released his first solo album in 1971 followed by *You Ain't Rollin' Your Roll Rite* in 1973, neither of which have been reissued. Meyer is pictured on the back cover with a ragtag gang of "transients"—about a dozen Texas musicians and their kids. Augie wrote all the tunes except three, including his take on Dylan's "Only a Hobo." Augie would play on Bob's *Love & Theft* decades later. Cosmic Tex-Mex hippie-country of the highest order.

Essra Mohawk : *Primordial Lovers* – Reprise

Mohawk's debut on Verve in 1969, *Sandy's Album Is Here at Last*, was released under her real name, Sandy Hurvitz, and produced by Frank Zappa. She was a "member" of the Mothers of Invention. I still don't dig her debut, but *Primordial Lovers*, from 1970, is kind of like a freer, unhinged Laura Nyro. This LP has funky breaks ("Spiral") and stunning tunes like "I Have Been Here Before," featuring Tim Buckley guitar collaborator Lee Underwood, a song which supposedly inspired David Crosby to write "Déjà Vu." Nice gatefold art and a lyric booklet too! Reissued well on CD by Rhino Handmade in 2000.

Bob Pickering : *Appaloosa Rider* – Capitol

Is this the worst-selling album in Capitol Records history? With no sales history listed on Popsike or Discogs, this is a 1973 outsider-country LP from the Henryetta, Oklahoma, native that has the quirky, skewed charm of a woozier John Hartford. It's co-produced by Whitey Thomas, possibly the same Whitey Thomas who played trumpet with Glenn Miller. It wouldn't surprise me if Pickering was completely tone deaf, but the results are strangely appealing, especially on the tunes with full string arrangements. In his liner notes he writes, "This may be my only shot. I'll consider it a success if it makes you smile." There's nothing about this LP that isn't weirder than fuck. A guy at the flea market gave it to me for free. Go ahead, hate me!

Duffy Power : s/t – GSF

My friend Sean recently sent me a YouTube of "The River" by Duffy Power from 1973, and it blew me down. Stuck at the very end of Side 2, the song has such a pained, deep atmosphere, with just acoustic guitar and a swelling string section. "My mother was violent towards me physically and mentally from the age of six," Power reveals in the 2007 CD reissue liner notes. "The first daydreams that I remember were of making a raft and sailing away down the Thames." An artist with a very early Beatles connection and a reedy falsetto, Power would not record again for decades. File next to Terry Reid's *River*.

John Simon : *John Simon's Album* – Warner Bros.

Warner Bros. Records in 1971. Sure, they had Hendrix and the Dead and Captain Beefheart, but they also had green-labeled oddball freak-outs like *Bill Martin's Concerto for Headphones and Contra Buffoon in Asia Minor*, John Randolph Marr, and this adventurous LP by Simon & Garfunkel/the Band producer John Simon. The material is quirky as hell, in a Biff Rose/Nilsson sort of way, with top-notch accompaniment from Muscle Shoals players, members of the Band, and a couple of Derek's Dominoes.

Joey Stec : s/t – Playboy

I got this 1976 LP from John Allen's stash at the WFMU Record Fair about 15 years ago. I've never seen a copy in any store, but it's readily gettable online. Stec was a member of '60s pop-psych group the Millennium, who recorded one album in 1968 on Columbia. Stec's solo LP was produced by Jimmy Miller (Rolling Stones) and features Dominoes Carl Radle and Jim Gordon, along with Bobby Keys. The songs are memorable, the playing is tight, and it sorta sounds like what would happen if Big Star cut a record with the Stones' sax player.

Ray Stinnet : *A Fire Somewhere* – Light in the Attic

Collectors know "The Dream"—you're searching for a record, you find it, and it is the coolest thing ever. Then you wake up depressed, because that record doesn't exist. The cover of Ray Stinnet's *A Fire Somewhere* looks like the record that's always in that dream—except it exists. Executive produced by Booker T. and recorded at Ardent Studios, the former guitarist for Sam the Sham & the Pharoahs was supposed to have his album released on A&M in 1971, but instead it moldered for forty years until 2012, when Light in the Attic rescued it with an over-the-top 2-LP package: tip-on gatefold jacket, big booklet, unreleased tracks, and a poster! Truth be told, this album isn't that great, but Light in the Attic undertaking such a massive rescue operation for an album like this is something I thought I'd only ever see in my dreams.

David Sylvian : *Secrets of the Beehive* – Virgin

1987. There wasn't much released in 1987 that sounded remotely like this (although Bryan Ferry's classy *Bete Noire* was released the same week), and when it came out, it just washed everything away for me. It still sounds perfect. Joined by David Torn, Ryuichi Sakamoto, Mark Isham, and Danny Thompson, Sylvian works his fragile (some might say, precious) post-Ferry/Walker croon around autumnal arrangements, slinking his way straight into your heart. A masterpiece.

Bobby Whitlock : *s/t* – Dunhill/ABC

Whitlock's work with the Stones, Derek & the Dominoes, and George Harrison speaks for itself—he was part of three of the greatest records in rock music history. But his first solo album also deserves a spin, with his husky, passionate Southern voice fronting crack players like Clapton, Bonnie Bramlett, the Dominoes' Carl Radle and Jim Gordon, and Bobby Keys. Reissued by the brilliant folks at Light in the Attic along with Whitlock's second album, *Raw Velvet*, in 2013.

Ron Wood & Ronnie Lane : *Mahoney's Last Stand* – Atco

Anything involving Ronnie Lane is worth listening to, and this fine forgotten 1976 soundtrack to a forgotten movie is no exception. A CD reissue surfaced in 1999—now an out-of-print and expensive collector's item. So start digging for this gem, full of great musicianship (Townshend, Ian McLagan, Bobby Keys, Rick Grech, Jim Price) and palpable camaraderie. Plus you gotta love a record with a song called "Chicken Wire" immediately followed by a song called "Chicken Wired."

Link Wray : *Be What You Want To* – Polydor

I got turned onto this on a road trip with Daniel Bachman. He'd play "All Cried Out" over and over again in the car. The song is just a monster weeper—gospel-tinged background vocals, deep strings, a horn section, rhapsodic piano parts. The song is credited to Deborah/Curtis on this 1973 LP, and to Thomas Jefferson Kaye on Kaye's album *First Grade*, so I wonder who actually wrote it. Anyway, produced by Kaye and recorded in San Francisco with Jerry Garcia, Peter Kaukonen, and tons of background singers, this one sits nicely next to the great LPs he recorded in a Maryland shack—A self-titled album (1971), the mysterious *Mordicai Jones* LP (1971), and *Beans and Fatback* (1973).

Vernon Wray : *Wasted* – Sebastian Speaks

Guitarist William Tyler earned himself yet another ticket to heaven (as if he needed another) when he reissued Vernon Wray's 1972 private-press solo album, *Wasted*, in 2010. In a reproduced press release, there's talk of Vernon's acting roles in four episodes of *Gunsmoke* and in Kristofferson's *Alice Doesn't Live Here Anymore*. I can't find any evidence of this or of his other solo album, *I'm a Superstar at My House*, which is the greatest album title I have ever heard. Brothers Doug and Link join in on funky burners and weepy moaners, all ragged but right.

Steve Young : *Rock Salt & Nails* – A&M

I was pretty psyched to find the Homestead Act's 1972 *Gospel Snake* LP recently, featuring a very young Steve Young. *Rock Salt & Nails* is country outlaw Young's 1969 debut LP, best known for the sparkling "Seven Bridges Road," later covered by the Eagles. Sitting in are James Burton, Hal Blaine, Gram Parsons, and Gene Clark. Influenced by Buddy Holly, Gene Clark, and Roy Orbison, you'd expect the guy-with-guitar-singing-his-rootsy-heart-out thing to get old after a few songs, but it never does.

Chapter 21:

Old-Time List

Here is a list of some old-time, blues, folk, Native American, and gospel LPs from my collection. It's not complete or comprehensive. They're listed in order of how I pulled them off the shelf, which is to say, in no order at all. They are grouped in a "roots" section in my linen-closet-cum-record-storage area.

To paraphrase Jerry Seinfeld, everything in your house is in various states of becoming garbage. Who knows what my daughters will wind up doing with it all. My hope is that they'll want to keep the collection intact and enjoy it, but I wonder how practical that will be for them. I know it might all wind up in a dumpster, just like the prodigious collection of 78 rpm records rescued and released on the Tompkins Square box set, *Work Hard, Play Hard, Pray Hard.* I've never collected 78s, because I wanted to avoid getting that particular disease. I am perfectly happy with a well crafted reissue CD or LP of archival material. I do appreciate the allure of holding and playing the original article, and I understand and respect the obsessive psyche of the 78 collector.

I lost a couple hundred records in Hurricane Sandy. I had left a bunch of stuff in the storage unit of my old building in New York when I moved to San Francisco. The basement flooded. After the flood, I called a moving company and told them to just bring me everything in the unit, regardless of condition. There were nine boxes of records, about 60 records in each box, stacked 3 across and 3 high. The boxes on the bottom were all waterlogged when they arrived, and they weighed about 100 pounds each. Most of the stuff in those boxes were rare blues and old-time LPs. Bracing myself, I looked inside the ravaged boxes, saw that the records were totally saturated with contaminated water, and didn't bother trying to rescue anything or catalog what was lost. I just hauled them out to the trash. Now when I see something I think I lost, I buy it, so I've slowly replaced a few of the more choice items. It seems only fitting to have lost so many blues LPs in a flood, the sad inspiration for many a blues song.

I also lost some nice memorabilia. I met Ray Davies during the Kinks' ill-fated one-album stint on Columbia, and he signed my *Great Lost Kinks Album* "I do not wholly approve of this album— Ray Davies." Ruined! I presented Ray with a pair of Doc Martens with Union Jacks on them; I wonder if he still has those. I lost box sets from Jeff Beck and Lou Reed that they had signed in front of me. Things like that. I rescued plenty of stuff too, and I'm grateful for that. Considering what people went through in the aftermath of Sandy, my travails were insignificant.

I did learn from the experience. I look at my collection differently. It used to seem like some indestructible totem, a shrine I had built in honor of my own good taste. After the flood, I realized that I could lose it all at any time. Once you get to a certain age, you realize there are records you own that you'll likely never play again before you die. Probably quite a few of them. Whereas when you're in your twenties, you don't think about your time being limited, how many more Mays or Septembers you might get to experience. Realizing this, you become haunted by your own possessions. You realize a certain portion of your used LP collection belonged to dead people with similar tastes as you. And all your records will someday belong to someone else.

LISTEN UP!

Ramblin' Thomas: *Chicago Blues 1928* – Biograph
Washington Phillips: *What Are They Doing in Heaven Today?* –
   Mississippi
Old Originals Vol. 1: *Old-Time Instrumental Music Recently Recorded in
   North Carolina and Virginia* – Rounder
John Ashby & the Free State Ramblers: *Fiddling by the Hearth* – County
Sanctified Singers, Part Two – Blues Classics
Fields Ward: *Bury Me Not on the Prairie* – Rounder
Old Love Songs & Ballads from the Big Laurel, North Carolina –
   Folkways
The Riendeau Family: *Old Time Fiddling from Old New England* –
   County
Blind Willie Johnson: 1929-1930 – RBF / Folkways
The Wonderful World of Old Time Fiddlers Vol. 1 – Vetco
The Wonderful World of Old Time Fiddlers Vol. 2 – Vetco
Emmett Miller and His Georgia Crackers: *The Old Masters*
Put No Blame on the Master: Jamaican Gospel Vol. II – Social Music
Harry McClintock: *Hallelujah! I'm a Bum* – Rounder
Georgia Fiddle Bands Vol. 2 – County
Blind Willie McTell: *Last Session* – Prestige Bluesville
The Original Carter Family from 1956 Radio Transcripts – Old
   Homestead
Henry Johnson: *The Union County Flash!* – Trix
Cortelia Clark: *Blues in the Street* – RCA
Fiddlin' John Carson: *The Old Hen Cackled and the Rooster's Gonna
   Crow* – Rounder
Bessie Johnson: 1928-1929 – Herwin
Mississippi Blues: 1927-1936 – Belzoni
Henry Thomas: *Sings the Texas Blues!* – Origin
Henry Thomas: *Ragtime Texas! Complete Recorded Works 1927-1929* –
   Herwin
Fred Van Eps And Vess Ossman: *Kings of the Ragtime Banjo* – Yazoo
K.C. Douglas: *A Dead-Beat Guitar and the Mississippi Blues* – Cook
Robert Pete Williams: *Free Again* – Prestige Bluesville

The Callahan Brothers – Old Homestead
Graham Townsend: *Le Violon/The Fiddle* – Rounder
Buddy Thomas: *Kitty Puss* – Rounder
Blind Willie McTell: *Atlanta Twelve String* – Atlantic
Home in West Virginia – *West Virginia Project Vol. 2* – Old Homestead
Gid Tanner and the Skillet Lickers – Vetco
Sic 'em Dogs on Me – Herwin
Arizona Dranes: *Barrel House Piano with Sanctified Singing* – Herwin
Cannon's Jug Stompers: *Complete 1927-1930* – Herwin
Bessie Jones: *So Glad I'm Here* – Rounder
Blues from the Western States – *1927-1949* – Yazoo
Blind Joe Taggart – *A Guitar Evangelist 1929-1931* – Herwin
The Rural Blues – *Sacred Tradition 1927-1930* – Herwin
Bottleneck Guitar Masterpieces: the Voice of the Blues – Yazoo
Country Blues Bottleneck Guitar Classics 1926-1937 – Yazoo
Pioneers of the Jazz Guitar – Yazoo
Blind Willie Johnson: *Praise God I'm Satisfied* – Yazoo
Blind Lemon Jefferson: *King of the Country Blues* – Yazoo
Tex-Arkana-Louisiana Country – *1929-1933* – Yazoo
Clifford Gibson: *Beat You Doin' It* – Yazoo
Memphis Jug Band – Yazoo
String Ragtime – *To Do This You Got to Know How* – Yazoo
The Dixon Brothers: *Beyond Black Smoke* – Country Turtle
Da Costa Woltz's Southern Broadcasters – County
The Louisiana Aces – Rounder
The Gospel Ship – *Baptist Hymns & White Spirituals from the Southern Mountains* – New World
Darby & Tarlton: *Jimmy Tarlton & Tom Darby* – Old Timey
The Devil Is Busy in Knoxville – Mississippi
Uncle Dave Macon – RBF / Folkways
Been Here All My Days – Mississippi
Jimmie Rodgers: *My Rough & Rowdy Ways* – RCA
Blind Lemon Jefferson – Milestone
Ma Rainey: *Ma Rainey's Black Bottom* – Yazoo
Ray & Ina Patterson: *Old Time Ballads & Hymns* – County
Fight On, Your Time Ain't Long – Mississippi

Life Is a Problem – Mississippi
Oh Graveyard, You Can't Hold Me Always – Mississippi
Amédé Ardoin: *The Original Recordings 1928-1938* – Old Timey
Bukka White: *Big Daddy* – Sutro Park
Fred McDowell / Furry Lewis: *When I Lay My Burden Down* – Sutro Park
Skip James: *The Complete 1931 Sessions* – Yazoo
Skip James: *Greatest of the Delta Blues Singers* – Melodeon
Skip James: 1931 – Mississippi
Skip James: *Devil Got My Woman* – Vanguard
Skip James: *Today!* – Vanguard
Guitar Wizards – 1926-1935 – Yazoo
Last Kind Words — 1926-1953 – Mississippi
I Don't Feel at Home in This World Anymore – 1927-1948 – Mississippi
Ed Haley: *Parkersburg Landing* – Rounder
Frank Hutchison: *The Train that Carried My Girl from Town* – Rounder
Memphis Minnie: *Gonna Take the Dirt Road Home* – Origin
Silas Hogan: *Trouble* – Excello
Rev. E.D. Campbell: *1927 – Complete Recordings* – Eden
Where the Soul of a Man Never Dies – Social Music
Must Jesus Bear the Cross Alone and All the World Go Free – Social Music
Wolf's at the Door – Lost Recordings from the Spirits of the South – Sutro Park
Bullfrog Blues – Mamlish
Robert Wilkins: *The Original Rolling Stone* – Herwin
Traveling Through the Jungle – Negro Fife and Drum Band Music from the Deep South – Testament
Blind Willie McTell: *Trying to Get Home* – Sutro Park
Lead Belly: *Huddie Ledbetter's Best* – Capitol
Lead Belly: s/t – Playboy
Ma Rainey: *Blame It on the Blues* – Milestone
Ma Rainey: *Broken-Hearted Blues* – Riverside
Carolina Tar Heels – Old Homestead
Roy Hall & His Blue Ridge Entertainers: *1938-1941* – County
Ola Belle Reed – Rounder

Peg Leg Howell: *The Legendary Peg Leg Howell* – Testament
Peg Leg Howell & His Gang – 1927-1930 – Origin
Woody Guthrie: *Dust Bowl Ballads* – Folkways
O'Bryant's Washboard Wonders: *1924-26 – Back Alley Rub* – Biograph
Dennis McGee: *The Early Recordings* – Morning Star
Kenny Baker: *Portrait of a Bluegrass Fiddler* – County
E.C. Ball: *With Orna Ball & The Friendly Gospel Singers* – Rounder
Tampa Red: *Guitar Wizard* – RCA
Riley Puckett: *Waitin' for the Evening Mail* – County
Son House: *Father of the Folk Blues* – Columbia
The Anglin Brothers: *The South's Favorite Trio* – Old Homestead
Negro Prison Songs from the Mississippi State Penitentiary – Tradition
Jelly Roll Morton: *Mr. Jelly Lord* – Riverside
Stuff Smith: *1936-1943 – Hot Fiddle Swing Classics* – Folklyric
The Allen Brothers: *The Chattanooga Boys* – Old Timey
The Friends of Old Time Music – Disc/Folkways
Stanley Brothers: *Earliest Recordings* – Revenant
Cajun Vol. 1 – Abbeville Breakdown – 1929-1939 – Columbia
Lonnie Johnson: *Steppin' the Blues* – Columbia
Sam McGee: *Grand Dad of the Country Guitar Pickers* – Arhoolie
Johnny Dodds – s/t – RCA
Rare Hot Chicago Jazz – 1925-1929 – Herwin
Bennie Moten's Kansas City Orchestra – 1923-1929 – Historical
Fred McDowell: *Amazing Grace* – Sutro Park
Mississippi Fred McDowell: *Somebody Keeps Callin' Me* – Antilles
Mississippi Fred McDowell: *I Do Not Play No Rock 'n' Roll* – Capitol
*Yonder Go That Old Black Dog – Blues, Spirituals, and Folksongs from
　Rural Georgia by Eddie Lee Jones and Family* – Sutro Park
Clawhammer Banjo – Old Time Banjo and Fiddle Tunes – County
*Gambler's Lament – Old Time Songs and Ballads from the Southern
　States* – Country Turtle
The East Texas Serenaders: *1927-1936* – County
The Georgia Yellow Hammers: *The Moonshine Hollow Band* – Rounder
Pernell Charity: *The Virginian* – Trix
Grayson & Whitter: *The Recordings of Grayson & Whitter* – County
Harry Smith's Anthology of American Folk Music, Vol. 4 – Revenant

Roscoe Holcomb & Wade Ward: *The Music of Roscoe Holcomb & Wade Ward* – Folkways
Native American Ballads – RCA
Ernest V. Stoneman and the Blue Ridge Corn Shuckers – Rounder
The Delmore Brothers: *Brown's Ferry Blues – 1933-1941* – County
The Delmore Brothers – Vol. 1 – Old Homestead
Texas Farewell – Texas Fiddlers – 1922-1930 – County
Red Fox Chasers – s/t – County
Texas-Mexican Border Music Vol. 5 – Folklyric
The Original Memphis Five – s/t – RBF
Way Down South in Dixie – Old Time Fiddle Band Music from Kentucky – Vol. 3 – Morning Star
Wish I Had My Time Again – Old Time Fiddle Band Music from Kentucky – Vol. 2 – Morning Star
Wink the Other Eye – Old Time Fiddle Band Music from Kentucky – Vol. 1 – Morning Star
Nashville – The Early String Bands Vol. 2 – 1925-1934 – County
Johnny Dodds & Kid Ory – s/t – Epic
Blind Blake: *Search Warrant Blues – 1926-1932* – Biograph
Hobart Smith: *Of Saltville, Virginia* – Folk-Legacy
Buell Kazee: *Sings & Plays* – Folkways
Old Time Fiddle Classics Vol. 2 – County
Old Time Fiddle Classics Vol. 1 – County
The Social Harp – Early American Shape-Note Songs – Rounder
An Introduction to Gospel Song – RBF
George Davis: *When Kentucky Had No Union Men* – Folkways
Let's Go Riding – Guitar Rags! Blues! Hokum! – Origin
The Fisk Jubilee Singers: *The Gold and Blue Album* – Folkways
Lonnie Johnson: *Tomorrow Night* – King
Earl Johnson and His Clodhoppers: *Red Hot Breakdown* – County
Fields Ward and His Buck Mountain Band: *Early Country Music* – Historical
Early Country Music – Vol. 2 – Historical
Wade Mainer & the Sons of the Mountaineers – 1937-1941 – County
Dave Apollon: *Mandolin Virtuoso* – Yazoo
Georgia Tom Dorsey: *Come On Mama Do That Rag – 1929-1932* – Yazoo

Bessie Jackson / Walter Roland: *1927-1935* – Yazoo
Blind Willie McTell: *1927-1935* – Yazoo
Blind Willie McTell: *1927-1933* – *The Early Years* – Yazoo
Mississippi John Hurt: *1928 Sessions* – Yazoo
Memphis Jamboree – *1927-1936* – Yazoo
Roots of Rock – Yazoo
Favorite Country Blues – *Guitar-Piano Duets* – *1929-1937* – Yazoo
Please Warm My Weiner – *Old Time Hokum Blues* – Yazoo
Bo Carter: *Greatest Hits* – *1930-1940* – Yazoo
Eddie Lang: *Jazz Guitar Virtuoso* – Yazoo
Papa Charlie Jackson: *Fat Mouth* – *1924-1927* – Yazoo
Dock Boggs: *Legendary Singer & Banjo Player* – Folkways
Dock Boggs: *Country Blues* – Folkways
Dock Boggs: *The Legendary Dock Boggs* – Verve/Folkways
Dock Boggs: *Legendary Singer & Banjo Player* – Disc
Ragtime 2 – *The Country* – *Mandolins, Fiddles, & Guitars* – RBF
Ragtime 1 – *The City* – *Banjos, Brass Bands, & Nickel Pianos* – RBF
Barefoot Bill: *Hard Luck Blues* – Mamlish
Ed Bell: *Mamlish Blues* – Mamlish
Charley Patton: *Founder of the Delta Blues* – Yazoo
Big Joe Williams: *Early Recordings* – *1935-1941* – Mamlish
The State Street Ramblers – *Vol. 1* – *1928* – Herwin
Rev. D.C. Rice: *Sanctified Singing with Traditional Jazz
        Accompaniment* – Herwin
The Blue Sky Boys: *The Sunny Side of Life* – Rounder
Drop on Down in Florida – *Recent Field Recordings of Afro-American
        Traditional Music* – Florida Folklife
Fiddlin' Edd Justus – *s/t* – Shadow
The Stripling Brothers : *The Lost Child & Other Original Fiddle Tunes
        Recorded* – *1928-1936* – County
Cotton Mills and Fiddles – Flyin'Cloud
Death Might Be Your Santa Claus – Legacy
Charlie Poole : *1926-1930* – Historical
The North Carolina Ramblers – *1928-1930* – Biograph
Charlie Poole: *The Legend of Charlie Poole* – County
Charlie Poole and the North Carolina Ramblers : *Vol. 2* – County

Charlie Poole and the North Carolina Ramblers : *Vol. 4* – County
Gid Tanner and His Skillet Lickers: *Hear the New Southern Fiddle and Guitar Records!* – Rounder
The Skillet Lickers: *Old Time Tunes Recorded 1927-1931* – County
The Skillet Lickers: *Old Time Fiddle Tunes And Songs From North Georgia Vol. 2* – County
Gid Tanner and His Skillet Lickers: *The Kickapoo Medicine Show* – Rounder
Harry Choates : *His Original 1946-1949 Recordings* – Arhoolie
Leroy Carr: *Blues Before Sunrise* – Columbia
The Blues Tradition – Notable Performances of Early Bluesmen – 1927-1932 – Milestone
I'm Wild About My Lovin' 1928-1930 – Historical
Harry Reser: *Banjo Crackerjax – 1922-1930* – Yazoo
Bo Carter: *1931-1940* – Yazoo
Alabama Blues – 1927-1931 – Yazoo
Furry Lewis – In His Prime – 1927-1928 – Yazoo
The Mississippi Shciks: *Stop and Listen* – Mamlish
Wade Ward : *Uncle Wade: A Memorial to Wade Ward, Old Time Virginia Banjo Picker – 1892-1971* – Folkways
James P. Johnson: *Father of the Stride Piano* – Columbia
Great Big Yam Potatoes: Anglo-American Fiddle Music from Mississippi – Mississippi Dept. of Archives and History
Play It Like You Did Back to George St. – An Anthology of Cincinnati Blues – 1924-1936 – Shake It
Texas Hoedown – County
Good Time Blues – St. Louis – 1926-1932 – Mamlish
Tennessee Strings – Rounder
J'etais au Bal – Music from French Louisiana – Swallow
Pink Anderson: *Carolina Blues Man* – Prestige Bluesville
Bille and Dede Pierce: *Blues and Tonks from the Delta* – Preservation Hall
Pierce Humphrey's Crescent City Joymakers – Riverside
King Oliver: *In New York* – RCA
Tampa Red: *Don't Jive Me* – Prestige Bluesville
The Country Blues – RBF

Frank Hovington: *Lonesome Road Blues* – Rounder
Jabbo Smith: *The Trumpet of the '20s* – Melodeon
Sam Chatmon: *The Mississippi Sheik* – Blue Goose
The Dixon Brothers: *Vol. 1* – Old Homestead
Eck Robertson : *Famous Cowboy Fiddler* – County
Roscoe Holcomb: *The High Lonesome Sound* – Folkways
Rufus Crisp – *s/t* – Folkways
Dillard Chandler: *The End of an Old Song* – Folkways
Allen Shelton: *The Original Banjo Man* – Outlet
Roane County Ramblers – Complete Recordings – 1928-29 – County
Mississippi John Hurt: *The Immortal* – Vanguard
Obray Ramsey: *Blue Ridge Banjo* – Washington
Betsy Rutherford: *Traditional Country Music* – Biograph
Frank Wakefield: *s/t* –Rounder
Harry and Jeanie West: *Country Music in Bluegrass Style* – Prestige
    International
Lead Belly: *Last Sessions Vol. Two* – Folkways
Anthology of American Folk Music – Volume Three: Songs – Folkways
Don Stover: *Things in Life* – Rounder
Joe Meadows: *West Virginia Fiddler* – Old Homestead
Lydia Mendoza: *Part 1: Early Recordings – 1928-1938* – Folklyric
The Kentuckians: The Solid Bluegrass Sound Of – Melodeon
L.B. Siler and the Round Mtn. Boys: *If That's the Way You Feel* –
    Programme Audio Records
Mississippi John Hurt: *Folk Songs and Blues* – Piedmont
Echoes of the Ozarks – Vol. 1 – Arkansas String Bands – 1927-1930 –
    County
Echoes of the Ozarks – Vol. 2 – Arkansas String Bands – 1927-1930 –
    County
Echoes of the Ozarks – Vol. 3 – County
Kelly Harrell & the Virginia String Band – s/t – County
The Cooke Duet – s/t – no label
Songs of Complaint & Protest – Library of Congress
Uncle Charlie Osborne: *Relics & Treasure* – June Appal
Little Brother Montgomery: *Crescent City Blues* – RCA
Blind Alfred Reed: *How Can a Poor Man Stand Such Times and Live?* –
    Rounder

Traditional Fiddle Music of Mississippi Vol. 2 – County
Mississippi Moaners: 1927-1942 – Yazoo
Ted Lundy and the Southern Mountain Boys: *The Old Swinging Bridge*
    – Rounder
Mountain Music of Kentucky – Folkways
John Jackson: *Blues and Country Dance Tunes*
From Virginia – Arhoolie
Old Time Ballads from the Southern Mountains, Recorded 1927-1931 –
    County

23-LP set – Indian Records, Inc.
Northern Arapaho Song
Arikara Songs
Blackfeet Songs
Northern Cheyenne War Dance Songs
Northern Cheyenne Songs
Southern Cheyenne Songs
Chippewa Cree (Rocky Boy) Songs
Crow Grass Dance Songs
Crow Tribal Songs
Gros Ventre and Assiniboine Songs
Old Traditional Kiowa Pow Wow Songs
Mandan-Hidatsa Tribal Songs
Omaha Tribal Songs
Shoshone-Bannock Pow Wow Dance Songs
Shoshone Tribal Pow Wow Songs
Popular Sioux Traditional Songs
Standing Rock Sioux Traditional Songs
Sioux War Dance Songs
Crow Creek Sioux Songs
Umatilla Traditional Tribal Songs
Songs of the Warm Springs Confederated Tribes
Winnebago Traditional Tribal Songs
Southern Cheyenne Peyote Songs

Tompkins Square Discography

Artist	Title	Sel. #
Roscoe Holcomb	San Diego State Folk Festival 1972	TSQ 5210
Bob Brown	Willoughby's Lament	TSQ 5135
Bob Brown	The Wall I Built Myself	TSQ 5111
Michael Chapman	Fish	TSQ 5197
John Hulburt	Opus III	TSQ 5159
Various Artists	Remembering Mountains: Unheard Songs by Karen Dalton	TSQ 5173
Various Artists	Imaginational Anthem Vol. 7	TSQ 5104
Various Artists	When I Reach That Heavenly Shore: Unearthly Black Gospel, 1926-1936	TSQ 5081
Bessie Jones	Get in Union	TSQ 5074
Alice Gerrard	Follow the Music	TSQ 5050
Smoke Dawson	Fiddle	TSQ 5036
James Blackshaw	Fantomas: Le Faux Magistrat	TSQ 5012
Dillard Chandler	The End of an Old Song	TSQ 2998
Ryley Walker	All Kinds of You	TSQ 2004
Various Artists	I Heard the Angels Singing: Electrifying Black Gospel from the Nashboro Label, 1951-1983	TSQ 2981
Ryley Walker	The West Wind	TSQ 2974
Daniel Bachman	Jesus I'm a Sinner	TSQ 2943

Various Artists	*Live at Caffe Lena: Music from America's Legendary Coffeehouse, 1967-2013*	TSQ 2967
Dino Valente	*Dino Valente*	TSQ 2929
Various Artists	*Let Me Play This for You: Rare Cajun Recordings*	TSQ 2912
Various Artists	*Turn Me Loose: Outsiders of Old Time Music*	TSQ 2905
Various Artists	*Imaginational Anthem Vol. 6: the Roots of American Primitive Guitar*	TSQ 2851
Charlie Poole & the Highlanders	*Charlie Poole & the Highlanders*	TSQ 2875
Don Bikoff	*Celestial Explosion*	TSQ 2837
Lena Hughes	*Queen of the Flat-Top Guitar*	TSQ 2813
Various Artists	*Imaginational Anthem Vols. 1-5*	TSQ 2790
N/A	*"Obscure Giants of Acoustic Guitar" trading-card set*	n/a
Various Artists	*Imaginational Anthem Vol. 5*	TSQ 2691
Various Artists	*Work Hard, Play Hard, Pray Hard: Hard Time, Good Time & End Time Music: 1923-1936*	TSQ 2783
Daniel Bachman	*Seven Pines*	TSQ 2752
Bill Wilson	*Ever Changing Minstrel*	TSQ 2684
Arizona Dranes	*He Is My Story: the Sanctified Soul of Arizona Dranes*	TSQ 2677
Harry Taussig	*Fate Is Only Twice*	TSQ 2745
Mark Fosson	*Digging in the Dust: Home Recordings 1976*	TSQ 2721
Various Artists	*Oh Michael, Look What You've Done: Friends Play Michael Chapman*	TSQ 2707
Hiss Golden Messenger	*Poor Moon*	TSQ 2660
Various Artists	*Aimer et Perdre: To Love & to Lose Songs, 1917-1934*	TSQ 2653
Calvin Keys	*Shawn-Neeq*	TSQ 2646

Various Artists	*This May Be My Last Time Singing: Raw African-American Gospel on 45RPM 1957-1982*	TSQ 2639
James Elkington & Nathan Salsburg	*Avos*	TSQ 2615
Various Artists	*To What Strange Place: the Music of the Ottoman-American Diaspora, 1916-1929*	TSQ 2608
Frank Fairfield	*Out on the Open West*	TSQ 2578
Ben Hall	*Ben Hall*	TSQ 2462
Ran Blake	*Grey December – Live in Rome*	TSQ 2592
Nick Jonah Davis	*Of Time and Tides*	TSQ 2547
Amede Ardoin	*Mama, I'll Be Long Gone: the Complete Recordings of Amede Ardoin 1929-1934*	TSQ 2554
Michael Chapman	*Trainsong: Guitar Compositions, 1967-2010*	TSQ 2530
William Tyler	*Behold the Spirit*	TSQ 2424
Various Artists	*People Take Warning! Murder Ballads & Disaster Songs, 1913-1938*	TSQ 2509
Prefab Sprout	*Let's Change the World With Music*	TSQ 2493
Sean Smith	*Christmas*	TSQ 2486
Various Artists	*Imaginational Anthem Vol. 4: New Possibilities*	TSQ 2448
Various Artists	*Bloody War: Songs 1924-1939*	TSQ 2479
Charlie Louvin	*Hickory Wind: Live at the Gram Parsons Guitar Pull, Waycross GA*	TSQ 2363
Various Artists	*Unheard Ofs & Forgotten Abouts*	TSQ 2387
Roland White	*I Wasn't Born to Rock 'N Roll*	TSQ 2400
Various Artists	*Beyond Berkeley Guitar*	TSQ 2394
Shawn David McMillen	*Dead Friends*	TSQ 2356
The Giuseppi Logan Quintet	*The Giuseppi Logan Quintet*	TSQ 2325
A Broken Consort	*Crow Autumn*	TSQ 2332
Various Artists	*Face a Frowning World: An E.C. Ball Memorial Album*	TSQ 2288

Various Artists	*Fire in My Bones: Raw, Rare + Otherworldly African American Gospel, 1944-2007*	TSQ 2271
Frank Fairfield	*Frank Fairfield*	TSQ 2257
Red Fox Chasers	*I'm Going Down to North Carolina: the Complete Recordings of the Red Fox Chasers [1928-31]*	TSQ 2219
Powell St. John	*On My Way to Houston*	TSQ 2233
Ben Reynolds	*How Day Earnt Its Night*	TSQ 2226
Tim Buckley	*Live at the Folklore Center, NYC – March 6, 1967*	TSQ 2189
A Broken Consort	*Box of Birch*	TSQ 2134
Peter Walker	*Peter Walker Long Lost Tapes 1970*	TSQ 2103
Ran Blake	*Driftwoods*	TSQ 2097
Charlie Louvin	*Sings Murder Ballads & Disaster Songs*	TSQ 2127
Max Ochs	*Hooray for Another Day*	TSQ 1059
Brad Barr	*The Fall Apartment*	TSQ 2011
Richard Crandell	*In the Flower of Our Youth*	TSQ 2035
Charlie Louvin	*Steps to Heaven*	TSQ 2059
Polk Miller	*Polk Miller & His Old South Quartette*	TSQ 2028
James Blackshaw	*Litany of Echoes*	TSQ 1783
Peter Walker	*Echo of My Soul*	TSQ 1752
Various Artists	*Imaginational Anthem Vol. 3*	TSQ 1905
Various Artists	*Imaginational Anthem Vols. 1-3 (Box Set)*	TSQ 1899
James Blackshaw	*Celeste*	TSQ 1837
James Blackshaw	*Sunshrine*	TSQ 1844
James Blackshaw	*Lost Prayers and Motionless Dances*	TSQ 1851
Various Artists	*People Take Warning! Murder Ballads & Disaster Songs 1913-1938*	TSQ 1875
Spencer Moore	*Spencer Moore*	TSQ 1950
James Blackshaw	*The Cloud of Unknowing*	TSQ 1967
Charlie Louvin	*Charlie Louvin*	TSQ 1042
Charlie Louvin	*Live at Shake It Records*	TSQ 1912

Various Artists	*Berkeley Guitar*	TSQ 5252
Robbie Basho	*Venus in Cancer*	TSQ 1820
Various Artists	*A Raga for Peter Walker*	TSQ 1622
Various Artists	*Imaginational Anthem Vol. 2*	TSQ 1424
Christian Kiefer & Sharron Kraus	*The Black Dove*	TSQ 1124
Harry Taussig	*Fate Is Only Once*	TSQ 1523
Shawn David McMillen	*Catfish*	TSQ 1721
Various Artists	*Imaginational Anthem Vol. 1*	TSQ 0531
Ran Blake	*All That Is Tied*	TSQ 1965
Charles Gayle	*Time Zones*	TSQ 2839
Bern Nix	*Low Barometer*	n/a
Suni McGrath	*Seven Stars b/w Fantasia 7"*	TSQ0531-7
Max Ochs	*Imaginational Anthem b/w Oncones 7"*	n/a

78 RPM Series

Lucinda Williams / Michael Chapman	*That Time of Night*	TSQ 12653
Joe Bussard	*Guitar Rag b/w Screwdriver Slide*	TSQ 71136
Luther Dickinson	*Zip-A-Dee-Doo-Dah/Beautiful Dreamer b/w Nobody Knows the Trouble I've Seen/Peace in the Valley*	TSQ 11873
Ralph Stanley	*Single Girl b/w Little Birdie*	TSQ 22527
Tyler Ramsey	*Raven Shadow b/w Black Pines*	TSQ 10972
Michael Hurley	*Watertrain b/w Black & Yellow Bee*	TSQ 22041

About the Author

Josh Rosenthal is a Grammy-nominated producer and founder of San Francisco-based record label Tompkins Square. Celebrating ten years in 2015, Tompkins Square has received seven Grammy nominations and wide acclaim for its diverse catalog of new and archival recordings. In his first book, *The Record Store of the Mind*, Rosenthal ruminates over unsung musical heroes, reflects on thirty years of toil and fandom in the music business, and shamelessly lists some of the records in his record collection.

Rosenthal lives in San Francisco and is the proud father of two daughters, Emma and Hazel.

Acknowledgements

Thanks to Emma and Hazel for conceptualizing the cover, Hazel for drawing the cover, and to them both for giving me a visual concept of my book, thus inspiring me on to completion. To my family and friends. To Susan Archie, Tompkins Square's long-suffering, Grammy-winning art director, for punching up the book. To my editor, Joslyn Hamilton, my book publicists Ken Weinstein and Rob Goodman, and Allison Davis and the team at INscribe, my eBook distributor.

Special thanks to all the folks I interviewed.

This book release coincides with the 10th Anniversary of my record label, Tompkins Square. I'm so fortunate to have had two great distribution partners in the US and UK for the entire ten-year run: INgrooves, based here in San Francisco, and Cargo Records in London. I'm also grateful to label art directors Joel Jordan (2005–2011) and Susan Archie (2011–present).

Thanks to everyone who has ever purchased, streamed, or stolen a Tompkins Square recording, and for all the many kind words of encouragement from fans of the label the world over.

CPSIA information can be obtained
at www.ICGtesting.com
Printed in the USA
FSOW04n0315010416
18593FS